ADRENALINE

2000

THE YEAR'S BEST STORIES OF
ADVENTURE AND SURVIVAL

ADRENALINE

2000

THE YEAR'S BEST STORIES OF ADVENTURE AND SURVIVAL

EDITED BY CLINT WILLIS

**Thunder's Mouth Press and
Balliett & Fitzgerald Inc.**

New York

An Adrenaline Book®

Published by
Thunder's Mouth Press
A Division of Avalon Publishing Group Incorporated
841 Broadway, 4th Floor
New York, NY 10003

and

Balliett & Fitzgerald Inc.
66 West Broadway, Suite 602
New York, NY 10007

Distributed by Publishers Group West

Associate Editor: Nate Hardcastle

Book design: Sue Canavan

frontispiece photo: © Weststock Photography

Manufactured in the United States of America

ISBN: 1-56025-299-5

Library of Congress Card Number: 00-108281

For Will Balliett

contents

p h o t o g r a p h s

introduction

Not so long ago, adventure writing occupied a modest niche in literature's library. Ten or 15 years back, when I came across a musty copy of Alfred Lansing's *Endurance* on a shelf at someone's beach house, I'd never heard of it. I read and enjoyed the book, and went looking for others like it. I found them: books like Lennard Bickel's *Mawson's Will* and Maurice Herzog's *Annapurna* and Sir Wilfred Thesiger's *Arabian Sands*. More often than not, they were out of print. When I found a copy in a library or at a second-hand bookshop it would have that 1950s feel to it—sturdy, boxy, with a dust jacket that managed to be a little lurid without being flashy.

Those books took me back to the pleasure that reading gave me when I was very young, capable of losing myself almost entirely in someone else's story. I have long associated that pleasure with so-called boys' books, the kind populated by characters who take chances in pursuit of some standard of excellence or goodness—characters such as Horatio Hornblower, Sherlock Holmes, Robin Hood or King Arthur.

Lately, more readers have discovered the lure of a well-told adventure story. This surge of interest in the stuff of adventure shouldn't surprise anyone who pays even a little attention to our popular culture, which has failed us in some pretty serious ways. Sellers of magazines, television, films, music and books will do anything to get our attention —but can't hold it. They promise to instruct and entertain us; instead they wear us out with trivial advice and useless information: which mutual funds to buy, which movie stars plan to marry each other, which cars offer the best acceleration for the money, which foods to avoid if we don't want to die an early death.

The best adventure writing tells us how to live. The stories in this book are not escapist literature; on the contrary, they confront readers with facts. These are survival stories in the deepest sense—stories about staying not just alive, but fully alive in the face of our own fragility.

By some standards, Edward Marriott has no business hunting for sharks in Nicaragua; he should be staring at a computer screen in an office somewhere in a developed country. The same goes for Michael Finkel, huddled with a crowd of dehydrated Haitian refugees in the hold of a leaky boat in the Atlantic Ocean, or Sy Montgomery, looking for pink dolphins in the Amazon. Instead, they're having adventures.

I'm going to say that an adventure is an experience that is in some way joyful and at least a little dangerous. The danger is connected to the joy. That might be because risk makes us pay attention: It keeps us deeply interested.

So do the 13 selections in this book, which constitute the best adventure writing published during the past year in books and magazines and on Web sites. The quality and range of the work reflect the public's growing interest in armchair adventure. This trend has provided an audience for writers who find their subjects and openings for their talent in activities such as shark hunting, mountain climbing, extreme skiing, cannibalism, crocodile attacks . . . the sort of thing that gets a person's blood pumping.

Bookstores are filled with books that lack narrative, by writers who want to tell us what they know without showing us how they came to know it. This book is loaded with story—the unfolding of events that bring knowledge or even wisdom. Here is Montgomery, after getting bad news on her Amazon trip:

Steve and I sat stunned. Dianne went outside and cried, then
came back and stared vacantly while smoking a cigarette. I sat
stupidly repeating, "I can't believe it. I can't believe it." We
did not know what to do with the grief, or with the horror, or
with the guilt. We had reveled in the danger of the Amazon,
thinking we were remote from it. We had observed it like a
work of art, like a drama on a stage, not thinking the river, the
mother of this place, could swallow one of us whole.

Val Plumwood is out paddling in the Australian wetlands when a
crocodile drags her into the water.

In that flash, I glimpsed the world for the first time 'from
the outside' as a world no longer my own, an unrecognizable bleak landscape composed of raw necessity, indifferent
to my life or death.

For Montgomery and Plumwood, experience is the beginning of a
new sort of relationship to the world—one that engages them in an
acceptance of things as they are. The rest of us might wish to arrive at
some version of that relationship. We don't need to visit the Amazon
or survive a crocodile attack to get there. We get there however we can,
making up our own stories as we go. Malcolm Cowley at around age
80 wrote about this process:

One project among many, one that tempts me and might
be tempting to others, is trying to find a shape or pattern in
our lives. There are such patterns, I believe, even if they are
hard to discern. Our lives that seemed a random and
monotonous series of incidents are something more than
that; each of them has a plot. Life in general (or nature, or
the history of our times) is a supremely inventive novelist
or playwright but he—or she?—is also wasteful beyond

belief and her designs are hidden under the . . . rubbish of
the years. She needs our help as collaborators. Can we clear
away the bundles of old newspapers, evading the booby
traps, and lay bare the outlines of ourselves?

Most of the writers whose work appears in this book are engaged in
just such work, whether or not they mean to be. They chronicle
experience—their own or, in a few cases, someone else's—that in its
intensity has the power to burn away the fog that often clouds our
days. What's left is clarity, the clarity you might experience short of
water in the desert or crossing a snow slope in the high Himalaya—or
at the birth of a child or the death of a friend. Our lives are one adventure after another.

Bear that in mind while you read the narratives in this book. These
writers aren't set apart simply by their willingness to go to dangerous
places, though some of them do. They stand out for what they find.
They occasionally find disaster. Mostly they find experience in all its
glory, and they bring it back to us in shapes that often are strikingly
familiar. In doing so, they fulfill one of a writer's highest ambitions:
They help us to recognize the outlines of our lives—which, when we
can manage to live in them, are more thrilling than any book.

—*Clint Willis*

from Savage Shore
by Edward Marriott

Edward Marriott (born 1966) makes a career of placing himself in harm's way. But Marriott is no simple thrill-seeker. His writing is moving and funny, in part because he's often scared. In 1995 he paid a visit to Nicaragua's Moskito Coast, where locals took him fishing for the voracious bull shark. The party used a dugout canoe and hand lines.

At Arturo's request, I'd brought bananas—fat, ripe claws, still on the stalk—and carried them through the tropical night, down tracks I now knew well, almost able to gauge the distance by the incline, the exact crunch and give of the rubble underfoot. Down the tight alleyway to Arturo's yard, I smelled the gutterswill again, less rich now than during the day, and felt my way along the walls of houses, testing each step before moving on, doubling the length of the journey so that by the time I arrived it was past four and Arturo, to my surprise, was already up, brushing his teeth with lagoon water, not five yards from the outflow from the open sewer.

He greeted me silently, mouth afroth. Together we bailed the dugout, heaping nets and hooks high in the prow, scraping at the swollen wood with coconut halves. We worked until the boat was dry and people in nearby shacks were coughing in their sleep. In Arturo's shack, through a square of grease-smoked glass, I glimpsed his wife moving about slowly, a slight shake to her movements: too many dawn starts, I guessed, too much broken sleep. And there was, as Arturo had predicted, just the faintest breeze tickling onshore, barely strong enough to ruffle the water, detectable only in a sweet cooling of the skin.

As yet, though, we had no engine. Arturo wanted to fish further out, ten miles south, and to do that he needed an outboard. His neighbor Elias had one, and had promised to come if they split the catch, but he was nowhere to be seen. Arturo made me wait and cut round the back of his shack, muttering to himself. It was ten minutes before he returned, and in those minutes came the first intimation of dawn: a lifting of the absoluteness of night, the first edges of things rising into focus. I carried the gasoline over to the dugout, found the paddles, laid out the bananas and the bread Arturo's wife had baked, and waited.

Ten minutes later, they both emerged, Elias running apologizing after Arturo, yawning continually, dressed only in his underpants, one hand on the sagging elastic. He'd overslept, but promised we'd be out there soon. He hurried to the water's edge and began lifting away palm branches from what I'd thought was a heap of refuse, and soon was heaving the outboard clear, setting it on its back beside the tank of gasoline. He maneuvered it one-handed, with seeming ease: hard to believe an outboard that weighed so little was as quick as he boasted. I watched, feeling the first flurry of concern, uncomfortably close to my bowels. Elias looked up, grinned, hoisted his underpants. "Five minutes," he said, and was gone again.

"We'll be going soon," Arturo said, nodding, looking east across the lagoon to the bar mouth and the slowly opening sky. Dawn was edging in, nudging a slip of palest gray along the horizon, letting me stagger about less blindly. Arturo had always impressed on me the importance of a pre-dawn start, and I detected under his current resolute optimism a fear that time was running by too fast; that Elias would be a half hour, not five minutes; that the other shark fishermen were already out there working the best reaches; that we'd miss our chance and, within hours, the weather would turn again. He began to sharpen his knives, blade to blade—long, determined strokes, ending in a conjuror's flourish. The first of the cockerels awoke, bleating red-throated, tremulous.

"Where's Elias?" Arturo muttered finally, sheathing the knives. He looked at his watch, shook it, held it to his ear. "Time to go."

We did what we could—dragged the dugout to the water's edge, sat the gasoline flat in the stern, wedged blocks in the hull to serve as seats, one behind the other—and were struggling with the outboard, our feet sliding in the mud, when Elias appeared, breathless but dressed, carrying a throw net and a clutch of hooks.

"I thought we'd need some more," he said, seeming even younger than earlier, his hair now slicked back; he was chewing a clod of white bread. He walked over and took the engine from me without explanation, and he and Arturo lowered it onto the flat-backed stern, spinning tight the butterfly screws. From there to the water it took all three of us, leaning full weight, to get the dugout to move at all; it inched heavily through the mud, leaving a shallow grave into which dark water rose uncertainly.

Elias was the last, pushing off from the stern while Arturo and I weighted the prow, leaning over each other in our efforts to cast off. When we were afloat, Elias heaved himself in, mud drooling from his knees and calves, the dugout shipping gouts of water till I scrambled to midships and, finally, we lay flat in the water, with barely an inch of clearance. Behind us, the edge-dwellers were waking: an old man took to his porch and peed noisily; Arturo's wife stood in her open doorway, blank-faced. Coconut palms were stenciled against the lightening sky. Elias wound a length of twine round the starting mechanism and knelt in the hull and pulled hard. The engine sputtered soggily. I leaned back toward Arturo.

"We're not too late?" I said. Though it was a relief, at last, to be off, I was troubled by other matters—this rickety transport, for one, and whether it would withstand a larger sea—but it was clear no good would come of airing them. This question, at least, was answerable.

Arturo laughed, pounded me on the back. "You worry too much."

The engine kicked in, a single-cylinder sneeze that spat oily smoke clear to the bank. Arturo congratulated Elias, settled on his bench seat, laid the red glove flat beside him. "You'll see," he grinned, as we juddered forward, in gear at last. "The shark—he waits for us."

To a shark hunter from the West—from North America, or Australia— equipped with 300hp cruiser and air-con cabin and satellite navigator and submarine radar and high-velocity harpoon, the approach of Arturo and his kind would have seemed laughably amateur. In Nicaragua, any man with a dugout and a hand line could turn shark hunter; it was not so much a romantic calling as a means of survival, a way to feed the family, since fins commanded high prices. The attendant danger was accepted because that was the way things had always been. In richer countries, where economic hardship seldom forced men to sea to hunt sharks, shark fishermen had become heroic figures, emblematic of a braver, simpler age.

This century's best-known shark hunter was William Young, a sturdy Californian adventurer, later naval captain, who spent his life fishing shark in Australia, Florida, and French Somaliland, but who settled in Honolulu. Known to the locals as "Kane Mano," Shark Hunter, Captain Young died aged eighty-seven, having killed, by his own estimate, a hundred thousand sharks: an average day's haul was twenty or thirty. In his dotage, reminiscing over the carnage that had been his life, his callused feet cradled in sharkskin pumps, he recalled how he'd first learned the trade: he'd kill a horse, drag it to sea, slit open its belly, then harpoon the circling sharks. To him, sharks were "arrogant," "cold," "rapacious."

From photographs, Young himself appears little more, though something else is evident, too: behind those Bakelite spectacles is a hard face, with dark, animal eyes. As he stands, clad in blood-smeared overalls, behind that strung-up fifteen-foot hammerhead, the impression is of a man who has never once questioned himself, nor anything he's done.

He died in 1962, his conscience untroubled. At that point, marine biologists had not yet isolated the shark as a threatened species; then, talk was still of the "war" with sharks, and what research there was focused on the protection of man, not fish. Shark deterrents, of variable efficacy, proliferated. The "bubble fence," invented by the owner of an eastern seaboard hotel in 1960, in response to a particularly vicious attack off the New Jersey coast, carried the boast that "sharks will not even cross it to get to a juicy steak." Which would have been excellent, if true, since the bubble fence—a perforated pipe, laid on the seabed, through which compressed air was pumped, creating a rising curtain of bubbles—was certainly cheap to produce. Unfortunately, as later tests showed, sharks parted this curtain as if it were so much gossamer.

Depth-charging, attempted first in 1958 off Margate, South Africa, was equally unsuccessful: sharks possess no swim bladder, and are thus impervious to anything other than a virtually direct hit. Indeed, the vibrations from a depth charge draw sharks almost as quickly as does the scent of blood: survivors from the U.S. destroyer *Frederick C. Davis,* torpedoed in the Atlantic on 25 April 1945, told of fellow seamen torn apart by sharks attracted to the scene by the detonation of depth charges on the sunken ship.

During the first years of World War II, the lack of an efficient, portable deterrent badly undermined the fighting spirit of U.S. forces. "Reports of shark attacks on members of our combat forces have created a wartime sea survival problem that can no longer be neglected," counseled an Army Air Corps bulletin. "The possibility of attack is a growing hazard to morale."

Triggered by President Roosevelt's personal intervention, urgent research began into the possibility of chemical deterrents. In the early 1940s, at Woods Hole Oceanographic Institute in Massachusetts, no less than seventy-nine different substances were tried out. Only one—copper acetate—proved effective, and this, blended with an inky dye, became Shark Chaser, issued to all servicemen and strapped to every life raft. It was indescribably malodorous, dead-rat funky; was, in fact, the closest chemical approximation of decomposed shark ever manufactured— which, to any half-canny fisherman, made perfect sense: no shark, however ravenous, will touch another that has been left to rot.

When all deterrents failed, and sharks broke through beach nets to kill sun-pinkened bathers and puppy dogs, men exacted disproportionate revenge. Two days after the fatal mauling of a fifteen-year-old Hawaiian surfer just before Christmas 1958, government officials and community leaders on Oahu called for nothing less than extermination of every shark that menaced their shores. Twenty-seven thousand dollars was raised to man and fuel a shark boat. Within the year, 697 sharks—snared on overnight half-mile lines—were captured and destroyed. They weren't even given the dignity of being mashed for fertilizer, the lowliest possible by-product: just incinerated, in great mounds, like the corpses of diseased cattle.

Yet now, four decades later, there was no figure more reviled by the marine biology establishment than the shark hunter. One in particular— a Queenslander, Vic Hislop, self-styled "Shark Man," with his sharktooth pendant and deep-pile chest hair, his quick line in self-justification, his highly lucrative and formidably gory "Shark Show"—has become almost an outlaw in Australia. The "authorities," he believes, are engaged in a full-scale coverup, obscuring from the public, to protect the tourist industry, the true extent of shark-related deaths off Australian coasts. In south Australia, where the great white is a protected fish, Hislop claims to have suffered police harassment, has regularly had his boat impounded. The authorities, in turn, accuse him of misleading journalists, of talking up the shark threat to keep himself and his bloodthirsty sideshow in the limelight.

In conversation Hislop comes across as garrulous, obsessed, paranoid. When I asked to meet him, he declined; when I persisted, he agreed only on condition that I pay him. I hedged; we ended up talking on the telephone. He'd grown to distrust journalists, he said: so many times he'd allowed them access to his life, had permitted camera crews to film him on the hunt, and every time he'd ended up being portrayed as a simple-minded, single-issue propagandist.

He sent me his "book," a self-published glossy brochure, in which he marshaled his arguments in full and lingered over past heroics. It was hard not to smile as the eye passed over yet another photograph of

Hislop—scrawny and diminutive, despite the Popeye posturing—leg up on yet another carcass, but there was something, some grain of the possible, in what he said. All those autopsies that read, "missing, presumed drowned"; all those swimmers and surfers whose friends had seen them sucked clean under, leaving no clue, no trace. What *had* happened to them? And what of Hislop? Had he, as he claimed, been cast out simply because his message was too unpalatable? It was not impossible.

By the time we'd reached the middle of the lagoon, still some way from the open sea, there was a slight chop on the water, the surface splintered into tiny corrugations, no longer oily-smooth. Arturo sat in the bow, I in the middle, Elias at the stern, with one hand on the tiller. We were kicking up a fine spray, which soaked us like drizzle; leaves of water spilled over the side and I bailed hard, nervous we'd founder, since we'd started with an inch in the hull and neither Elias nor Arturo seemed especially concerned.

In this spectral light I could just make out the shapes of other dories, their sails like origami triangles, inching toward the sea in the windless pre-dawn. There were twenty, perhaps more, but they made no noise, and glimmered in and out of sight, moving separately and then in convoy, floating in the pale haze as if through smoke, after a battle. When our engine died—just the fuel line coming loose, though the diagnosis took Elias a while—the voices of the other fishermen carried clear across the water, all their early-morning rumblings about cloud formations and the day's prospects, along with the hard crackle of the plastic sheeting as they roped their sails tight, the kiss of their paddles on the water, their labored breathing.

We stopped, engine off, in the lee of the mangroves at the far side of the lagoon. We needed prawns, Arturo explained, untangling the throw net: prawns would serve as bait for snapper and whitejack, which, in turn, gaffed bloody and alive, would lure the sharks. He stood in the prow, gathering the skirts of the net, taking the first corner in his teeth, laying the net in folds across his arm, then, with his breath held in, he cast it spinning over the bow. It landed a perfect circle, the lead-weighted circumference pulling the filaments down through the murk. When he pulled it up, guiding it back to the edge of the dory, it came effortlessly, shedding water from its topknot, the weights gathering the bottom shut. Only when he held it up, clear of the water, did I see that there were scores of tiny prawns in the netting, blue-gray and wriggly, snared by their whiskers.

"Ha!" Arturo said, triumphant, shaking out the net into the bottom of the boat. "A good day is coming."

The prawns spun free, bouncing off the sides of the hull; each time he repeated the maneuver they clustered more thickly round my feet, swilling about in the oily floodwater in the bottom of the hull. Arturo became ever more jubilant, convinced that their abundance was a sign—proof of the harvest to come.

As we crossed from the lagoon to the ocean, emerging from the lee of Bluff Island, the hull began to fill alarmingly. Out in this swell, the dugout, even at low revs, was shipping water over the bow and gunwales. I shouted back to Elias, pointing at my feet, which were awash to the ankles; he grinned, indicated the bailer. "A little bit of water," he said. "*Es normal.*"

Here, where the lagoon met the sea, the currents boiled and surged. It took a while to breach this section, the propeller biting air in a frantic whine as we nosed off the back of each swell, but rhythm came easier once we were clear. While I bailed, just about keeping pace with the in-fill, Arturo stretched his back and massaged his knees, using the spare bailer to ladle up the prawns, sieving them through his fingers.

"Just here," he announced abruptly.

Elias, sleepy from the start, jolted upright. "Already?"

I stopped bailing. Arturo twisted round, waved a finger at both of us. "The sea horse. This is where I see the sea horse." He eyed us eagerly, as if expecting some clamorous response. I waited. Finally, when it was clear Elias wasn't planning to speak up, I said, "Sea horse?"

"Big storm day," Arturo said, nodding. He turned back to face the sea, gesturing toward the wide horizon, toward the first nudgings upward of a huge dawn sun. He threw his voice like an orator, waving wildly with a shark hook. "I see a big reeling of water and a great animal stuck out his head and was gone."

"You were out here? In a storm?"

He held the hook in front of my face, as a teacher might, growing short-tempered. "So I get up near to where it come out and when I'm there it come right out again and it's braying as a horse, same as a horse bray—'neeigh!'—and then it was gone again. It really was a sea horse—same mane as a horse, same head, same big ears." And his eyes were wide as a horse's after all this, wholly earnest, defying disbelief. Eventually, during a lull in the engine and before the next swell hit, Elias spoke.

"Arturo, *hombre*, enough. The light is coming. Can't you see?" And he heaved the boat toward the sea again and, still grinning, opened the throttle into the waves.

Further to sea, with the pelicans banking for shore, Elias leveled our course; we were running parallel to the coastline, at least two miles distant from the dark sand and wind-beaten coconut palms that formed the beachhead. Elias would watch four, five waves ahead, turning windward or away, gunning the engine or easing off, to minimize the pitch and yaw, but still we took on water, regularly, evenly, never less than inches-deep about our feet. I bailed, but less anxiously: we were out here now; the sky, now dawn had fully come, seemed to threaten nothing more than flat, absolute heat; nothing was looming; the far rim of cumulus seemed easeful, unhurried. But whenever I dropped my shoulders and, forgetting, emptied less determinedly, water filled steadily. "Eduardo!" Arturo would shout, looking round. "Your job!"

He was crouched forward in the prow, knees to his chest, backside uncomfortably on our anchor of rude-welded rods. With a scrubber of steel wool he was working through the six-inch shark hooks, concentrating on the point and barb, buffing till the steel showed through again. His equipment was aging and eclectic: the link sections, the "trace" between hook and line, which in the collection of a better-off shark fisherman would have comprised three-foot strips of tempered steel wire, were, in his case, corroded sections of chain, scavenged from other machinery.

From here, far offshore, the coast stretched to infinity: south to Costa Rica, Panama, Colombia; north to Pearl Lagoon, Cape Gracias, Honduras, the United States. It was at Pearl Lagoon, some days earlier, that the mayor, like the old logger who'd entrusted me with his letter for the Queen, had pleaded with me, as an Englishman, to mobilize my government to rid his people of "the Spaniards." If I did not, he warned, revolution was inevitable. "If these Spaniards don't stop thieving all our natural resources—all our timbers and fish—then we will have no choice but to fight. Every man here will fight."

Up those inland waterways, north from Bluefields, where once Dutch and English buccaneers hid their schooners from the Spanish overlords, where spreading mangroves and shifting sandbars constantly kept fishermen and campesinos on their guard, the bull shark lurked. Pearl Lagoon had a narrow, silted bar, dividing ocean from freshwater lagoon, and its fishermen spoke of it with dread.

Hard to imagine, traveling this coast and hearing such stories, that any shark could have ever been dismissed as "wretched" or "cowardly," but a U.S. Army manual, published before World War II, attempted just such vapid reassurance. "The shark is a cowardly fish which moves about slowly, and is easily frightened by surprises in the water, noise, movement and unusual shapes. This last point alone would be enough for a shark not to attack man." And, should one confound expectation and do just that, then all the alert marine had to do was pull a knife and "open up its stomach . . . you cause water to enter—that will kill it almost instantaneously."

Misunderstood creatures, feared and worshiped in equal measure. In the Solomon Islands, before the missionaries came, sharks were kept as captive gods, corralled in sacred caverns, appeased by regular human sacrifice. William Ellis, an early-nineteenth-century missionary, observed similar practices in the Archipel de la Société: "Temples were erected in which priests officiated, and offerings were presented to the deified sharks, while fishermen and others, who were much at sea, sought their favour."

Ancient Hawaiians, too, valued the shark, but more for its potential as entertainment: at Pearl Harbor, Hawaiian kings ordered underwater jousts between ravenous, penned-in sharks and gladiators armed only with shark-teeth swords. In the 1920s, Fijians were observed "shark-charming," a skill unheard of anywhere else. A French missionary, who'd witnessed islanders kissing sharks into submission, reported, more than a little stunned: "It's some occult power they have which I can't define, but once the native kisses it, that shark never moves again."

There were no such eccentricities with the bull shark. All the Costeños comprehended was that most basic rule, that a dorsal fin above the surface meant a hungry shark, though undisturbed calm was, conversely, no guarantee of safety. Like the great white, the bull shark as often foraged underwater, breaking the surface only at the last moment, jaws stretched to a perfect, serrated oval.

It was as stealthy as it was unpredictable, taking squid, sea urchin, crab, stingray, porpoise, whale, other shark, and each other: if one bull shark was injured in a food fight, the others would tear it to pieces in seconds. Its memory for blood was unerring, and it was impossible to read, "always inclined," according to a 1962 paper in the *Journal of the Royal Naval Medical Service*, "to be offensive . . . a particularly ferocious species which will attack large fish without apparent provocation and not for food."

Only gradually, and with the accumulation of years of data from marine biologists, coast guards, and fishermen, was a full portrait of the bull shark beginning to emerge. Off the shores of Natal, in South Africa, where once it was assumed that the near-mythical great white was responsible for most deaths, it now appeared that the pig-eyed bull shark, a good deal more compact, with its disproportionately large incisors, accounted for something like four times the number of victims. It was the hardiest of all tropical sharks, the most resilient to change, and it was able to survive many years in captivity with less stress than any other. Its depredations on the Ganges, preying on the half-burned bodies thrown from sacred ghats, were most often blamed on the Ganges shark, *Glyphis gangeticus*, but this in truth was a needle-toothed softie, a mere plankton-sifter by comparison.

As to why all this should be, there was little agreement. Certainly the bull shark's taste for both fresh and brackish water had brought it into close and regular contact with animals and men, and where the pickings are easy, so sharks make their home. A hundred years ago, Charles Napier Bell, a longtime Bluefields resident, recorded in his memoirs that "there is no harbour in the world more dangerous for sharks than Greytown"—modern-day San Juan del Norte, the settlement at the mouth of the San Juan, for which I was headed—and so it remained.

In these waters the bull shark scavenged ceaselessly, swallowing whole anything that tumbled from the bank: orange peel, empty rum bottles, stones, twigs. Along the turbid coast, and in the heavily silted rivers and mangrove waterways, with visibility often down to zero, it had developed a preternatural olfactory sense: at a hundred meters, a single drop of blood was lure enough.

And now we were heading south, to a lone cay so small it was still invisible, ancestral property of the Rama Indians, who, whenever the ocean was calm enough, would paddle across from the mainland to tend their microplantation and fish for shark. The lee of the island, Arturo said, was rich with fish, though he had discovered this only by accident, stranded late one afternoon when the wind had turned on him: the next dawn, casting from the rocks, waiting for better weather, he'd landed three big sharks. He wasn't sure why the cay had proved so abundant, what aquatic alchemy had produced such a swarming, but had made sure of one thing: he'd told no other shark fishermen, and though they had grown suspicious, and often quizzed him and Elias, none of them had an outboard and so never managed to follow the two men much further than the bar.

Ideally, he said, we should have made it there at dawn, but things had taken longer than anticipated. But he remained confident, yelling out at first glimpse of the cay—a distant thumb-smudge splintered by the heat haze—breaking off to point out flying fish, which flitted weightless across the water, flashing like chain mail. We drank luke-warm coffee from Arturo's flask, and above the noise of the engine threw out theories about what best attracted shark.

Blood, we all knew, was the surest lure, even in minute quantity; so too, Arturo held, were vomit, offal, garbage, and carrion—all rank-smelling, signaling easy pickings. Elias, who'd seen a friend taken on Bluefields bar, believed there was something in the flailings of pan-icked or inexperienced swimmers that triggered a shark's aggression: perhaps because the vibrations felt like those of a wounded fish.

From what I'd learned, it seemed that almost anything could pro-voke attack, anything unusual, particularly any large impact: more sailors, according to one breathtaking statistic, were taken by sharks in the worst World War II shipwrecks than had been killed in attacks close to shore in all of recorded history.

Sharks, so the thinking goes, have hearing acute as a trip wire, and the commotion of a ship going down or a plane scything into the sea draws them from hundreds of miles away. The torpedoing off Natal on 18 November 1942 of the English troopship *Nova Scotia*, for example, left 850 dead, from a total of 1,042; according to survivors' estimates, more than half—young men, able swimmers all, adrift in bath-warm seas—were taken by sharks.

The sinking of the Philippine ferry *Doña Paz* on 20 December 1987 was more sanguinary still: the ship, though authorized to carry only 608 passengers, was that night wedged with between 3,000 and 4,000 villagers returning home for New Year fiestas. At ten that evening the ferry was rammed portside by an oil tanker. Both vessels exploded. Those who weren't burned alive jumped into the raging sea, aslick with flame. Only twenty-five survived; over the next few days, three hundred shark-mutilated corpses were found littered on island shores, and for weeks afterward, Philippine fishermen reported finding body parts in the belly of almost every shark they landed.

In the crescent lee of the island Elias cut the engine; we drifted toward a steep, rocky beach. Though the day was near windless, there was a heavy swell, which smashed to broken foam on the red cliffs seaward. It was not much of a place—five hundred yards long, crested with stunted coconut and banana trees, with a high-tide scurf of plastic sandals and bleached aluminium drink cans and hard-dried seaweed.

"Iguana Cay!" Arturo shouted, standing upright in the prow. We nosed toward the beach, pitching in the swell, Elias behind me yelling instructions—when to jump, remember to take the rope. The water was warm here, a generous turquoise, opaque with sea life.

Grabbing the rope, Arturo jumped for shore, disappearing to his waist, paddling his arms against the suck of the swell, making it to the dry rocks soaked and breathing heavily. He beckoned me to follow, ordering Elias to stay out, drop anchor, and set the bait lines. Arturo was grinning now, as if just pleased to have made it this far. While I hesitated on the bow, wondering whether to launch off heedless, or lower myself more gently and swim for it, he held the rope loose, letting the dugout rest easy a few yards offshore. When I finally leapt forward, expecting a last-yard flounder to land, I sank to my neck. Something brushed my calf. I kicked into breast stroke, fired with panic and the certainty that, in this warm gloop, I'd get no warning of a shark, just that bleak numbness as my leg went.

"Shark," I panted as I crawled onto the beach. I struggled breathless to my feet, tried to smile.

"If you'd come two days ago," Arturo said, ignoring my flailings, giving me his hand, "you could have had this."

He pointed to the remains of a fire, set at the crest of the beach, on flat, slatelike rocks. Scattered through the cold ashes were the bones of a hammerhead, about six feet long. The head—skin stretched tight, graypurplish in color—looked unlike any earthly living thing, an alien mutant with smoked-glass eyes set at the far edges of an airfoil skull. It would have been caught off these rocks by the Rama Indians, Arturo said, roasted and eaten the same day, its sandpapery hide cut into strips and used "to scrub the smoke from the bottom of pots." What was left of the spine—featherweight disks of ivory cartilage—would serve as counters on a homemade checkerboard. The smell, though the fish had been stripped clean and only its barest outline remained, was as potent as if from weeks of decay, sun-stewed to ulcerous softness. With a stick, I lifted the head and out of the scimitar mouth, frozen ajar, crawled fat flies, too lazy to take to the air, their wings and feet wet with feasting.

Arturo was up at the far end of the beach, trousers rolled to his knees, the material drying in streaks. He'd cut himself a spear from the bush and was sharpening one end to a pencil point.

"Iguana," he said. "Sharks eat anything, but they love iguana." This cay, he said, was thick with them, hence its name; they had been stranded here when the island split from the mainland. He grinned, confident in his mastery of history. "Millions of years ago this was the coast." He stabbed his spear into the red-clay cliff. "Come. Let's hunt."

He walked ahead, negotiating the narrow strip of dry rocks under the cliff, and I followed. We left the beach behind us as we headed for the point. Further on, the rocks became boulders, black as lead and coated with white deposit. Every few yards Arturo would stop, hold his spear above his head, and lecture me, the sea warm as tea about our ankles. For centuries, he said, the cay had been Rama property. The Indians cultivated bananas and coconuts, hunted shark and, rarer these days, the hawksbill turtle, with its perfect, mottled carapace. They'd be out here every three weeks or so, whenever the weather allowed, fishing from two or three dories, onto which they'd heap their plunder and paddle hard, on uncertain seas, back to the mainland.

Iguana Cay, Arturo believed, constituted the most abundant fishing area of the whole Miskito Bank. And, so far, it remained his and the Ramas' secret: even Maximo, when I'd asked him to name the best sharking grounds, had cited Punta Gorda, a rocky promontory some way further south. So: given all this, I wanted to know, why did the Ramas let Arturo—a Miskito with Creole blood, hardly a natural ally—fish these gold-dust waters?

"How can they stop me?" he said, spearing into the shallows, after a darting of color. "I'm here and then I'm gone. I have an engine—not one of them has an engine. This is the way it is. There's nothing they can do."

Further on, as we came out of the lee, Arturo gave a little holler and fell to his knees. "What did I say?" He was speaking as much to himself as to me, chuckling like a happy-fed animal. As he stood up again and I came alongside I saw he'd speared a lizard of some sort. It hung limply and smelled poisoned, as bad as the hammerhead on the beach.

"It's dead," I said, meaning that it had been dead a while, surely too long to be of much use to us. "It stinks. What is it?"

Arturo looked at me sorrowfully, as if amazed all over again at my failure to learn. "Iguana."

"I thought they needed to be fresh."

"Sharks eat anything." He gripped it by the tail, lifted it off the spike, yelled across to Elias in the dugout. "Catch this!" And with one broad arc he slung the iguana nose-first, high into the sky. It flew a perfect trajectory, diving legs out toward Elias, who waited, arms wide, a good forty yards from our rocks. It was a near-flawless throw, missing Elias's lap by inches, hitting the gunwale and smacking the water, waiting there a second before coughing out bubbles and sinking into the blue. Elias dropped his line, plunged in his arm, and caught the iguana, water drooling from its open jaws.

"Keep it," Arturo shouted. "There'll be more."

At the point, where the high-tide mark was a spine of plastic debris and the sea wind felt more muscular, scurrying low through the banana trees, I came upon something far odder: a bag made from what looked like burlap, no bigger than two cupped hands, hung from a low-jutting root. It was weighted full, and was greasy to the touch; inside was a honey-colored mass.

"Shark liver," Arturo said, coming from behind, knocking it with the end of his spear.

"From the hammerhead?"

"Probably." It had been left here, some way from the carcass, to discourage rodents. Shark oil, Arturo added, setting off again across the rocks, "cures asthma, lots of illness we don't know about."

He was relishing this chance to act the guide, to work me over with his knowledge. Observing me balk at the very fact of garbage in a place this remote, he turned sensitive environmentalist. "This," he shook his head gravely, "is the modern face of paradise." He played to my weakness for shark lore, summoning wilder and ever-more-implausible stories, watching with pleasure as I gaped, incredulous. When we startled to flight a covey of leather-winged birds, big and black as ravens, and I asked him what they were, he led me away from the shore, toward the banana trees, and at every step would pick up a leaf, or a seedpod, and list its medicinal uses and aphrodisiac properties. Young coconut leaf, he said, made fine tea. Another—"bird wine"—was "medicine for the liver: when you drink it, your pee is like water."

In a clearing, he cut a sapling, long as a jousting lance, and lunged upward into the canopy of a coconut palm till three coconuts thumped to earth: hard green ovals, the size of rugby balls. He picked up each in turn, ground their points into the base of the tree trunk, then tore away the husks. "Who needs knives?" he said, taking a rock to the first, naked-whiskered nut, passing it to me, holding it up like a goblet. "Go on, drink."

This small cay, he said, had everything a man could need: palms for roofing, a type of year-round grape, even a tangled ground cover that produced whorls of cotton. The seaward edge was a shallow slant of red rock, graveled with the shells of tiny crabs, up which the ocean hissed and moaned. And at this point, growing tired, Arturo tried to cut back to the beach, but here the plantation was at its most overgrown, the banana trees choked with creepers and underbrush grown hard as wire.

"The morning's getting hotter," he muttered impatiently, as if it were somehow my fault. "We've got to get on."

As we came round the point once more, back into the lee of the island, Elias was standing in the boat, waving and shouting. He wanted us back on board and was yelling at us to run. He waved an arm at the water immediately around him, barked a further flurry of indecipherable yelps, and Arturo, shouting something back, broke into a run, leaping from boulder to boulder.

The tide had risen steadily, making the way back to the beach treacherous, with few dry footings, but he moved fast and lightly, one hand against the cliff for balance, standing, finally, in the shallows on the beach, hauling on the anchor rope. I was slower, and less sure, and by the time I reached the beach Arturo was already aboard and Elias had restarted the engine.

We anchored mid-bay, fifty yards offshore, the westerly gradually building, pushing us hard against the anchor, making the lines sing. The bait lines were nylon, with lead sinkers, with a single-barbed hook skewered through the pale jelly flesh of two prawns. Elias and Arturo lassoed theirs out effortlessly, and it took me a little while longer to learn this, how to have the line flying weightless through the palm, how to draw it back through the water at that certain depth, how to strike—knowingly, not too fast—and, just as crucial, how to play the part of the gnarled sea dog, impassive, none too easily impressed, unchanging as the sun.

For ten, fifteen minutes, we hooked fish as fast as we could get the lines out. Even I, the novice, whom Elias and Arturo eyed uncertainly, could do no wrong; I'd strike too early, or not at all, and still would haul up catch: red snapper, whitejack, hammering their tails in the oily slop about our ankles. The snapper, Arturo said, playing in another, just feet from the boat, was Jesus' fish, the one that fed the five thousand, and still bore his fingerprints: twin dark smudges, either side of the spine, just behind the dorsal fin. And he clasped the fish between flat palms, its gills still flexing, looked hard into its bleak ball-bearing eyes, and spat into its oval pout.

"That's good luck." He winked and tossed the snapper, mouthing furiously, into the squirming hull.

"When I was a kid," he said later—soaked through but beaming, big hands paying back the line as delicately as a seamstress, having just landed the biggest snapper so far—"all the creeks in Bluefields, the whole lagoon, all down this coast, all were infested with sharks. You couldn't swim nowhere. But then, in the fifties and sixties, they started to buy them for their fins and meat and the sharks started to get wild, to disappear."

"You mean the sharks somehow knew what was happening?" We'd both hauled in and were just sitting there, growing stiff on our haunches, rocking in the swell, the sea knocking hollow against the hull. "They understood?"

Arturo held up a finger. "In certain ways," he said, turning to check on Elias's line, then testing mine too, "they are smart animals. They have a way to survive just like we do. Whenever you kill the animal, and it bleeds, it never goes to that place again."

"But here?" He'd returned to this cay many times: why had the sharks not yet worked this out?

"Some places"—he tapped a finger against his nose—"they will always come back to." Iguana Cay, with its unique confluence of marine life, the way the undersea shelf rose up here, delivering abundance and variety on a scale unknown anywhere else along the Miskito Coast, would always prove irresistible. He leaned forward. "Let me tell you something. Listen to this, then tell me what you think."

He talked, keeping his line taut. "A few months ago, I was out here, in this very spot, with Elias." He nudged Elias with his mahogany fish club; Elias, looking down, smiled. Arturo was baiting up again as he spoke, and as he stood to cast his line I noticed dark movement beneath the surface, midway between us and the shore, working transverse, closing on us.

"Arturo," I said, wanting him to look too, but he was warming to his story, and would not be diverted.

"So we were here, four in the morning, we'd spent the night on the cay. Very dark, the moon was new." He was watching his line now, but dreamily, only half focused. "And all of a sudden, after an hour of nothing, we hook a shark of a hundred and fifty pounds. Big enough,

I tell you, but not a monster. I've got it on the rope, it's hooked well and good, and it fights a big fight. I'm on my knees, Elias is keeping the boat steady. . . ."

At the edge of my vision I saw the dark shape again, and this time nearer the beach; Elias, whose line was paid out that way, jolted upright and started round. Arturo, oblivious, talked on.

"Did you see that, Arturo?" I blurted.

Arturo stopped still, let his line hang loose in his hands. "What?"

"A big fish. Shark?" I pointed to where I'd seen the movement, but now there was nothing; now I was seeing shadows everywhere, the surface of the water splintered into sky, beach, red cliff, its own deep turquoise.

"Shark?" Arturo repeated, looking across my head to Elias. "Shark?"

Elias nodded. "*Creo, pero no estoy seguro.* I'm not sure."

"*Muy bien,*" Arturo said, softening. "So we haul in. We've got enough bait." There was a sudden shimmy on his line, a guitar-string quiver, but he continued at the same pace, hand over hand, and started where he'd left off, playing out the story as he wound in his line: unhurried, deliberate, conscious.

"So, after fifteen minutes, perhaps twenty," he went on, "I'm getting the shark close to the boat. I can see him down there, diving and fighting, but I know he's getting tired. I've got the rope, I'm sitting down, he's getting closer and closer. And then—" He clapped his hands together, opened his palms to the sky; his voice rose, rapturous. "Then the water gets BIG, I can't see what's happening, everything goes white and churned up and when it calms down the line's gone slack." He paused. Elias was motionless, turned toward Arturo, his line loose over his knees, mouth open.

"So what do I do?" Arturo continued, his eyes enormous. I can feel weight, but no movement. What's happened to this shark?" Again, that pause. "Only one way to find out: pull on the rope, hard as God allows." He grinned at Elias, who snorted into the back of his hand. "It comes up fast, oh my God too fast, and the sea turns from blue to red and at the last moment, just when I realize, just when it's too late, the whole thing is flying out of the water toward me."

"The whole shark?"

"No! Just the head! The whole rest of it was bitten off. Just the head is left on my hook, just the head flies out of the water and lands in my lap."

Elias was shaking with silent laughter. "Just the head," he repeated, in a hoarse whisper. "Just the head." He reached across, knuckled Arturo in the ribs.

At that moment, no more than ten yards ahead of us, the sea turned to milkshake. Arturo, in the middle, jolted forward, threw an arm against the gunwale to steady himself, his bait line sprang free of the water, loosing drops all down its length. Then it snapped. No whip crack, no dramatic high note, just a tangle of soggy nylon thread, half in the boat, half out. The water, still again momentarily, broke one last time: a sharp, dark outline cut free, then disappeared into foam of its own creation, like a diver's flippers, giving one last kick.

"*Sangre de Dios,*" Arturo breathed. "Get those shark lines out."

Yet for the next half-hour, with all three lines baited with snapper, all was quiet. We said little, Arturo and Elias convinced a strike was imminent. Arturo laid his red glove over the gunwale in front of him, and from time to time touched it with reverence.

"Arturo?"

"*Sí?*"

"What happens if we hook a three-hundred, four-hundred-pound shark? What good's your glove going to be then?"

"My glove," he sighed, "is so the rope don't burn my hand. A big shark will haul the canoe round and round as he looks for deep water." He smiled, guardedly. "We're going to have to play him really hard." We'd fight it to the beach, land and kill it there; after that, somehow, we'd heave it into the dugout and make for the mainland.

Two pelicans were circling us, almost colorless against the sky, cutting low over the cay and back again, making an odd clicking sound; they moved their wings little, setting and readjusting to the warm updrafts, passing between us and the sun, maintaining their distance.

It was getting hotter: I had only a baseball cap for shade and kept shifting the peak round, trying to protect my neck. Unused to such intense direct sun, my face and neck liquid with sweat, I tried to scoop up seawater to cool me down, but at the surface it was almost blood temperature and the salt when it dried made me even thirstier. Arturo, seeing me struggle, offered coffee from his flask: "Hot is good, it cools you down." Which was fine in theory, but didn't take into account the quantity of sugar he'd stirred in; so I sipped, and thanked him, and handed it quickly back.

Arturo speared the iguana onto an extra hook, its belly splitting easily as soaked paper, a guff of bad-egg air as the innards bulged through. He threw it from the bow and it hit the water heavily, floating tail-up for a few seconds before sinking abruptly, in a cough of bubbles. He looped the line around the plank on which he sat.

"It's really going to go for that?" Here, where there was no shortage of fresh snapper and succulent whitebait?

Arturo turned, smiled. "Well, we'll see."

In my imagination, the monster I'd glimpsed out there in the shallows would have had no problem with a putrefying iguana, could indeed, if the mood struck it, have swallowed the dugout, all three of us, the outboard and gas tank, whole, with one dilation of its industrial-sized gullet.

Ever since childhood I had feared and been drawn to the ocean, its unseen depths, and when long ago had learned of *Carcharodon megalodon*, the prehistoric shark, this fear seemed nothing less than reasonable. Here was a fish whose fossilized teeth were six inches long; whose gape, face on, measured a good ten feet in diameter; whose length, nose to tail, reached well over a hundred feet. Or "reaches," rather, since it is argued that *megalodon* is no more extinct than "megamouth," a soot-colored plankton sifter unknown to science until 1976, when a fourteen-foot specimen was snagged in netting by a U.S. Navy research boat. The evidence for *megalodon*'s continued existence is inconclusive, but certainly plausible: early in this century, some four incisors were dredged from the bottom of the Pacific—"real" teeth, not fossils—

which could not have been down there for long, since early dredging equipment was only robust enough to scrape the shallowest trench. So, I imagined, somewhere down there, beyond the tropical cays and reefs and turtle grounds, the great fish lurked still, seldom surfacing from the very deep, and only then for swift, spectacular meals: whole lines of shrimp pots, half a seal colony.

However, neither Arturo, gazing out across the water, nor Elias, lying back against the engine with his cap pulled low over his face, seemed to share any of my sense of foreboding. This was Arturo's livelihood and, over the decades, as shark had become scarcer and the price of fins had risen, he'd turned ever more wily, lying to the other fishermen when they'd pressed him for his favorite spots, setting deliberately misleading trails, dropping clues that led his rivals in the exact opposite direction from the one toward which he was headed. And as the business had changed, so had the fishermen: in the 1960s, when fins were plentiful and were off-loaded for a mere twenty-five cents a pound, they all worked together, secure in the knowledge that there was enough for everyone. Now, with fins scarcer, and fetching upwards of thirty-five dollars a pound, the fishermen operated alone, suspicious of one another, jealously protective of whatever special knowledge they had acquired, drying their catch in secret, smuggling the fins to Maximo under cover of darkness.

With the heat of the sun and the slop of machine oil and rotten water, the fish in the hull were beginning to smell; the snappers were blanching, their eyes gone puffy, tiny whorls of excreta trailing out behind. Arturo, in a low murmur that had almost sent Elias to sleep and was close to achieving the same effect on me, was reminiscing about the old days of plenty, mentioning names I'd never heard, places I'd never been.

It filled me with sadness, this downward curve in fortunes that had been his working life, this struggle to eke a living from ever-diminishing resources, but whenever I started to offer sympathy, he shook his head, stopped me with an upheld hand. Just listen, his silent gesture instructed me. Hear me out.

• • •

Suddenly, with a yelp, Elias was awake. He'd tied his line round his wrist and now, desperately, was struggling against pressure to work it free. "I've got one, I've got one," he jabbered, the line tight toward the beach. Eventually he managed to untie it and throw it loose, but the slack disappeared in an instant. He wrapped the engine rag round his hand and braced himself, the line flexing into deep water off the stern, so tight it shivered the surface.

"What is it?" I was leaning over, trying to catch its shadow. But Elias didn't seem to hear; he was focused, taking line as the fish stalled, paying out again as it cut underneath us. When it surfaced—Elias arched against it, his back bowed with the strain—it came very fast, thrashing against the side of the boat: sinewy, black, a big cobra's jaw, straining at the hook.

"Barracuda!" Elias shouted, jubilant. He ordered me to stay back, and he and Arturo wrestled it aboard. It was three or four feet long, thick as a fire hose, with a wolf's fangs and a menacing underbite. Its tall pounded our legs; its teeth snapped at the air. Arturo gripped the club, about to complete the kill, but seemed suddenly as mesmerized as I, immobile, watching the great fish slowly die. It seemed unlike anything I'd ever seen or imagined, an unholy hybrid of serpent and mile-deep sightless groper, distorted almost to humanness by its great vampire mouth.

As it lay there, sucking in ever slower, its gill leaves breezing smaller and smaller flutters, I felt my line tug once, then twice: persistent, heavyweight fumblings.

"Arturo . . . ," I said, testing the tension, unsure. "What's this? What do I do?" Strike? Leave alone?

Arturo, up in the prow, didn't answer. He was holding his line between thumb and forefinger and concentrating hard. I saw his hand clench, unclench, and he reached for the glove, forced in his fingertips and yanked it on with his teeth.

"Shark?" I said, speaking as much to myself as to him. I'd had a heavier take, then a deadweight, not what I expected it to feel like.

"Possibly." He grinned, toothy as the barracuda. "Oh, yes, just possibly." His line was running fast through his glove, slack spooling from his lap. And then again, harder this time, I felt my line go, burning my skin as it ripped away.

"Let it run!" Arturo shouted at me, still focused hard on his own. "Let it take it and tire itself out."

I tore off my cap, forced it flat into my hand as protection, but in the half-second it took to change grip I lost my last five meters of line and it sprang hard against its backstop, the plank seat, out of my hand.

"What now?"

"Take it up," Arturo said, doing the same himself, hand over hand. "It won't take long."

Mine played erratically—compliant, then brutish, sometimes almost teasing. Shark, Arturo said: we must have hit a number, all hunting, all at the same time. We'd have got three if Elias hadn't been struggling to untangle his line. I wondered about his diagnosis, though: I was no strongman, yet was able to fight it with my own hands.

Elias, in the stern, had dropped his line and was instructing me, miming the necessary actions, how much pressure I should be applying, when to tighten up and when to play it easy. He ran salt water through his hair, pasted it flat to his skull, and leaned close to me; I could feel his heat, the smell of last night's beer and frijoles.

"There!" He pointed off the stern, no more than ten yards: a pale racing of color, like a seal's back, just below the surface.

"That's it." Arturo beamed. "What did I say?" His fish was hard by the boat now, his line plumbing vertically into the sun-slanted water. I stole glances at him, realizing this might be my only lesson, but every time I did so I lost grip of my own line, letting run too much slack so that the fish dived fast the next moment and slammed hard against the gunwale. Arturo seemed able to watch both at once—checking on me, following his own weaving line as he drew it ever nearer—and when he swept his fish into the boat it was with a simple, unbroken movement.

It hit the bottom writhing: a four-foot shark with filmy cat's eyes and a tail that smashed about wildly, soaking me with fish-scaly water. The extra weight sank us perilously low and at every swell now we were shipping water. Elias grabbed the bailer; the water he slung out was dark, smeared with prawns and entrails of snapper and tubercular clots of engine oil.

"You, now," Arturo said, ignoring his own shark, which lay agasp in the hull, hook still through its bottom jaw.

"What do I do?" It felt as though it was directly below us, switching direction like a caged animal.

"It's getting tired." He leaned forward, shielded his eyes from the sun. "Bring it up. Slowly."

I could have drawn in quicker, but I could feel my muscles cramping. Arturo was right: the fish did seem to be slowing, and only once did it draw away strongly enough for the line to pull through my hand. As I brought it closer, it seemed almost to be cowering from us, pulling the line back under the hull as it stuck to the boat's shadow.

"Bring it in now," Arturo said, hands braced on the edge of the boat.

"But I can't see it."

"It's there. Lift it out."

I half stood, just enough to see where the line entered the water. The shark was there, split lengthways by our shadow, hanging motionless as if it knew exactly the way this was going. I could feel it trembling down the wire, and knew it could feel me too, both of us new to this, both anxious rookies. After all my dreams of hooking a monster, this one seemed disappointingly small, something of a consolation prize, docilely waiting.

I wrapped the line round both hands and pulled hard. The shark was heavy, and its head tilted stiffly, rucking creases across its back. It was so still, and the underside of its throat and belly was pale as linen in the sunlight just below the surface. The hook glittered as I hoisted the fish toward vertical.

"Finish it quickly," Arturo muttered. "Get it out."

But I couldn't. I leaned harder against it, my knees on the gunwale, but could bring it no further than the surface. Maneuvering it underwater, weightless, had been easy: hauling it aboard, fighting its true weight, felt impossible. The shark itself, half comatose, did nothing to help: basking in the warmth, sun on its back, bewildered and exhausted by the struggle, it was resting against me, its weight against the hook.

"Give me a hand," I said, but Arturo, anticipating, was already at my shoulder, ordering Elias to the other side of the boat.

"Come on," he said. "Now! You pull!" And he knelt in the boat, in the blood and oil and fish scales, and plunged his arms into the water. With his face almost submerged he grabbed the shark round its middle, shouted at me to lift and together we hoisted it clear of the water. "Now in the boat!" he shouted. "Quick!"

Halfway over, the shark hammered sideways, knocking me to the floor. Arturo still had a hold on its tail, but it was flailing crazily now, its jaw locked open, strips of snapper caught in its teeth. I tried to stand, but the boat was rocking and taking water and I was dizzied by the knock, so I stayed where I was, certain they were both about to land on me. The shark was corkscrewing through Arturo's grasp, like a too-big child not wanting to be dressed. Arturo trod backward and slumped into the prow and the mess of netting and, forced back by the weight of the fish, sat down heavily, the shark kicking away from him. For a second, it lay still on the bottom of the boat. Elias, looking up from bailing, hooted.

"Bastard," Arturo breathed, his chest heaving.

"How are we going to get back?" Elias said. The stern was leaking fast. Left much longer, the shark would have been able to swim free.

"Take in the anchor," Arturo snapped. We'd pull onto the beach, off-load nonessentials. "Where's my club?" He groped behind himself, through the heap of netting, scooped a hand through the hull-slop. I saw it before he did: floating near Elias's feet, half-submerged, clean and dark as a bone. I hooked it with my foot and lifted it out.

Arturo knelt in the hull between the two sharks. His, landed ten minutes earlier, had stilled; mine, startled momentarily on capture, was now beating about wildly again, one arching muscle, drumming the side of the boat. Its head was up, showing the hook and the bloodless wound through its underjaw, torn ragged by its fighting. It shouldered forward, then slid back toward the stern, and its skin against my calves was like emery paper.

"Hold it there," Arturo ordered, twisting round to get an angle on its skull. I tried to steady it round its middle, leaning my whole weight forward, but it surged and pounded. Arturo forced his knee onto its back until only its tail was moving and struck it on the snout, between the eyes; through its body I felt a shiver of electricity. Again and again he clubbed it, until and beyond the point when it was clearly dead and had ceased to even twitch. There was no blood, nothing to suggest pain, no rolling of the eyes, just a soft indent where he'd hammered it repeatedly. He closed his eyes halfway through, and when he handed back the club, his head was still bowed. He lay back in the bow, on the rubbish and bottles and netting, pulled his cap down over his eyes and folded his arms tight across his chest. His hands were shaking.

We left the anchor buried in undergrowth and drained the dugout on the beach as best we could. It was after midday now, and too hot to continue fishing. Yet, just off the cay, heading for the mainland, Elias hooked another. He'd been trailing his line experimentally, using the last, most fetid snapper as bait. The shark he hauled in was bovine, almost comatose, though a good foot longer than the other two. It was a nurse shark, Arturo said—the color of the seafloor, freckled with pale spots. Arturo reached over the side and he and Elias heaved it aboard.

He shook his head, disappointed. "Not dangerous. He lives in the rocks, eats lobster, crabs." Yet, stranded at our feet, half the snapper still in its mouth, it clung on longer than the other two, its gills whispering in and out until we were almost home. Seeing it there, purblind, helpless, I wished we'd put it back, since its seal-soft fins were worthless and its meat was fatty and cloying, but Arturo wanted to show it to his neighbors' children, let them tug its fleshy whiskers and run their fingers along its milk teeth, so we wedged it in the hull. Arturo sharpened his knife on its side, flipping the blade in the sunlight, his eyes unfocused, shoulders heavy.

• • •

It was hard to imagine, having witnessed the ease of Arturo's baited-hook technique, that shark fishermen had ever practiced anything else, but in Micronesia, until midway through this century, hunters used snares woven from plant fibers. Tied like a noose, the snare was lowered from a canoe, and seashells were rattled in the water to draw the shark, which was then teased through the loop by the lure of bloody meat. It took time, this method, and patience too, since any panicky movements startled off the fish: slowly, with a steady hand, the noose was drawn over the head, and was tightened as it passed the gill slits. Maoris, who prized unchipped center teeth as earrings, perfected the method: hooks, they knew, wreaked dental mayhem.

Early hooks were of bone or wood. Hawaiian chieftains bequeathed their skeletons for the carving of hooks, although, throughout the islands, bones of great fishermen were judged equally propitious. To prepare wooden hooks, young ironwood branches were lashed into tight Us, and released only when they'd hardened into shape. And always, whatever their constituent materials, the hooks were speared with the oiliest and bloodiest bait fish. Sharks can sniff food at five hundred meters—one part mammal blood, according to researchers, in a hundred million parts water—and even their eyesight, once thought weaker than that of most fish, was, in poor light, a good ten times more sensitive than man's.

We took a different way back, a shorter route to shore, heading for the south entrance to the Bluefields lagoon. We rode with the swell, which had strengthened since we'd been fishing and now tipped us firmly back, with a sense of barely contained power. In part this change of route was of necessity, since to return northward would have meant taking the swell side-on, but in part it was because Arturo wanted to fish for prawn alongside the mangroves again, and these southern mangroves were the best.

Pelicans followed us, watching for floundering fish where the water shallowed and boiled. With each swell, each shove toward shore, the sea lost its luminous turquoise and became darker and muddier.

Arturo, up in the bow, was shouting back orders to Elias: keep straight, hard left now, that's it, steady. The shallower we got, the more opaque the water became. Arturo tried to avoid riding the waves, but at points this was impossible, and we'd crest with a great howl as the outboard reared out of the water. And then, beyond the bar, in an instant the water was deep again and I smelled the dirt of the warm land, saw once more the grackles overhead above the forest and felt relieved, more than I'd ever guessed I'd feel, to be heading for the safety of streets and buildings.

Through the lagoon mouth, into the lagoon itself: the water was a mile wide here, and with forest so brightly green the color looked painted on. Above the canopy towered spikes, like outsize telegraph poles—all that remained of the coconut palms that had survived the hurricane, a decade earlier.

"Everything you see," Arturo said, indicating the new forest, the way it crowded the water's edge, "all of it has pushed up since the big storm."

"Even the mangroves?" They seemed so sturdy, immovable, their claw roots thick as a man's legs.

"When the hurricane came," he answered, turning back to face the front, "everything went down. Only five houses in Bluefields remained standing. And the forest—all that was destroyed. From the town you could see straight out to sea—no roofs or walls stood in your way."

Ahead I noticed three dories, smaller than ours, struggling under tarpaulin sails. They scarcely seemed to be moving at all, and their sails sagged motionless.

I watched all this half-dreaming, aware that soon I'd be moving on, tracking the bull sharks south, to the San Juan River, and beyond. I wanted Arturo to join me—had wanted this, in fact, ever since he'd said he had family there. San Juan del Norte, the settlement at the river mouth, was by all accounts a pirate town, not much different now than it had been two and a half centuries before, and I figured Arturo could ease my way. He'd intimated more than once that he'd been planning just this trip for a few years now, but the opportunity had never arisen. I suspected something else: a wound, some rift let fester. As we closed on the dories I asked again. How about it, I said, casually as I could manage, why not? Here's the chance you never had. He knew I'd help with the travel—that much we'd discussed already.

He turned back to face me, smiled as if he hadn't heard. "See those boats?" He hooked a thumb across the bow. "Rama Indians."

They looked a scanty lot, in tattered clothing, sitting two to a canoe. They stopped their paddling to watch us approach.

"Morning," Arturo called out, in English. Elias cut the engine and we coasted level. One of the Indians reached out a hand to grab our boat; the dories slid together, swollen timbers creaking. Two of their boats were empty, but in the furthest, a slug-fit in the hull, was a considerable-sized shark, half on its side, its long-muscled tall fin dragging in the water. It was the color of clay shot with lead, and its mouth, ripped sideways by the hook, was clamped shut: ugly, pitiable, like a prizefighter being stretchered from the ring. In a final show of disrespect they'd heaped their netting and old bait on top, and sat with their feet up on its hide.

"Some shark," Arturo said, kneeling up to see better, his eyes wide. "Where did you catch it?"

They glanced from one to another, suddenly fidgety. "Out there," one said.

Arturo grinned. "Out where?" He scanned their faces, acting blithe, as if it was all a big joke.

"To sea." This was the first man talking, the one who'd pulled us alongside. He rested his jaw in his hand.

"To sea—that so? We've been out all morning. Never saw you all." Arturo was sizing up the big shark, muttering to himself. No one answered him; I could sense them steal glances our way, comparing the catches.

"Iguana Cay? You been out there?" The Rama was smiling as he said this, chewing something in his cheek.

"No, no," said Arturo, too quickly, but they were all eyeing him now, hands on their paddles, laid flat across their dugouts. "What you going to do with the shark?" he added, flustered. "Take it to Maximo?"

"Take it home first." The Rama laughed and was echoed by the rest:

mouthfuls of broken teeth, blackened, holed, mostly missing. He picked up his paddle and dug the surface. "Show the ladies."

I asked Arturo why he'd lied, especially since, by his own admittance, the Rama well knew he fished their cay, but he did not answer. We rode the hour back in silence, and not until we reached the wet mud landing at his house, and were unloading the sharks in front of the children, did I try him again.

"How long," I began, as we dragged the dugout from the water, into the same mud furrow from which it came. "How long's the weather going to last? How long will it be good for?"

He straightened, leaving mud prints on the gunwale. "Have fun today? Consider yourself a shark fisherman now?" Elias, fuel tank in one hand, gas line in the other, was mumbling good-bye, ignoring Arturo.

"Yes," I said, to them both. Elias turned to go. "I'm off too,"

I said to Arturo. "Perhaps tomorrow. As soon as I work out how to get to San Juan del Norte." He was leaning over the sharks, measuring them in hand spans. I spoke to his back. "And you, Arturo? You coming?"

"Ah," he said. "The question." He laid a hand on my shoulder, pushed us out of the sun, under an overhang. He screwed up his eyes, roused phlegm in his throat, spat noisily at a garbage pail. "You don't worry about me. I'll be there."

Desperate Passage

by Michael Finkel

Much adventure literature is the stuff of macho thrill-seeking: adrenaline rushes and bragging rights. Michael Finkel (born 1969) aims higher with this piece. Finkel and photographer Chris Anderson in May, 2000 boarded a 23-foot boat with 44 Haitians, who hoped to escape their impoverished island for a new life in the United States. Finkel's account conveys his empathy and fear, as well as his wonder at the risks people take for a chance at the American Dream.

Down in the hold, beneath the deck boards, where we were denied most of the sun's light but none of its fire, it sometimes seemed as if there were nothing but eyes. The boat was 23 feet long, powered solely by two small sails. There were 41 people below and 5 above. All but myself and a photographer were Haitian citizens fleeing their country, hoping to start a new life in the United States. The hold was lined with scrap wood and framed with hand-hewn joists, as in an old mine tunnel, and when I looked into the darkness it was impossible to tell where one person ended and another began. We were compressed together, limbs entangled, heads upon laps, a mass so dense there was scarcely room for motion. Conversation had all but ceased. If not for the shifting and blinking of eyes there'd be little sign that anyone was alive.

Twenty hours before, the faces of the people around me seemed bright with the prospect of reaching a new country. Now, as the arduousness of the crossing became clear, their stares conveyed the flat helplessness of fear. David, whose journey I had followed from his hometown of Port-au-Prince, buried his head in his hands. He hadn't moved for hours. "I'm thinking of someplace else," is all he would reveal. Stephen, who had helped round up the passengers, looked anxiously out the hold's square opening, four feet over our heads, where he could see a corner of the sail and a strip of cloudless sky. "I can't swim," he admitted softly. Kenton, a 13-year-old boy, sat in a puddle of vomit and trembled as though crying, only there were no tears. I was concerned about the severity of Kenton's dehydration and could not shake the thought that he wasn't going to make it. "Some people get to America, and some people die," David had said. "Me, I'll take either one. I'm just not taking Haiti anymore."

It had been six weeks since David had made that pronouncement. This was in mid-March, in Port-au-Prince, soon after Haiti's national elections had been postponed for the fifth time and the country was entering its second year without a parliament or regional officials. David sold mahogany carvings on a street corner not far from the United States Embassy. He spoke beautiful English, spiced with pitch-perfect sarcasm. His name wasn't really David, he said, but it's what people called him. He offered no surname. He said he'd once lived in America but had been deported. He informed me, matter-of-factly, that he was selling souvenirs in order to raise funds to pay a boat owner to take him back.

David was not alone in his desire to leave Haiti. In the past six months, Haitians have been fleeing their country in numbers unseen since 1994, when a military coup tried to oust Jean-Bertrand Aristide, who was president at the time. Haiti's poverty level, always alarming, in recent years has escalated even higher. Today, nearly 80 percent of Haitians live in abject conditions. Fewer than one in 50 has a steady wage-earning job; per capita income hovers around $250, less than one-tenth the Latin American average. Haitians once believed that Aristide might change things, but he was no longer in power, and the endless delays in elections, the recent spate of political killings, and the general sense of spiraling violence and corruption has led to a palpable feeling of despair. In February, the State Department released the results of a survey conducted in nine Haitian cities. Based on the study, two-thirds of Haitians—approximately 4,690,000 people—"would leave Haiti if given the means and opportunity." If they were going to leave, though, most would have to do so illegally; each year, the United States issues about 10,000 immigration visas to Haitian citizens, satisfying about one-fifth of 1 percent of the estimated demand.

To illegally enter America, Haitians typically embark on a two-step journey, taking a boat first to the Bahamas and then later to Florida. In the first five months of this year, the United States Coast Guard has picked up 883 Haitians, most on marginally seaworthy vessels. This is almost twice the number caught in all of 1999. Late April was an especially busy time. On the 22nd, the Coast Guard rescued 200 Haitians after their boat ran aground near Harbor Island, in the Bahamas. Three days later, 123 Haitian migrants were plucked from a sinking ship off the coast of Great Inagua Island. Three days after that, 278 Haitians were spotted by Bahamian authorities on a beach on Flamingo Cay, stranded after their boat had drifted for nearly a week. By the time rescuers arrived, 14 people had died from dehydration; as many as 18 others had perished during the journey. These were merely the larger incidents. Most boats leaving Haiti carry fewer than 50 passengers.

Such stories did not deter David. He said he was committed to making the trip, no matter the risks. His frankness was unusual. Around foreigners, most Haitians are reserved and secretive. David was boastful and loud. It's been said that Creole, the lingua franca of Haiti, is 10 percent grammar and 90 percent attitude, and David exercised this ratio to utmost effectiveness. It also helped that he was big, well over six feet and bricked with muscle. His head was shaved bald; a sliver of mustache shaded his upper lip. He was 25 years old. He used his size and his personality as a form of self-defense: the slums of Port-au-Prince are as dangerous as any in the world, and David, who had once been homeless for more than a year, had acquired the sort of street credentials that lent his words more weight than those of a policeman or soldier. He now lived in a broken-down neighborood called Projet Droullard, where he shared a one-room hovel with 13 others—the one mattress was suspended on cinder blocks so that people could sleep not only on but also beneath it. David was a natural leader, fluent in English, French, and Creole. His walk was the chest-forward type of a boxer entering the ring. Despite his apparent candor, it was difficult to know what was really on his mind. Even his smile was ambiguous—the broader he grinned the less happy he appeared.

The high season for illegal immigration is April through September. The seas this time of year tend to be calm, except for the occasional hurricane. Early this May I mentioned to David that I, along with a photographer named Chris Anderson, wanted to document a voyage from Haiti to America. I told David that if he was ready to make the trip, I'd pay him $30 a day to aid as guide and translator. He was skeptical at first, suspicious that we were working undercover for the C.I.A. to apprehend smugglers. But after repeated assurances, and after showing him the supplies we'd brought for the voyage—self-inflating life vests (including one for David), vinyl rain jackets, waterproof flashlights, Power Bars, and a first-aid kit—his wariness diminished. I offered him an advance payment of one day's salary.

"O.K.," he said. "It's a deal." He promised he'd be ready to leave early the next morning.

David was at our hotel at 5:30 a.m., wearing blue jeans and sandals and a T-shirt, and carrying a black plastic bag. Inside the bag was a second T-shirt, a pair of socks, a tin bowl, a metal spoon, and a Bible. In his pocket was a small bundle of money. This was all he took with him. Later, he bought a toothbrush.

David opened his Bible and read Psalm 23 aloud: *Yea, though I walk through the valley of the shadow of death,* and then we walked to the bus station, sidestepping the stray dogs and open sewers. We boarded an old school bus, 36 seats, 72 passengers, and headed north, along the coast, to Île de la Tortue—Turtle Island—one of the three major boatbuilding centers in Haiti. David knew the island well. A year earlier, he'd spent a month there trying to gain a berth on a boat. Like many Haitians who can't afford such a trip, he volunteered to work. Seven days a week, he hiked deep into the island's interior, where a few swatches of forest still remained, and hacked down pine trees with a machete, hauling them back to be cut and hammered into a ship. For his efforts, David was served one meal a day, a bowlful of rice and beans. After 30 days of labor there was still no sign he'd be allowed onto a boat, so he returned to his mahogany stand in Port-au-Prince.

The bus rattled over the washboard roads and the sun bore down hard, even at 7 in the morning, and the men in the sugarcane fields were shirtless and glistening. A roadside billboard, faded and peeling, advertised Carnival Cruise Lines. "Les Belles Croisières," read the slogan—the Beautiful Cruises. At noon, we transferred to the bed of a pickup truck, the passing land gradually surrendering fertility until everything was brown. Five hours later the road ended at the rough-edged shipping town of Port-de-Paix, where we boarded a dilapidated ferry and set off on the hourlong crossing to Île Tortue, a fin-shaped wisp of land 20 miles long and 4 miles wide. Here, said David, is where he'd begin his trip to America.

There are at least seven villages on Île Tortue—its population is about 30,000—but no roads, no telephones, no running water, no electricity, and no police. Transportation is strictly by foot, via a web of thin trails lined with cactus bushes. David walked the trails, up and down the steep seafront bluffs, until he stopped at La Vallée, a collection of huts scattered randomly along the shore. On the beach I counted 17 boats under construction. They looked like the skeletons of beached whales. Most were less than 30 feet long, but two were of the same cargo-ship girth as the boat that had tried a rare Haiti-to-Florida nonstop in January but was intercepted by the Coast Guard off Key Biscayne, Florida. Three hundred ninety-five Haitians, 14 Dominicans, and 2 Chinese passengers were shoehorned aboard, all of whom were returned to Haiti. According to survivors' reports, 10 people had suffocated during the crossing, the bodies tossed overboard.

The boats at La Vallée were being assembled entirely with scrap wood and rusty nails; the only tools I saw were hammers and machetes. David said a boat left Île Tortue about once every two or three days during the high season. He thought the same was true at the other two boatbuilding spots—Cap-Haïtien, in the northeast, and Gonaïves, in the west. This worked out to about a boat a day, 40 or more Haitians leaving every 24 hours.

The first step in getting onto a boat at Île Tortue, David said, is to gain the endorsement of one of the local officials, who are often referred to as elders. Such approval, he explained, is required whether you are a foreigner or not—and foreigners, especially Chinese, occasionally come to Haiti to arrange their passage to America. A meeting with the elder in La Vallée was scheduled. David bought a bottle of five-star Barbancourt rum as an offering, and we walked to his home.

The meeting was tense. David, Chris, and I crouched on miniature wooden stools on the porch of the elder's house, waiting for him to arrive. About a dozen other people were present, all men. They looked us over sharply and did not speak or smile. When the official appeared, he introduced himself as Mr. Evon. He did not seem especially old for an elder, though perhaps I shouldn't have been surprised; the average life expectancy for men in Haiti is less than 50 years. When Haitian men discuss serious matters, they tend to sit very close to one another and frequently touch each other's arms. David placed both his hands upon Mr. Evon and attested, in Creole, to the availability of funds for the trip and to our honesty.

"What are your plans?" asked Mr. Evon.

"To go to America," David said. "To start my life."

"And if God does not wish it?"

"Then I will go to the bottom of the sea."

That evening, several of the men who had been present during our interview with Mr. Evon came to visit, one at a time. They were performing what David called a "vit ron"—a quick roundup, trying to gather potential passengers for the boat they were each affiliated with. David chose to work with an amiable man named Stephen Bellot, who claimed to be filling a ship that was likely to leave in a matter of days. Stephen was also a member of one of the more prominent families on Île Tortue. He was 28 years old, lanky and loose-limbed, with rheumy eyes and a wiggly way of walking that made me think, at times, that he'd make an excellent template for a cartoon character. In many ways, he seemed David's opposite. Where David practically perspired bravado, Stephen was tentative and polite. His words were often lost in the wind, and he had a nervous habit of rubbing his thumbs across his forefingers, as if they were little violins. He had been raised on Île Tortue and, though he'd moved to Port-au-Prince to study English, he seemed to lack David's city savviness. In Port-au-Prince, Stephen had worked for several years as a high school teacher—chemistry and English were his specialties. He was paid $35 a month. He'd returned to Île Tortue six months ago in order to catch a boat to America. The prospect of leaving, he admitted, both inspired and intimidated him. "I've never been anywhere," he told me. "Not even across the border to the Dominican Republic." He said he'd set up a meeting with a boat owner the next day.

The boat owner lived on the mainland, in Port-de-Paix. Stephen's mother and brother and grandmother and several of his cousins lived in a small house nearby, and Stephen took us there while he went off to find the captain. An open sewer ran on either side of the two-room cinder-block home; insects formed a thrumming cloud about everyone's head. There was a TV but no electricity. The lines had been down for some time, and nobody knew when they'd be repaired. Sleep was accomplished in shifts—at all times, it seemed, four or five people were in the home's one bed. The sole decoration was a poster advertising Miami Beach. We waited there for 11 hours. The grandmother, bone thin, sat against a wall and did not move. Another woman scrubbed clothing with a washboard and stone. "Everyone in Haiti has been to prison," David once said, "because Haiti is a prison."

The captain arrived at sunset. His name was Gilbert Marko; he was 31 years old. He was wearing the nicest clothing I'd seen in Haiti—genuine Wrangler blue jeans, a gingham button-down shirt, and shiny wingtips. He had opaque eyes and an uncommonly round head, and tiny, high-set ears. There was an air about him of scarcely suppressed intensity, like a person who has recently eaten a jalapeño pepper. The meeting went well. David explained that his decision to leave had not been a hasty one—he mentioned his previous trip to Île Tortue and his time in America. Stephen said we all understood the risks. Both David and Stephen declared their support for us. This seemed good enough for Gilbert. He said he'd been to the Bahamas many times. He had seven children by five women and was gradually trying to get everyone to America. He spoke excellent English, jingly with Bahamian rhythms.

His boat, he said, was new—this would only be its second crossing. There would be plenty of water and food, he insisted, and no more than 25 passengers. He was taking family members and wanted a safe, hassle-free trip. His boat was heading to Nassau, the Bahamian capital. The crossing could take four days if the wind was good, and as many as eight days if it was not. We'd have no engine.

Most people who make it to America, Gilbert explained, do so only after working in the Bahamas for several months, usually picking crops or cleaning hotel rooms. According to Gilbert, the final segment of the trip, typically a 90-minute shot by powerboat from the Bimini Islands, Bahamas, to Broward Beach, Florida, costs about $3,000 a person. Often, he said, an American boat owner pilots this leg—10 people in his craft, a nice profit for a half-day's work.

Eventually, talk came around to money for Gilbert's segment of the trip. Nothing in Haiti has a set price, and the fee for a crossing is especially variable, often depending on the quality of the boat. Virtually every Haitian is handing over his life savings. The price most frequently quoted for an illegal trip to the Bahamas was 10,000 gourdes—about $530. Fees 10 times as high had also been mentioned. Rumor on Île Tortue was that the two Chinese passengers on the Key Biscayne boat had paid $20,000 apiece. Gilbert said that a significant percentage of his income goes directly to the local elders, who in turn make sure that no other Haitian authorities become overly concerned with the business on Île Tortue.

After several hours of negotiations, Gilbert agreed to transport Chris and me for $1,200 each, and David and Stephen, who were each given credit for rounding us up, for $300 each.

Gilbert had named his boat *Believe in God*. It was anchored (next to the *Thank You Jesus*) off the shore of La Vallée, where it had been built. If you were to ask a second grader to draw a boat, the result would probably look a lot like the *Believe in God*. It was painted a sort of brackish white, with red and black detailing. The mast was a thin pine, no doubt dragged out of the hills of Île Tortue. There was no safety gear, no maps, no life rafts, no tool kit, and no nautical instruments of any type save for an ancient compass. The deck boards were mis-aligned. With the exception of the hold, there was no shelter from the elements. Not a single thought had been given to comfort. It had taken three weeks to build, said Gilbert, and had cost $4,000. It was his first boat.

Gilbert explained that he needed to return to Port-de-Paix to purchase supplies, but that it'd be best if we remained on the boat. The rest of his passengers, he said, were waiting in safe houses. "We'll be set to go in three or four hours," he said as he and his crew boarded a return ferry.

Time in Haiti is an extraordinarily flexible concept, so when eight hours passed and there was no sign of our crew, we were not concerned. Night came, and still no word. Soon, 24 hours had passed since Gilbert's departure. Then 30. David became convinced that we had been set up. We'd handed over all our money and everyone had disappeared. Boat-smuggling cons were nothing new. The most common one, David said, involved sailing around Haiti and the Dominican Republic two or three times and then dropping everyone off on a deserted Haitian island and telling them they're in the Bahamas. A more insidious scam, he mentioned, involved taking passengers a mile out to sea and then tossing them overboard. It happens, he insisted. But this, said David, was a new one. He was furious, but for a funny reason. "They stole all that money," he said, "and I'm not even getting any."

• • •

David was wrong. After dark, Gilbert and his crew docked a ferry along-side the *Believe in God*. They had picked up about 30 other Haitians—mostly young, mostly male—from the safe houses, and the passengers huddled together as if in a herd, each clutching a small bag of personal belongings. Their faces registered a mix of worry and confusion and excitement—the mind-jumble of a life-altering moment. Things had been terribly delayed, Gilbert said, though he offered no further details. I saw our supplies for the trip: a hundred-pound bag of flour, two 55-gallon water drums, four bunches of plantains, a sack of charcoal, and a rooster in a cardboard box. This did not seem nearly enough for what could be a weeklong journey, but at least it was something. I'd been told that many boats leave without any food at all.

The passengers transferred from the ferry to the *Believe in God*, and Gilbert sent everyone but his crew down to the hold. We pushed against one another, trying to establish small plots of territory. David's size in such a situation was suddenly a disadvantage—he had difficulty contorting himself to fit the parameters of the hold and had to squat with his knees tucked up against his chest, a little-boy position. For the first time since I'd met him he appeared weak, and more than a bit tense. Throughout our long wait, David had been a study in nonchalance. "I'm not nervous; I'm not excited; I'm just ready to leave," he'd said the previous day. Perhaps now, as the gravity of the situation dawned on him, he realized what he was about to undergo.

"Wasn't it like this last time you crossed?" I asked. David flashed me an unfamiliar look and touched my arm and said, "I need to tell you something," and finally, in the strange confessional that is the hold of a boat, he told me a little of his past. The first time he'd gone to America, he said, he'd flown on an airplane. He was 9 years old. His mother had been granted an immigration visa, and she took David and his two brothers and a sister to Naples, Florida. Soon after, his mother died of AIDS. He had never known his father. He fell into bad company, and at age 17 spent nine months in jail for stealing a car. At 19, he served a year and five days in jail for selling marijuana and then was deported. That was six years ago. In Naples, he said, his friends had called him

Six-Four, a moniker bestowed because of his penchant for stealing 1964 Chevy Impalas. He admitted to me that if he returned to Naples, where his sister lived, he was concerned he'd have to become Six-Four again in order to afford to live there. In America, he mentioned, there is shame in poverty—a shame you don't feel in Haiti. "People are always looking at the poor Haitians who just stepped off their banana boat," he said. This was something, he suggested, that Stephen might find a painful lesson.

The view from the hold, through the scuttle, was like watching a play from the orchestra pit. Gilbert handed each crew member an envelope stuffed with money, as if at a wedding. Nobody was satisfied, of course, and an argument ensued that lasted into the dawn. Down in the hold, where everyone was crushed together, frustration mounted. Occasionally curses were yelled up. When it was clear there was no more money to distribute, the crew demanded spots on the boat for family members. Gilbert acquiesced, and the crew left the ship to inform their relatives. Soon there were 35 people on board, then 40. Hours passed. There was no room in the hold to do anything but sit, and so that is what we did. People calmed down. Waiting consumes a significant portion of life in Haiti, and this was merely another delay. The sun rode its arc; heat escaping through the scuttle blurred the sky. A container of water was passed about, but only a few mouthfuls were available for each person. Forty-two people were aboard. Then 46. It was difficult to breathe, as though the air had turned to gauze. David and Stephen could not have been pressed closer to each other if they'd been wrestling. There had been murders on these journeys, and suicides, and suffocations. Now I could see why. "We came to this country on slave boats," David said, "and we're going to leave on slave boats."

There was a sudden pounding of feet on the deck and a man—an old man, with veiny legs and missing teeth—dropped headfirst into the hold. Gilbert jumped after him, seized the old man by his hair, and flung him out. I heard the hollow sounds of blows being landed, and then a splash, and the attempted stowaway was gone.

Everything was quiet for a moment, a settling, and then there was again commotion on deck, but it was choreographed commotion, and the sails were raised, a mainsail and a bed-sheet-size jib, two wedges of white against the cobalt sky. We'd already been in the hold 10 hours but still the boat did not leave. There was a clipped squawk from above, and the rooster was slaughtered. Then Gilbert came down to our quarters—he'd tied a fuchsia bandanna about his head—and crawled to the very front, where there was a tiny door with a padlock. He stuck his head inside the cubby and hung a few flags, sprayed perfumed water, and chanted. "Voodoo prayers," said David. When Gilbert emerged he crawled through the hold and methodically sprinkled the top of everyone's head with the perfume. Then he climbed onto the deck and barked a command, and the *Believe in God* set sail.

The poorest country and the richest country in the Western Hemisphere are separated by 600 miles of open ocean. It's a treacherous expanse of water. The positioning of the Caribbean Islands relative to the Gulf Stream creates what is known as a Venturi effect—a funneling action that can result in a rapid buildup of wind and waves. Meteorologists often call the region "hurricane alley." For a boat without nautical charts, the area is a minefield of shallows and sandbars and reefs. It is not uncommon for inexperienced sailors to become sucked into the Gulf Stream and fail to reach their destination. "If you miss South Florida," said Cmdr. Christopher Carter of the Coast Guard, who has 16 years' experience patrolling the Caribbean, "your next stop is North Carolina. Then Nova Scotia. We've never found any migrants alive in Nova Scotia, but we've had ships wash ashore there."

Initially, the waves out past the tip of Île Tortue were modest, four or five feet at most, the whitecaps no more than a froth of curlicues. Still, the sensation in the hold was of tumbling unsteadiness. The hold was below the waterline, and the sloshing of the surf was both amplified and distorted—the sounds of digestion, it occurred to me, and I thought more than once of Jonah, trapped in the belly of a whale. When the boat was sideswiped by an especially aggressive wave, the stress against the hull invariably produced a noise like someone stepping on a plastic cup. Water came in through the cracks. Every time this happened, David and Stephen glanced at one another and arched their eyebrows, as if to ask, Is this the one that's going to put us under? When building a boat, David had said, it was common to steal nails from other ships, hammer them straight, and reuse them. I wondered how many nails had been pulled from our boat. As the waves broke upon us, the hull boards bellied and bowed, straining against the pressure. There was a pump aboard, a primitive one, consisting of a rubber-wrapped broom handle and a plastic pipe that ran down to the bottom of the hold. Someone on deck continuously had to work the broom handle up and down, and still we were sitting in water. The energy of the ocean against the precariousness of our boat seemed a cruel mismatch.

Nearly everyone in the hold kept their bags with them at all times; clearly, a few of the possessions were meant to foster good luck. One man repeatedly furled and unfurled a little blue flag upon which was drawn a vévé—a symbolic design intended to invoke a Voodoo spirit. Stephen fingered a necklace, carved from a bit of coconut, that a relative had brought him from the Bahamas. David often held his Bible to his chest. I had my own charm. It was a device called an Emergency Position-Indicating Radio Beacon, or EPIRB. When triggered, an EPIRB transmits a distress signal to the Coast Guard via satellite, indicating its exact position in the water. I was assured by the company that manufactured the beacon that if I activated it anywhere in the Caribbean, help would be no more than six hours away. The EPIRB was a foot tall, vaguely cylindrical, and neon yellow. I kept it stashed in my backpack, which I clasped always in my lap. Nobody except Chris, the photographer, knew it was there.

The heat in the hold seemed to transcend temperature. It had become an object, a weight—something solid and heavy, settling upon us like a dentist's X-ray vest. There was no way to shove it aside. Air did not circulate, wind was shut out. Thirst was a constant dilemma. At times, the desire to drink crowded out all other notions. Even as Gilbert was sending around a water container, my first thought was when we'd have another. We had 110 gallons of water on board, and 46 people. In desert conditions, it's recommended that a person drink about one gallon per day. It was as hot as any desert down there. Hotter. That meant we had a two-day supply. But we were merely sitting, so perhaps half a gallon would be enough. That's four days. The trip, though, could take eight days. If it did we'd be in serious trouble.

Finding a comfortable position in the hold was hopeless. The hull was V-shaped, and large waves sent everyone sliding into the center, tossing us about like laundry. I exchanged hellos with the people around me—Wesley and Tijuan and Wedell and Andien—but there seemed nothing further to say. Every hour, an electronic watch chirped from somewhere in the dark. One man read from a scrap of a paperback book, Chapters 29 through 33 of a work called "Garden of Lies." From here and there came the murmurs of sleep. The occasional, taut conversations between Stephen and David consisted primarily of reveries about reaching America. David said that he wanted to work in the fields, picking tomatoes or watermelon. His dream was to marry an American woman. Stephen's fantasy was to own a pickup truck, a red one.

The rules of the boat had been established by Gilbert. Eight people were allowed on deck at once; the rest had to remain in the hold. Six spots were reserved by Gilbert and the crew. The other two were filled on a rotating basis—a pair from the deck switched with a pair from the hold every 20 minutes or so. This meant each person would be allowed out about once every six hours. A crowded deck, Gilbert explained, would interfere with the crew and rouse the suspicions of passing boats. More important, people were needed in the hold to provide ballast—too much weight up top and the boat would tip.

Of the 46 people on the boat, 5 were women. They were crammed together into the nether reaches of the hold, visible only as silhouettes. The further back one crawled into the hold, the hotter it got. Where the women were it must have been crippling. Occasionally they braided one another's hair, but they appeared never to speak. They were the last to be offered time on deck, and their shifts seemed significantly shorter than those of the men.

The oldest person on the boat was a 40-year-old passenger named

Desimeme; the youngest was 13-year-old Kenton. The average age was about 25. Unlike the migrants of the early 90's, who tended more heavily to be families and rural peasants, most Haitian escapees are now young, urban males. The reason for this shift is probably an economic one. In recent years, according to people on Île Tortue, the price for a crossing has become vastly inflated, and women and farmers are two of Haiti's lowest-paid groups.

Two hours after leaving, the seasickness began. There was a commotion in the rear of the hold, and people started shouting, and a yellow bucket—at one time it was a margarine container—was tossed below. It was passed back. The man who was sick filled it up, and the bucket was sent forward, handed up, dumped overboard, and passed back down. A dozen pairs of hands reached for it. The yellow bucket went back and forth. It also served as our bathroom, an unavoidable humiliation we each had to endure. Not everyone could wait for the bucket to arrive, and in transferring the container in pitching seas it was sometimes upended. The contents mingled with the water that sloshed ankle-deep about the bottom of the hold. The stench was overpowering.

One of the sickest people on board was Kenton, the 13-year-old boy. He lay jackknifed next to me in the hold, clutching his stomach, too ill to grab for the bucket. I slipped him a seasickness pill, but he was unable to keep it down. Kenton was a cousin of one of the crew members. He had been one of the last people to board the boat. In the scramble to fill the final spots, there was no room for both him and his parents, so he was sent on alone. His parents, I'd overheard, had promised that they'd be on the very next boat, and when Kenton boarded he was bubbly and smiling, as if this were going to be a grand adventure. Now he was obviously petrified, but also infused with an especially salient dose of Haitian mettle—as he grew weaker he kept about him an iron face. Never once did he cry out. He had clearly selected a favorite shirt for the voyage: a New York Knicks basketball jersey.

This did not seem like the appropriate time to eat, but dinner was ready. The boat's stove, on deck, was an old automobile tire rim filled with charcoal. There was also a large aluminum pot and a ladle. The meal consisted of dumplings and broth—actually, boiled flour balls and hot water. Most people had brought a bowl and spoon with them, and the servings were passed about in the same manner as the bucket. When the dumplings were finished, Hanson, one of the crew members, came down into the hold. He was grasping a plastic bag that was one of his personal possessions. Inside the bag was an Île Tortue specialty—ground peanuts and sugar. He produced a spoon from his pocket, dipped it into the bag, and fed a spoonful to the man nearest him, carefully cupping his chin as if administering medicine. Then he wormed his way through the hold, inserting a heaping spoon into everyone's mouth. His generosity was appreciated, but the meal did little to help settle people's stomachs. The yellow bucket was again in great demand.

Hours trickled by. There was nothing to do, no form of diversion. The boat swayed, the sun shone, the heat intensified. People were sick; people were quiet. Eyes gradually dimmed. Everyone seemed to have withdrawn into themselves, as in the first stages of shock. Heads bobbed and hung, fists clenched and opened. Thirst was like a tight collar about our throats. It was the noiselessness of the suffering that made it truly frightening—the silent panic of deep fear.

Shortly before sunset, when we'd been at sea nearly 12 hours, I was allowed to take my second stint on deck. By now there was nothing around us but water. The western sky was going red and our shadows were at full stretch. The sail snapped and strained against its rigging; the waves, at last, sounded like waves. Gilbert was standing at the prow, gazing at the horizon, a hand cupped above his eyes, and as I watched him a look of concern came across his face. He snapped around, distressed, and shouted one word: "Hamilton!" Everyone on deck froze. He shouted it again. Then he pointed to where he'd been staring, and there, in the distance, was a ship of military styling, marring the smooth seam between sea and sky. Immediately, I was herded back into the hold.

A Hamilton, Stephen whispered, is Haitian slang for a Coast Guard ship—it's also, not coincidentally, the name of an actual ship. The news flashed through the hold, and in reflexive response everyone crushed deeper into the rear, away from the opening, as though this would help avoid detection. Gilbert paced the deck, manic. He sent two of the crew members down with us, and then he, too, descended. He burrowed toward his cubby, shoving people aside, unlocked the door and wedged himself in. And then he began to chant, in a steady tone both dirgelike and defiant. The song paid homage to Agwe, the Voodoo spirit of the sea, and when Gilbert emerged, still chanting, several people in the hold took up the tune, and then he climbed up and the crew began chanting, too. It was an ethereal tune, sung wholly without joy, a signal of desperate unity that seemed to imply we'd sooner drift to Nova Scotia than abandon our mission. Some of these people, it seemed, really were willing to sacrifice their lives to try and get to America. Our captain was one of them.

Over the singing came another sound, an odd buzz. Then there were unfamiliar voices—non-Haitian voices, speaking French. In the hold, people snapped out of their stupor. Stephen grabbed his necklace. David chewed on the meat of his palm. I stood up and peeked out. The buzz was coming from a motorized raft that had pulled beside us. Six people were aboard, wearing orange life vests imprinted with the words U.S. COAST GUARD. Gilbert was sitting atop one of our water drums, arms folded, flashing our interlopers a withering look. Words were shouted back and forth—questions from the Coast Guard, blunt rejoinders from Gilbert.

"Where are you headed?"

"Miami."

"Do you have docking papers?"

"No."

"What are you transporting?"

"Rice."

"Can we have permission to board?"

"No."

There was nothing further. In the hold everyone was motionless. People tried not to breathe. Some had their palms pushed together in prayer. One man pressed his fingertips to his forehead. Soon I heard the buzz again, this time receding, and the Coast Guard was gone. Gilbert crouched beside the scuttle and spoke. This had happened on his last crossing, he said. The Coast Guard just comes and sniffs around. They were looking for drugs, but now they've gone. Then he mentioned one additional item. As a precaution, he said, nobody would be allowed onto the deck, indefinitely.

The reaction to this news was subtle but profound. There was a general exhalation, as if we'd each been kicked in the stomach, and then a brief burst of conversation—more talking than at any time since we'd set sail. The thought of those precious minutes on deck had been the chief incentive for enduring the long hours below. With Gilbert's announcement, something inside of me—some scaffolding of fortitude—broke. We'd been at sea maybe 14 hours; we had a hundred to go, minimum. Ideas swirled about my head, expanding and consuming like wildfire. It was nighttime, but I felt hotter than ever. I was marinated in sweat. I thought of drowning, I thought of starving, I thought of withering from thirst.

Then, as if he'd read my mind, David took my right hand and held it. He held it a long time, and I felt calmer. He looked at my eyes; I looked at his. This much was clear: David wasn't willing to heed his own words. He wasn't prepared to die. He was terrified, too. This wasn't something we discussed until much later, though he eventually admitted it.

When David let go of my hand, the swirling thoughts returned. I wrestled with the idea of triggering the EPIRB. People were weak—I was weak—and it occurred to me that I had the means to save lives. But though pressing the button might lead to our rescue, it would certainly dash everyone's dreams. There was also the concern that I'd be caught setting it off, the repercussions of which I did not want to ponder. I made a decision.

"Chris," I said. I was whispering.

"Yes."

"I'm going to use the thing."

"Don't."

"Don't?"

"No, don't. Wait."

"How long?

"Just wait."

"I don't think I can."

"Just wait a little."

"O.K. I'll wait a little."

I waited a little, a minute at a time. Four more hours passed. Then, abruptly, the buzz returned. Two buzzes. This time there was no conversation, only the clatter of Coast Guard boots landing on our deck. At first, it seemed as though there might be violence. The mood in the hold was one of reckless, nothing-to-lose defiance. I could see it in the set of people's jaws, and in the vigor that suddenly leapt back into their eyes. This was our boat; strangers were not invited—they were to be pummeled and tossed overboard, like the old man who had tried to stow away. Then lights were shined into the hold, strong ones. We were blinded. There was no place for us to move. The idea of revolt died as quickly as it had ignited. Eighteen hours after we'd set tail, the trip was over.

Six at a time, we were loaded into rubber boats and transported to the Coast Guard cutter *Forward*, a ship 270 feet long and nine stories high. It was 4 o'clock in the morning. Nobody struggled, no weapons were drawn. We were frisked and placed in quarantine on the flight deck, in a helicopter hangar. Three Haitians were so weak from dehydration that they needed assistance walking. The Coast Guard officers were surprised to see journalists on board, but we were processed with the other Haitians. We were each supplied with a blanket, a pair of flip-flops, and a toothbrush. We were given as much water as we could drink. We were examined by a doctor. The *Forward*'s crew members wore two layers of latex gloves whenever they were around us.

The *Forward*'s commanding officer, a 19-year Coast Guard veteran named Dan MacLeod, came onto the flight deck. He pulled me aside. The Coast Guard, he said, had not lost sight of our boat since we'd first been spotted. He'd spent the previous four hours contacting Haitian authorities, working to secure an S.N.O.—a Statement of No Objection—that would permit the Coast Guard to stop a Haitian boat in international waters. When David and Stephen learned of this, they were furious. There is the feeling among many Haitians of abandonment by the United States—or worse, of manipulation. American troops helped restore Aristide to power, then they vanished. Now, because there is democracy in Haiti, the United States has a simple excuse for rejecting Haitian citizenship claims: Haitians are economic, not political migrants. For those Haitians who do enter America illegally—the United States Border Patrol estimates that between 6,000 and 12,000 do so each year—it is far better to try to seep into the fabric of the Haitian-American community than to apply for asylum. In 1999, 92 percent of Haitian asylum claims were rejected.

As soon as the Haitian government granted permission, the Coast Guard had boarded our boat. Though illegal migrants were suspected to be on board—two large water barrels seemed a bit much for just a crew—the official reason the boat had been intercepted, Officer MacLeod told me, was because we were heading straight for a reef. "You were off course from Haiti about two degrees," he said. "That's not bad for seat-of-the-pants sailing, but you were heading directly for the Great Inagua reef. You hadn't altered your course in three hours, and it was dark out. When we boarded your vessel you were 2,200 yards from the reef. You'd have hit it in less than 40 minutes."

Our boat running against a reef could have been lethal. The hull, probably, would have split. The current over the reef, Officer MacLeod informed me, is unswimmably strong. The reef is as sharp as a cheese grater. The EPIRB would not have helped.

Even if we'd managed to avoid the reef—if, by some good fortune, we'd changed course at the last minute—we were still in danger. Officer MacLeod asked me if I'd felt the boat become steadier as the night progressed. I said I had. "That's the first sure sign you're sinking," he said. There was more. "You were in three-to-four-foot seas. At six-foot seas, you'd have been in a serious situation, and six-foot seas are not uncommon here. Six-foot seas would've taken that boat down." When I mentioned that we'd expected the trip to take four or five days, Officer MacLeod laughed. "They were selling you a story," he said. In the 18 hours since leaving Haiti, we had covered 30 miles. We'd had excellent conditions. The distance from Haiti to Nassau is 450 miles. Even with miraculous wind, it could have taken us 10 days. The doctor on board said we'd most likely have been dealing with fatalities within 48 hours.

The next day, it turned out, was almost windless. It was hotter than ever. And the seas were choppy—seven feet at times, one officer reported. Another high-ranking officer added one more bit of information: a Coast Guard ship hadn't been in these waters at any time in the past two weeks. The *Forward* happened to be heading in for refueling when we were spotted.

Our trip, it appeared, had all the makings of a suicide mission. If there had been no EPIRB and no Coast Guard, it's very likely that the *Believe in God* would have vanished without a trace. And our craft, said Officer MacLeod, was one of the sturdier sailboats he has seen— probably in the top 20 percent. Most boats that make it, he mentioned, have a small motor. I wondered how many Haitians have perished attempting such a crossing. "That's got to be a very scary statistic," said Ron Labrec, a Coast Guard public affairs officer, though he wouldn't hazard a guess. He said it's impossible to accurately determine how many migrants are leaving Haiti and what percentage of them make it to shore. But given the extraordinary number of people fleeing on marginal sailboats, it seems very likely that there are several hundred unrecorded deaths each year. Illegal migration has been going on for decades. It is not difficult to imagine that there are thousands of Haitian bodies on the bottom of the Caribbean.

We spent two days on the *Forward*, circling slowly in the sea, while it was determined where we would be dropped off. On May 16, everyone was deposited on Great Inagua Island and turned over to Bahamian authorities. Chris and I were released and the Haitians were placed in a detention center. The next day they were flown to Nassau and held in another detention center, where they were interviewed by representatives of the United Nations High Commission for Refugees. None were found to qualify for refugee status.

As for the *Believe in God*, the boat came to a swift end. The night we were captured, we stood along the rail of the flight deck as the *Forward*'s spotlight was trained on our boat. It looked tiny in the ink-dark sea. The sail was still up, though the boat was listing heavily. Officer MacLeod had just started telling me about its unseaworthiness. "Watch," he said. As I looked, the mast leaned farther and farther down, as if bowing to the sea, until it touched the water. Then the boat slowly began to sink.

Two weeks later, all 44 Haitians were flown from Nassau to Port-au-Prince. They received no punishment from Haitian authorities. The next morning, Gilbert returned to Île Tortue, already formulating plans for purchasing a second boat and trying to cross once more. Stephen also went home to Île Tortue, but was undecided as to whether he'd try the journey again. David went back to Port-au-Prince, back to his small mahogany stand, back to his crumbling shack, where his personal space consisted of a single nail from which he hung the same black plastic bag he'd had on the boat. He said he felt lucky to be alive. He said he would not try again by boat, not ever. Instead, he explained, he was planning on sneaking overland into the Dominican Republic. There were plenty of tourists there and he'd be able to sell more mahogany. He told me he was already studying a new language, learning from a Spanish translation of *The Cat in the Hat* that he'd found in the street.

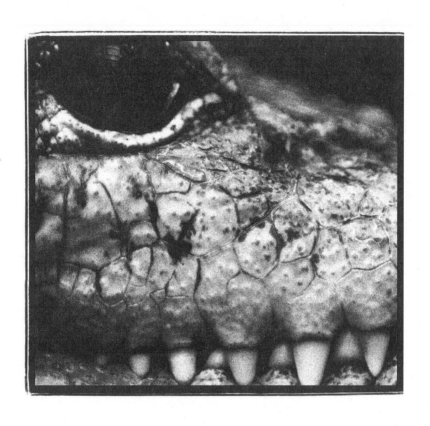

Being Prey

by Val Plumwood

Val Plumwood has been a pioneer in the field of ecofeminist philosophy for thirty years. In her 1993 book Feminism and the Mastery of Nature *Plumwood defined wilderness as a place where plants and animals are "free to work things out according to self-determined patterns." Nine years earlier, she had discovered firsthand what can happen when a crocodile exercises that freedom.*

In the early wet season, Kakadu's paperbark wetlands are especially stunning, as the water lilies weave white, pink, and blue patterns of dreamlike beauty over the shining thunderclouds reflected in their still waters. Yesterday, the water lilies and the wonderful bird life had enticed me into a joyous afternoon's idyll as I ventured onto the East Alligator Lagoon for the first time in a canoe lent by the park service. "You can play about on the backwaters," the ranger had said, "but don't go onto the main river channel. The current's too swift, and if you get into trouble, there are the crocodiles. Lots of them along the river!" I followed his advice and glutted myself on the magical beauty and bird life of the lily lagoons, untroubled by crocodiles.

Today, I wanted to repeat that experience despite the drizzle beginning to fall as I neared the canoe launch site. I set off on a day trip in search of an Aboriginal rock art site across the lagoon and up a side channel. The drizzle turned to a warm rain within a few hours, and the magic was lost. The birds were invisible, the water lilies were sparser, and the lagoon seemed even a little menacing. I noticed now how low the 14-foot canoe sat in the water, just a few inches of fiberglass between me and the great saurians, close relatives of the ancient dinosaurs. Not long ago, saltwater crocodiles were considered endangered, as virtually all mature animals in Australia's north were shot by commercial hunters. But after a decade and more of protection, they are now the most plentiful of the large animals of Kakadu National Park. I was actively involved in preserving such places, and for me, the crocodile was a symbol of the power and integrity of this place and the incredible richness of its aquatic habitats.

After hours of searching the maze of shallow channels in the swamp, I had not found the clear channel leading to the rock art site, as shown on the ranger's sketch map. When I pulled my canoe over in driving rain to a rock outcrop for a hasty, sodden lunch, I experienced the unfamiliar sensation of being watched. Having never been one for timidity, in philosophy or in life, I decided, rather than return defeated to my sticky trailer, to explore a clear, deep channel closer to the river I had traveled along the previous day.

The rain and wind grew more severe, and several times I pulled over to tip water from the canoe. The channel soon developed steep mud banks and snags. Farther on, the channel opened up and was eventually blocked by a large sandy bar. I pushed the canoe toward the bank, looking around carefully before getting out in the shallows and pulling the canoe up. I would be safe from crocodiles in the canoe—I had been told—but swimming and standing or wading at the water's edge were dangerous. Edges are one of the crocodile's favorite food-capturing places. I saw nothing, but the feeling of unease that had been with me all day intensified.

The rain eased temporarily, and I crossed a sandbar to see more of this puzzling place. As I crested a gentle dune, I was shocked to glimpse the muddy waters of the East Alligator River gliding silently only 100 yards away. The channel had led me back to the main river. Nothing stirred along the riverbank, but a great tumble of escarpment cliffs up on the other side caught my attention. One especially striking rock formation—a single large rock balanced precariously on a much smaller one—held my gaze. As I looked, my whispering sense of unease turned into a shout of danger. The strange formation put me sharply in mind of two things: of the indigenous Gagadgu owners of Kakadu, whose advice about coming here I had not sought, and of the precariousness of my own life, of human lives. As a solitary specimen of a major prey species of the saltwater crocodile, I was standing in one of the most dangerous places on earth.

I turned back with a feeling of relief. I had not found the rock paintings, I rationalized, but it was too late to look for them. The strange rock formation presented itself instead as a telos of the day, and now I could go, home to trailer comfort.

As I pulled the canoe out into the main current, the rain and wind started up again. I had not gone more than five or ten minutes down the channel when, rounding a bend, I saw in midstream what looked like a floating stick—one I did not recall passing on my way up. As the current moved me toward it, the stick developed eyes. A crocodile! It did not look like a large one. I was close to it now but was not especially afraid; an encounter would add interest to the day.

Although I was paddling to miss the crocodile, our paths were strangely convergent. I knew it would be close, but I was totally unprepared for the great blow when it struck the canoe. Again it struck, again and again, now from behind, shuddering the flimsy craft. As I paddled furiously, the blows continued. The unheard of was happening; the canoe was under attack! For the first time, it came to me fully that I was prey. I realized I had to get out of the canoe or risk being capsized.

The bank now presented a high, steep face of slippery mud. The only obvious avenue of escape was a paperbark tree near the muddy bank wall. I made the split-second decision to leap into its lower branches and climb to safety. I steered to the tree and stood up to jump. At the same instant, the crocodile rushed up alongside the canoe, and its beautiful, flecked golden eyes looked straight into mine. Perhaps I could bluff it, drive it away, as I had read of British tiger hunters doing. I waved my arms and shouted, "Go away!" (We're British here.) The golden eyes glinted with interest. I tensed for the jump and leapt. Before my foot even tripped the first branch, I had a blurred, incredulous vision of great toothed jaws bursting from the water. Then I was seized between the legs in a red-hot pincer grip and whirled into the suffocating wet darkness.

Our final thoughts during near-death experiences can tell us much about our frameworks of subjectivity. A framework capable of sustaining action and purpose must, I think, view the world "from the inside," structured to sustain the concept of a continuing, narrative self; we remake the world in that way as our own, investing it with meaning, reconceiving it as sane, survivable, amenable to hope and resolution. The lack of fit between this subject-centered version and reality comes into play in extreme moments. In its final, frantic attempts to protect itself from the knowledge that threatens the narrative framework, the mind can instantaneously fabricate terminal doubt of extravagant proportions: *This is not really happening. This is a nightmare from which I will soon awake.* This desperate delusion split apart as I hit the water. In that flash, I glimpsed the world for the first time "from the outside," as a world no longer my own, an unrecognizable bleak landscape composed of raw necessity, indifferent to my life or death.

Few of those who have experienced the crocodile's death roll have lived to describe it. It is, essentially, an experience beyond words of total terror. The crocodile's breathing and heart metabolism are not suited to prolonged struggle, so the roll is an intense burst of power designed to overcome the victim's resistance quickly. The crocodile then holds the feebly struggling prey underwater until it drowns. The roll was a centrifuge of boiling blackness that lasted for an eternity, beyond endurance, but when I seemed all but finished, the rolling suddenly stopped. My feet touched bottom, my head broke the surface, and, coughing, I sucked at air, amazed to be alive. The crocodile still had me in its pincer grip between the legs. I had just begun to weep for the prospects of my mangled body when the crocodile pitched me suddenly into a second death roll.

When the whirling terror stopped again I surfaced again, still in the crocodile's grip next to a stout branch of a large sandpaper fig growing in the water. I grabbed the branch, vowing to let the crocodile tear me apart rather than throw me again into that spinning, suffocating hell. For the first time I realized that the crocodile was growling, as if angry. I braced myself for another roll, but then its jaws simply relaxed; I was free. I gripped the branch and pulled away, dodging around the back of the fig tree to avoid the forbidding mud bank, and tried once more to climb into the paperbark tree.

As in the repetition of a nightmare, the horror of my first escape attempt was repeated. As I leapt into the same branch, the crocodile seized me again, this time around the upper left thigh, and pulled me under. Like the others, the third death roll stopped, and we came up next to the sandpaper fig branch again. I was growing weaker, but I could see the crocodile taking a long time to kill me this way. I prayed for a quick finish and decided to provoke it by attacking it with my hands. Feeling back behind me along the head, I encountered two lumps. Thinking I had the eye sockets, I jabbed my thumbs into them with all my might. They slid into warm, unresisting holes (which may have been the ears, or perhaps the nostrils), and the crocodile did not so much as flinch. In despair, I grabbed the branch again. And once again, after a time, I felt the crocodile jaws relax, and I pulled free.

I knew I had to break the pattern; up the slippery mud bank was the only way. I scrabbled for a grip, then slid back toward the waiting jaws. The second time I almost made it before again sliding back, braking my slide by grabbing a tuft of grass. I hung there, exhausted. *I can't make it,* I thought. *It'll just have to come and get me.* The grass tuft began to give way. Flailing to keep from sliding farther, I jammed my fingers into the mud. This was the clue I needed to survive. I used this method and the last of my strength to climb up the bank and reach the top. I was alive!

Escaping the crocodile was not the end of my struggle to survive. I was alone, severely injured, and many miles from help. During the attack, the pain from the injuries had not fully registered. As I took my first urgent steps, I knew something was wrong with my leg. I did not wait to inspect the damage but took off away from the crocodile toward the ranger station.

After putting more distance between me and the crocodile, I stopped and realized for the first time how serious my wounds were. I did not remove my clothing to see the damage to the groin area inflicted by the first hold. What I could see was bad enough. The left thigh hung open, with bits of fat, tendon, and muscle showing, and a sick, numb feeling suffused my entire body. I tore up some clothing to bind the wounds and made a tourniquet for my bleeding thigh, then staggered on, still elated from my escape. I went some distance before realizing with a sinking heart that I had crossed the swamp above the ranger station in the canoe and could not get back without it.

I would have to hope for a search party, but I could maximize my chances by moving downstream toward the swamp edge, almost two miles away. I struggled on, through driving rain, shouting for mercy from the sky, apologizing to the angry crocodile, repenting to this place for my intrusion. I came to a flooded tributary and made a long upstream detour looking for a safe place to cross.

My considerable bush experience served me well, keeping me on course (navigating was second nature). After several hours, I began to black out and had to crawl the final distance to the swamp's edge. I lay there in the gathering dusk to await what would come. I did not expect a search party until the following day, and I doubted I could last the night.

The rain and wind stopped with the onset of darkness, and it grew perfectly still. Dingoes howled, and clouds of mosquitoes whined around my body. I hoped to pass out soon, but consciousness persisted. There were loud swirling noises in the water, and I knew I was easy meat for another crocodile. After what seemed like a long time, I heard the distant sound of a motor and saw a light moving on the swamp's far side. Thinking it was a boat, I rose up on my elbow and called for help. I thought I heard a faint reply, but then the motor grew fainter and the lights went away. I was as devastated as any castaway who signals desperately to a passing ship and is not seen.

The lights had not come from a boat. Passing my trailer, the ranger noticed there was no light inside it. He had driven to the canoe launch site on a motorized trike and realized I had not returned. He had heard my faint call for help, and after some time, a rescue craft appeared. As I began my 13-hour journey to Darwin Hospital, my rescuers discussed going upriver the next day to shoot a crocodile. I spoke strongly against this plan: I was the intruder, and no good purpose could be served by random revenge. The water around the spot where I had been lying was full of crocodiles. That spot was under six feet of water the next morning, flooded by the rains signaling the start of the wet season.

In the end I was found in time and survived against many odds. A similar combination of good fortune and human care enabled me to overcome a leg infection that threatened amputation or worse. I probably have Paddy Pallin's incredibly tough walking shorts to thank for the fact that the groin injuries were not as severe as the leg injuries. I am very lucky that I can still walk well and have lost few of my previous capacities. The wonder of being alive after being held—quite literally—in the jaws of death has never entirely left me. For the first year, the experience of existence as an unexpected blessing cast a golden glow over my life, despite the injuries and the pain. The glow has slowly faded, but some of that new gratitude for life endures, even if I remain unsure whom I should thank. The gift of gratitude came from the searing flash of near-death knowledge, a glimpse "from the outside" of the alien, incomprehensible world in which the narrative of self has ended.

I had survived the crocodile attack, but not the cultural drive to represent it in terms of the masculinist monster myth: the master narrative. The encounter did not immediately present itself to me as a mythic struggle. I recall thinking with relief, as I struggled from the attack site, that I now had a good excuse for being late with an overdue article and a foolish but unusual story to tell a few friends. Crocodile attacks in North Queensland have often led to massive crocodile slaughters, and I feared that my experience might have put the creatures at risk again. That's why I tried to minimize publicity and save the story for my friends alone.

This proved to be extremely difficult. The media machine headlined a garbled version anyway, and I came under great pressure, especially from the hospital authorities, whose phone lines had been jammed for days, to give a press interview. We all want to pass on our story, of course, and I was no exception. During those incredible split seconds when the crocodile dragged me a second time from tree to water, I had a powerful vision of friends discussing my death with grief and puzzlement. The focus of my own regret was that they might think I had been taken while risking a swim. So important is the story and so deep the connection to others, carried through the narrative self, that it haunts even our final desperate moments.

By the same token, the narrative self is threatened when its story is taken over by others and given an alien meaning. This is what the mass media do in stereotyping and sensationalizing stories like mine—and when they digest and repackage the stories of indigenous peoples and other subordinated groups. As a story that evoked the monster myth, mine was especially subject to masculinist appropriation. The imposition of the master narrative occurred in several ways: in the exaggeration of the crocodile's size, in portraying the encounter as a heroic wrestling match, and especially in its sexualization. The events seemed to provide irresistible material for the pornographic imagination, which encouraged male identification with the crocodile and interpretation of the attack as sadistic rape.

Although I had survived in part because of my active struggle and bush experience, one of the major meanings imposed on my story was that the bush was no place for a woman. Much of the Australian media had trouble accepting that women could be competent in the bush, but the most advanced expression of this masculinist mindset was *Crocodile Dundee*, which was filmed in Kakadu not long after my encounter. Two recent escape accounts had both involved active women, one of whom had actually saved a man. The film's story line, however, split the experience along conventional gender lines, appropriating the active struggle and escape parts for the male hero and representing the passive "victim" parts in the character of an irrational and helpless woman who has to be rescued from the crocodile-sadist (the rival male) by the bushman hero.

I had to wait nearly a decade before I could repossess my story and write about it in my own terms. For our narrative selves, passing on our stories is crucial, a way to participate in and be empowered by culture. Retelling the story of a traumatic event can have tremendous healing power. During my recovery, it seemed as if each telling took part of the pain and distress of the memory away. Passing on the story can help us transcend not only social harm, but also our own biological death. Cultures differ in how well they provide for passing on their stories. Because of its highly privatized sense of the individual, contemporary Western culture is, I think, relatively impoverished in this respect. In contrast, many Australian Aboriginal cultures offer rich opportunities for passing on stories. What's more, Aboriginal thinking about death sees animals, plants, and humans sharing a common life force. Their cultural stories often express continuity and fluidity between humans and other life that enables a degree of transcendence of the individual's death.

In Western thinking, in contrast, the human is set apart from nature as radically other. Religions like Christianity must then seek narrative continuity for the individual in the idea of an authentic self that belongs to an imperishable realm above the lower sphere of nature and animal life. The eternal soul is the real, enduring, and identifying part of the human self, while the body is animal and corrupting. But transcending death this way exacts a great price; it treats the earth as a lower, fallen realm, true human identity as outside nature, and it provides narrative continuity for the individual only in isolation from the cultural and ecological community and in opposition to a person's perishable body.

It seems to me that in the human supremacist culture of the West there is a strong effort to deny that we humans are also animals positioned in the food chain. This denial that we ourselves are food for others is reflected in many aspects of our death and burial practices—the strong coffin, conventionally buried well below the level of soil fauna activity, and the slab over the grave to prevent any other thing from digging us up, keeps the Western human body from becoming food for other species. Horror movies and stories also reflect this deep-seated dread of becoming food for other forms of life: Horror is the wormy corpse, vampires sucking blood, and alien monsters eating humans. Horror and outrage usually greet stories of other species eating humans. Even being nibbled by leeches, sandflies, and mosquitoes can stir various levels of hysteria.

This concept of human identity positions humans outside and above the food chain, not as part of the feast in a chain of reciprocity but as external manipulators and masters of it: Animals can be our food, but we can never be their food. The outrage we experience at the idea of a human being eaten is certainly not what we experience at the idea of animals as food. The idea of human prey threatens the dualistic vision of human mastery in which we humans manipulate nature from outside, as predators but never prey. We may daily consume other animals by the billions, but we ourselves cannot be food for worms and certainly not meat for crocodiles. This is one reason why we now treat so inhumanely the animals we make our food, for we cannot imagine ourselves similarly positioned as food. We act as if we live in a separate realm of culture in which we are never food, while other animals inhabit a different world of nature in which they are no more than food, and their lives can be utterly distorted in the service of this end.

Before the encounter, it was as if I saw the whole universe as framed by my own narrative, as though the two were joined perfectly and seamlessly together. As my own narrative and the larger story were ripped apart, I glimpsed a shockingly indifferent world in which I had no more significance than any other edible being. The thought, *This can't be happening to me, I'm a human being. I am more than just food!* was one component of my terminal incredulity. It was a shocking reduction, from a complex human being to a mere piece of meat. Reflection has persuaded me that not just humans but any creature can make the same claim to be more than just food. We are edible, but we are also much more than edible. Respectful, ecological eating must recognize both of these things. I was a vegetarian at the time· of my encounter with the crocodile, and remain one today. This is not because I think predation itself is demonic and impure, but because I object to the reduction of animal lives in factory farming systems that treat them as living meat.

Large predators like lions and crocodiles present an important test for us. An ecosystem's ability to support large predators is a mark of its ecological integrity. Crocodiles and other creatures that can take human life also present a test of our acceptance of our ecological identity. When they're allowed to live freely, these creatures indicate our preparedness to coexist with the otherness of the earth, and to recognize ourselves in mutual, ecological terms, as part of the food chain, eaten as well as eater.

Thus the story of the crocodile encounter now has, for me, a significance quite the opposite of that conveyed in the master/monster narrative. It is a humbling and cautionary tale about our relationship with the earth, about the need to acknowledge our own animality and ecological vulnerability. I learned many lessons from the event, one of which is to know better when to turn back and to be more open to the sorts of warnings I had ignored that day. As on the day itself, so even more to me now, the telos of these events lies in the strange rock formation, which symbolized so well the lessons about the vulnerability of humankind I had to learn, lessons largely lost to the technological culture that now dominates the earth. In my work as a philosopher, I see more and more reason to stress our failure to perceive this vulnerability, to realize how misguided we are to view ourselves as masters of a tamed and malleable nature. The balanced rock suggests a link between my personal insensitivity and that of my culture. Let us hope that it does not take a similar near-death experience to instruct us all in the wisdom of the balanced rock.

Be Your Own Donkey
by Rolf Potts

Rolf Potts' (born 1970) work often chronicles his somewhat comical exploits backpacking around the world on "five cents (or so) a day." One trip landed him short of water two days into the Libyan Desert. Too bad those guys back in Farafra wouldn't sell him a donkey.

By the afternoon of my second day in the Libyan Desert, I finally found the sense of isolation I'd been looking for. The faint white ridge-line that marked the far edge of Dakhla Oasis 37.5 miles to the north had just dropped beneath the horizon, and I found myself adrift in a sterile sea of yellow dunes. Inspired by the gorgeous absence of everything but curves and light, I unslung my pack, tossed it into the sand and sat down for a much-needed breather.

Though it seemed innocuous at the time, this was probably the act that turned the next 10 hours of my life into a wearying mix of self-loathing and dull paranoia.

Up until that moment, my hike into the sandy fringe of the world's largest desert had been full of simple discovery and fascination. In the utter emptiness of the landscape, I found myself vividly aware of slight details: telltale irregularities in the texture of the sand; the metallic ping of the odd rocks beneath my boots; a lone ant marching up a dune, its abdomen tilted skyward. I noted a complete lack of odor in the air; I watched the rippled shadows of the landscape dissolve at midday, then deepen again in the afternoon.

This all changed just before sunset, when I opened my pack to find my gear slathered in a sodden brine of damp grit and filmy garbage. Beneath this water-slicked gear, I found my last bottle of Bakara mineral water—its thin, plastic shell burst open in the middle, its contents mostly gone. Unthinking, I sloshed the excess water out from the bottom of my pack and started spreading things out to dry in the sand.

It wasn't until I'd begun to tally my gear that I realized the problem: Two days into the desert, I had only one bottle of drinking water remaining, and that bottle was half-empty.

There are some moments in life when unexpected situations call for momentous, life-changing acts of resourcefulness and endurance. This was not one of them. Granted, I was hiking into one of the emptiest areas in the world: To my south and west, nothing but sand and rocks lay between me and the distant, barren borders of Sudan and Libya. To my north, however, a village called Mut—the southernmost outpost of Egypt's Dakhla Oasis—was no more than a 12-hour trudge away. Outright stupidity on my part excluded, I'd not likely be forced to jettison my gear, drink my own urine or flag down passing airplanes in the effort to survive.

Rather, my situation was far more representative of prosaic day-to-day life: It didn't require outright heroism so much as it required thankless, forgettable drudge work. A 12-hour forced march to Mut on a half-liter of water was certainly doable; it just wasn't desirable.

Sitting in the sand, the day going dark, I pondered other options. The only unknown factor at the time was what lay to my east. The map in my guidebook (which, I'll confess, was not designed to aid desert trekking) showed a dotted line dropping south out of Mut—evidence of the old caravan route that once arced down to the distant sands of Sudan. By my own estimation, I could cut due east in the cool of the night and arrive at the caravan road in less than five hours. If this road were still in use, I could wait there the next morning and hitch a ride on a truck (or, I'd secretly hoped, on a camel), thus neatly avoiding the tedious slog to Mut. On the other hand, if this road were disused I would double both my hiking distance and my odds of being forced to swill my own urine.

Gathering up my gear, I took an eastward bearing off my compass and rolled the dice.

Except for certain situations involving science, warfare or divine prophecy, there is never really any practical reason to go wandering off into the desert—and this is probably the very reason why so many people are inclined to do it.

Nearly 2,500 years ago, the Greek historian Herodotus wrote that, among the Masamon tribe of western Egypt, there lived some "wild young fellows, who planned amongst themselves all sorts of extravagant adventures, one of which was to explore the Libyan Desert and try to penetrate further than they ever had before." These youths, Herodotus noted, eventually came upon an isolated oasis, where they were attacked and imprisoned by a marauding band of dwarves.

Twenty-five centuries later, the idea of exploring lifeless stretches of sand for no good reason still carries a visceral appeal—dull dangers of dehydration and attack-dwarves notwithstanding.

In the deserts of the Arabic world, much of this mythic appeal has been perpetuated by the tales of classic explorers such as T.E. Lawrence, Wilfred Thesiger and Sir Richard Burton. When I traveled into the western sands of Egypt, however, I had yet to study the exploits of these steely, turban-wearing Brits. Rather my desert canon consisted primarily of eclectic American fare: Edward Abbey's Utah solitaire; the cinematic fantasies of George Lucas and Steven Spielberg; wisecracking vultures in *Far Side* cartoons; NASA photos of Mars. Perhaps as a result of this, my inclination toward epic exploration in the Libyan Desert was offset by equal inclinations toward fantasy and irreverence.

Thus, my first impulse upon arriving in the desert town of Farafra was to buy a donkey and ride it into the sandy unknown.

On paper, riding a donkey into the desert is a perfectly legitimate low-tech adventure. Not only are donkeys less expensive than camels and more authentic than Jeeps, I figured I could sell my beast at the end of the trip and break even for the experience.

As any layman who's tried it will know, however, shopping for donkeys in Egypt is a resoundingly humiliating experience. Not only does the American higher education system leave its graduates with very few practical skills in assessing the market value of pack animals, it would seem that the inhabitants of Egypt's oases aren't used to selling their livestock to foreigners. During my first morning of wandering through the dusty outskirts of Farafra, I spent two hours startling and bewildering farmers before I finally found someone who was interested in my proposition.

After a lot of sign language, a smiling old farmer hauled a load of green reeds from the back of his donkey and motioned for me to get on. Once I'd swung my legs onto the beast, the farmer smacked it on the rear and I went bouncing idiotically down the dirt road.

The donkey stopped soon after, so I climbed off and flashed the farmer a thumbs-up. I wasn't really sure what to do next (slam the doors? kick the tires?), so I decided to cut straight to the bargain. "OK," I said to the farmer. "Bikam? How much do you want for it?" I wasn't ready to buy it, necessarily, but I wanted to get a feel for price.

"Pen," he said.

Not sure what he meant, I took out a pen and some paper so he could write down the price. Smiling, he handed the paper back and pocketed the pen. As the farmer merrily returned to his work, it dawned on me that I had just purchased one 20-second donkey ride.

Since this flavor of commerce wasn't likely to get me very far, I tried to indicate that I actually wanted to purchase the entire animal with cash. Every time I waved some money around in an effort to pantomime my desire, however, the farmer just shook his head and gestured to the donkey. "Pen!" he repeated cheerfully.

Motioning my intention to come back, I jogged over to my hotel to find a translator. Mohammed, a temperamental middle-aged fellow who worked the front desk, was my only option at the time. After exchanging a few pleasantries, I got down to business.

"I need you to help me buy a donkey," I told him.

Mohammed scowled. "Why you want to buy a donkey?"

"I want to ride it into the desert."

"A Jeep or camel is better. I'll arrange you a trip."

"I'm not really interested in that; I want to try to do it on my own."

Mohammed raised an eyebrow in irritation. "You know how to keep a donkey?"

"What do you mean?"

"Food! Water! So it does not die!"

I realized I hadn't considered this. "No," I said. "Is it difficult?"

The grumpy clerk grinned at me sarcastically. "You want a desert trip by yourself?" he said, walking his fingers across the countertop. "You be your own donkey!"

Though I never did any more donkey shopping in the Egyptian oases, it took me two days before I had rationalized the disappointment and moved on to other options.

By that time, I'd continued on to Dakhla—the southwestern-most of Egypt's big oases—and I was sharing a dorm room at the Al Qasr Hotel with a German political science student named Tomas. Tomas enjoyed the tale of my Farafra donkey encounter, but he couldn't seem to understand my initial motive.

"Why did you want to buy a donkey?" he asked me.

"So I could travel into the desert," I said.

"Why did you want to travel into the desert?"

"So I could be away from things. I wanted to go to a place where nothing has ever lived. I wanted to be isolated."

"Isolated? What about the donkey?"

"Well, the donkey would just be a funny detail. You know, part of the challenge."

"So the isolation part wasn't really that important."

"No, I wanted to be isolated," I said to Tomas, still reluctant to admit that my donkey quest was based more on impulse than design. "I guess the donkey would have been part of that isolation, considering I really don't know much about donkeys."

"So did you want to be isolated or did you just want to feel isolated?"

"I wanted to be isolated," I said stubbornly.

"Yes, but really. How is being isolated all that different from feeling isolated?"

After 15 minutes of simple logic, Tomas had talked me into dreaming up a new journey—a walking trek into the Great Sand Sea.

Unlike the rest of the Libyan Desert, where blowing sands mix with dry buttes and rocky moonscape, the Great Sand Sea is nothing but dunes. Covering an enormous sprawl of territory along the Egypt-Libya border, this area went unexplored and uncharted for centuries because of its complete isolation and lack of water. In 1874, the first man to cross these dunes—a German geographer named Gerhard Rohlfs—nearly died in his attempt to lead 17 camels over 420 continuous miles of waterless desert. "It was as if we were on a wholly lifeless planet," wrote Rohlfs of the experience. "If one stayed behind a moment and let the caravan out of one's sight, a loneliness could be felt in the boundless expanse such as brought fear, even in the stoutest heart . . . Here, in the sand ocean, there is nothing to remind one of the great common life of the earth but the stiffened ripples of the last simoon; all else is dead."

Conveniently for my own purposes, a thin tongue of the Great Sand Sea stretches out into the western fringe of Dakhla Oasis. Here, I'd hoped, I could enjoy this feeling of boundless isolation without the danger of being isolated. Here, in relative safety, I could be my own donkey.

Using my guidebook map, I plotted a course that would start in Al Qasr village on the northern fringe of Dakhla, curve west and south through the desert, then boomerang back into the southern oasis village of Mut three days later.

Packing enough food and water to last the duration of the journey, I struck out for the dunes the following morning.

Tomas joined me for the first leg of the hike, since he was interested in exploring the Al-Muzawaka tombs two hours west of Al Qasr. There, we found a small network of caves that had been hollowed out by some long-ago inhabitants of the oasis. Unlike the famous tombs of Egypt's Nile valley, there were no admission booths, souvenir stands or rifle-toting guards at the site. The only soul we saw there was an old man who walked out from a lone stone house to take us by the arm and shine a flashlight into the caves. When we tipped him 50 piasters each, he smiled and took us to an open-faced cave that contained five dusty, brittle adult mummies.

Beyond Al-Muzawaka, Tomas followed me into the first cluster of yellow dunes before turning back for Al Qasr. For the rest of the afternoon, I maintained a sloppy southwestern bead, zagging my way up and over the grand piles of sand. Still within sight of the oasis, the desert sand was abuzz with activity: shiny blue beetles, fat black flies, faded pink garbage bags. Every so often, the sand would yield broken pieces of pottery or heavy brown stones.

As recently as 50 years ago, explorers in this part of the Egyptian desert were likely to find all sorts of artifacts preserved in the sand, from flint knives to broken ostrich shells to rock paintings. Mixed in with the pre-historic relics were evidence of more recent visitors: camel bones, bits of clothing, human skeletons. Just last year, a group of American tourists crossing the desert near Bahariyya found the remains of three German soldiers—all members of a flight crew that had disappeared on an exploratory mission during World War II.

Though I'd secretly hoped to find something ancient, desiccated or macabre in the desert, I never was that lucky. At one point, I found a copper bullet slug in the sand and put it in my pocket, thinking perhaps I'd drill a hole in it and hang it on a necklace. Five minutes later I found two more bullet slugs, then another. By the time I'd collected seven bullet slugs, they didn't seem so special any more, so I threw them all away.

The sun went down after 6, and—since I had no stove and there was obviously no firewood—I set in for the night in the lee of a huge dune. After spooning up a can of tuna for dinner, I pulled out my sleeping bag and stared at stars until I fell asleep. I woke up at first light and resumed my journey.

For the most part, the curved sameness of the Great Sand Sea precludes narrative. My second day in the dunes proceeded much like the first—the only difference being that the insects became fewer and the view of Dakhla's ridge-line became fainter as the day went on. I filled the emptiness of the landscape with my wandering mind, stopping occasionally to take compass bearings or photograph my footprints.

In a weird way, though, I don't really recall making much progress until I opened up my water-soaked backpack at dusk and found myself with a tough decision on my hands.

Though I didn't know it at the time, the area beyond my little tongue of the Great Sand Sea was once thought to be a possible location for an elusive oasis town called Zerzura. Reputedly a place of palms, fresh-water springs and white birds, Zerzura's location never could be pinned down once explorers started systematically mapping the desert 100 years ago. Early Arab historians placed it south of Siwa Oasis near the Libyan border; early British adventurers placed it west of Dakhla. Murray's 1899 "Guide to Egypt" placed it in four different locations in the hinterland of the Egyptian southwest. Over the years, various wanderers, bandits and pilots claimed to have seen Zerzura while headed elsewhere, but none could ever find his way back.

In his classic 1935 book "Libyan Sands," British explorer Ralph Bagnold (who was a member of the British Long Range Desert Group loosely portrayed in *The English Patient*) conceded that Zerzura would probably always be a lost oasis, having long ago been mapped under a different name and absorbed into the Egyptian geography. Still, he held on to the idea that it was out there waiting to be rediscovered in one form or another.

"I like to think of Zerzura as an idea for which we have no apt word in English," he wrote in the conclusion to his book, "meaning something waiting to be discovered in some out-of-the-way place, difficult of access, if one is enterprising enough to go out and look; an indefinite thing, taking different shapes in the minds of different individuals according to their interests and wishes."

This in mind, I suppose I discovered my Zerzura when I lost my water bottle in the depths of my pack. What had before been an adventure of fancy had now turned into a matter of real consequence. My Lucas-Spielberg reveries gave way to reality, and I discovered the desert all over again.

Of course, this is an assessment of hindsight. Under the pressure of the decision itself, I wasn't so philosophical as I trudged my way east. Having been raised to make the more conservative choice in this type of situation (i.e., enduring the direct slog to Mut), I found myself unconsciously veering to the north. Every so often I would catch myself and resume my eastbound progress.

Hiking through the desert under the light of the moon was quite similar to hiking the dunes in daylight. The only difference was that the air was cool, the sand was gray and the mood was spooky. After a while my footfalls didn't sound like they were coming from my own feet any more; I kept turning around to see if I was being followed. Even sudden patches of soft sand would give me an occasional start in the dim silence.

Eventually, my paranoid habit of veering north caught up with me, when—just short of midnight—I found a Jeep track in the sand. Since I'd been hiking what I thought was east for nearly six hours, I assumed that I'd reached the caravan road. In retrospect, this was a silly assumption: Given that Mut is the last sizable human outpost in that corner of Egypt, it would make sense that a southbound road toward Sudan would be large and well-maintained. At the time, however, I wasn't so confident. Not sure what to do, I snuggled into the slope of a nearby dune and waited for someone to show up.

After a 10-minute doze, I heard what sounded like footsteps coming my way. Suddenly nervous, I dug my head-lamp out of my pack. The sound got louder, then stopped. It started again, stopped again, then started once more, even louder than before. It sounded like someone was stumbling through the sand in a ragged pair of scuba-flippers. Too spooked to say anything, I turned on the head-lamp and stood there with my fists clenched—looking, no doubt, like some kind of spelunker-ninja madman. Finally, I spotted the culprit: a heavy paper-and-plastic cement bag, drifting its way down the Jeep track on a hiccuping migration to Sudan. I turned off my head-lamp and sat back down.

As I listened to the cement bag flop off into the night, I caught the hint of another sound: a truck downshifting somewhere in the distance. Shouldering my pack, I crossed the Jeep track and continued east. Within 30 minutes, I could see a set of headlights; an hour later I was standing on the blacktop caravan road to Mut. My eastbound gamble had paid off: I'd found my lost oasis in the form of an asphalt road. In an indulgent show of celebration, I took a long pull from my water bottle.

Finding a flat spot far enough from the road so the nighttime trucks wouldn't disturb me, I spread out my sleeping bag and dozed for a few hours.

Just past dawn, I packed up my gear and hitched a ride to the only place there was to go in that humble fringe of the Libyan Desert.

from Journey of the Pink Dolphins
by Sy Montgomery

Nature writer Sy Montgomery canoed down the Amazon River in search of pink dolphins, which have inspired local legends of seduction, paradise and death. She learned to her sorrow and enlightenment what the jungle's inhabitants already knew: "Death is no freak in the Amazon, but a companion with whom one walks daily . . ."

By now, we had established a morning routine: After shaking our shoes out, evicting giant cockroaches, Dianne and I would wander into the dining hall to check on the movements of the creatures in camp. "Where is the tarantula?" Last night, it had been observed crawling along the porch toward our room, to Dianne's immense dismay. ("What's worse than finding a tarantula in your room?" I had asked her. "Nothing in this universe," she had replied. "Nope," I said. "It's losing a tarantula in your room.") Later, it had retreated to a corner in the kitchen.

"Where is the vampire bat?" Steve had caught it, with his quick, ungloved hands, in Jerry's room, and now it was flying around in the dining hall. "Where is the whip scorpion?" This animal is actually not a scorpion at all but a spider, half again as big as a tarantula, with nine-inch antennae, and folded, hairy front arms to seize insects. "I do not like this whip scorpion *at all*," Dianne had commented. But Steve had released it in the dining hall, and now, he said, "it could be anywhere."

"Where is the poisonous caterpillar?" Steve had collected it from a tree, brushing it with a stick off the leaf it had been eating into one of the plastic containers he always carried for such occasions. The caterpillar has long yellow hairs and white stripes; its venom, Steve said, is as toxic as a coral snake's. He had confined it in a can marked PELI-GROSO but now it was inexplicably gone.

So many creatures here seem armed for Armageddon: They must contend with the fact that at any moment something may be trying to eat you, to strangle you, to sting you or bite you, to suck your blood or lay its eggs in your flesh. Even the great bird-hunting tarantulas had something to fear—the female tarantula wasp. Fully five inches long and purple-black, she flies in search of these huge hairy spiders, in order to sting her victim into paralysis and lay her eggs in its flesh. When the larvae hatch, they feed upon the body of the still-living spider, and when they are old enough, chew their way out of the body.

And yet, there is a strange and exciting beauty to this orgy of hunting and feeding. Each night, in our canoe, we visited a hollow snag that poked up out of the water quite near the lodge like the chimney of a drowned house. We usually came to check on the tarantula who lived there, and we could almost always count on seeing him hunting outside the rim of the hollow. But now, suddenly, he grabbed at something with his forelegs. What was it? The creature raced around the other side of the trunk, like a squirrel. Moises swung the boat around to see. The spider's intended victim was an inch-long orange assassin bug, named for its deadly hunting weapon—a hypodermic proboscis with which it injects its prey with venom. The assassin had just speared a large beetle, but in its haste to escape the tarantula, it scurried away with the beetle impaled on its poisonous spear.

No one appreciated these dramas more than Steve. His stories often began with sentences like, "One day I was out harvesting ants for my scorpion, when . . ." or "The only time I was bitten by a poisonous snake, I'd got this call from my boss at Snake Control. . . ." Outside of Orlando, where he had a home much like our lodge, built over a swamp, Steve had amassed an impressive collection of stinging, biting, poisonous predators. As well as snakes and scorpions, he had a two-foot tegu lizard with a blue tongue, who, he realized, "would love to kill me." The only animal in his menagerie he truly adored was his skunk ("One time when my skunk was combing through my hair, looking for something to eat . . ." began one of his stories). He had bought her because he was afraid of spiders, and skunks love to eat spiders. But, with the same great mental discipline required of a student of the martial arts, Steve had taught himself to enjoy and admire spiders for the very violence he had originally feared.

As he had taught himself the graceful moves of tai chi chuan and karate kata, he taught himself to see the grace in the violence of nature. And this was why he loved the Amazon. It was part of why Dianne and I loved it, too: this vast operatic drama of life and death, where beauty and cruelty twine tight. There is a wholeness to the spider's bite, the assassin bug's poison, the tarantula wasp's sting. None are evil or pointless; rather, the opposite is true. All are fulfilling roles which evolution had taken millions of years to perfect.

But we, of course, were spectators in that drama. For all the biting, stinging creatures here, for all the spines and branches, for all the unseen fish with sharp teeth and poisonous spines, Dianne and I felt comfortable and safe. True, my pale skin had burned badly in the sun; even Dianne's nut-brown California tan was now peeling off her nose like shoe leather. True, we had so many insect bites that scratching them became a form of passive entertainment, like watching TV. I woke up sometimes in bloody sheets from scratching bites in my sleep. But nothing worse had befallen us.

And although we still couldn't identify individuals, we were making some progress in our dolphin observations. One spectacular morning, we had found Charro Lake alive with dolphins—perhaps a dozen bufeos and perhaps as many tucuxis—and recorded 160 surfacings in a single hour. Two bufeos even swam into the shallows, in order to get closer to us. Later we discovered they were swimming in only four feet of water, jammed with submerged branches. Though we'd read bufeos generally ignore tucuxis, that morning the two species were clearly interacting. Fifteen times in one half-hour period, we saw tucuxis and bufeos in very close proximity, and four times we saw a baby tucuxi surface next to an adult bufeo, the sleek little gray head beside the large, pink, bulbous one.

At one point that day, a pink face erupted from the water bearing a fish sideways in the jaws. The dolphin shook the fish like a dog shaking a sock. In dogs, this is a kill gesture, meant to break the neck of a small prey item; so for the dolphin the shake may have broken the bones in the fish's body so it could not struggle. The dolphin then repositioned the fish in its jaws so it slid down the throat headfirst.

By timing and numbering our observations, we were able to see some patterns. The bufeos were generally most active for periods that averaged half an hour (although sometimes they stretched to forty-one minutes), followed by periods of rest of roughly the same time. They were most active in the morning; by noon, we often found, they moved away, perhaps to the rivers.

Once, we thought we saw a dolphin sleeping. For eight minutes, between eleven twenty-nine and eleven thirty-seven one morning, in a shallow spot along a grassy bank, we saw an individual rise, slow and low, almost once a minute at the exact same spot. Later we learned that bufeos prefer to sleep in shallow waters, often (disconcertingly, for aquarium patrons) upside down. It is thought, in fact, one reason most of the hundred or so bufeos that had been imported to aquaria between 1950 and 1976 quickly died is that they had no access to shallow waters where they could rise to the surface easily.

We made this observation at a village named Huasi, the busy crossroads of two waterways where bufeos, tucuxis, and people often met. Along with Charro Lake, this was one of our most productive observation areas. We could count on seeing dolphins there almost every day, and here we clearly observed how the hunting techniques of tucuxis and bufeos differ: the tucuxis always hunted in groups, seeming to herd schools of fish toward one another, while the bufeos pursued fish singly.

In addition to the dolphins, children were always coming and going in canoes to the noisy, stilted school. One day, at recess, we saw two little girls holding baby caimans in their hands like Barbie dolls. Bored with their reptilian toys, the bolder girl suggested, *"Vamanos a ver los gringos!"* ("Let's go watch the gringos!") and paddled over to stare at us intently for half an hour as we recorded data on our check sheets. Opposite the school, adults gathered on an island bus stop, awaiting the *collectivo*, the "water bus," to Iquitos. When the boat arrived, again we saw a marked difference in the behavior of bufeos and tucuxis: several bufeos came close to investigate, though the tucuxis stayed away. When the water bus pulled away, the bufeos frolicked in the wake and blew air noisily.

With a thick sheaf of observation sheets recording everything we saw, we would return from each outing to Paul's immaculate lodge and feel as if we were coming home. With its good food, cozy beds, cold-water showers pumped from the river, and his attentive staff who had become our friends, the lodge was a cocoon of comfort and safety. We began to feel that nothing bad, nothing pointless or terrible, could ever happen here.

But on the day of our week's anniversary in camp, we saw that we were wrong.

We were headed to Charro Lake that dripping morning. On the way, we passed the *Francis Antonio,* the thrice-weekly *collectivo* from Sall Pedro to Iquitos. By six-fifteen, the boat's thatched roof was already piled high with logs, bundles of yarina fronds, and twelve lumpy burlap sacks of charcoal. A slaughtered peccary was slung, hammocklike, in the rear of the boat, while most of the passengers sat forward, gazing out the windows. Three roosters perched there, their gold and green tail feathers streaming like wet ribbons in the drizzling rain. The roosters would be roasting by day's end, I thought. I felt sorry for the caimans, sorry for the peccary, sorry for the roosters; but the people, too, of course, are players in the drama of hunting and killing here, and for this they are no more guilty than tarantulas or jaguars.

Next we passed through a canal. Vultures, with their black lizard heads and naked necks, perched watching from the tops of drowning trees, waiting for death to feed them. Moises said dead animals float by this corridor, strangled by vegetation. All life, I began to think, is savage here.

But soon, one of Moises' shortcuts brought us face-to-face with innocents. In the thorny crown of a mimosa protruding two feet above the water's surface, Moises spotted a cup-shaped nest only slightly larger than a hummingbird's. Our canoe sideswiped the tree at the very moment he spotted the nest, and its single, speckled, half-inch egg popped out into our canoe.

Had we broken the tiny egg?

We heard anguished calls from the edge of the drowning bushes. We couldn't see them, but we knew the callers were the parents of that egg. They had seen what had happened. They knew what was at stake: their entire universe was, at that moment, at risk of flying apart.

Suddenly, the vulnerability and perfection of that egg nearly made me weep. Frances Hodgson Burnett has written of the "immense, tender, terrible, heart-breaking beauty and solemnity of Eggs." In *The Secret Garden*, Burnett wrote: "If there had been one person in that garden who had not known through all his or her innermost being that if an Egg were taken away or hurt the whole world would whirl round and crash through space and come to an end—if there had been even one who did not feel it and act accordingly there could have been no happiness even in that golden springtime air."

Surely the egg was life's first love: Mates come and go, but to the egg, life has remained steadfast. Love, I thought, may have originated with the nest—one built perhaps a quarter-billion years ago by one of the reptilian ancestors of birds and crocodiles, the thecodonts, who may have guarded eggs and fed their nestlings 185 million years before *Tyrannosaurus rex*. Surely, I thought, that reptile brain had known to fear the destruction of her eggs. Love's twin is fear, fear that the loved one might be hurt, or taken away. And like love, it is ancient and abiding: it is the architect of the nest, built to protect the beloved. So this ancient fear is with us still, so old it is inseparable from the most profound and lasting of loves. In this Amazon world where everything seems at once to be gorging and mating and hunting, where life feeds routinely on death, still, the parents of eggs and nestlings, parents of babies and children, feel their anguish no less. A savage world, I realized, is no less loving, no less anguished.

Dianne lifted the egg. Miraculously, it was unbroken. As we replaced the egg in its perfect cradle, we saw the parents: two white-banded antbirds, fat as juncos, with dark feathers pin-striped with white lines. They were hopping anxiously, calling back and forth to one another amid the dense foliage twenty yards from the tree, to which they had fled upon our approach.

Later we passed the large, leaf-lined communal nest of the greater ani, a black, thick-billed bird with prominent white eyes. The nest had been built with the efforts of five or six adults, much like the homes of the people who live here. Several females laid and incubated their eggs together. Surrounded by a cloud of mosquitoes, the babies screamed and the males flicked their paddle tails and growled at us bravely.

The day proved too rainy to observe dolphins, so we retreated to the lodge. We were waiting for Mario's mother to come. When we had met at their spacious thatched home in San Pedro, Ilda had generously promised to show us weaving one day, and she was scheduled to come right after lunch. Dianne and Steve and Jerry and I passed the time pleasantly, leafing by lamplight through the eclectic library of field guides and novels and handbooks. In *Where There Is No Doctor*, a guide written by a health worker in rural Mexico, I read under the heading "Foul or Disgusting Remedies Are Not Likely to Help" that leprosy cannot be cured by a drink made of rotting snakes, nor syphilis cured by eating a vulture. Further, it advised, to cure goiter, don't tie a crab to the lump; don't smear it with the brains of a vulture; do not apply human feces; and do not try to cure it by rubbing it with the hand of a dead child.

By noon, the sky was still fat with rain. The air hung thick as a wet flannel sheet. Mario's mother was late, but we assumed that, in the manner of people who don't live by the clock, she would eventually arrive. Moises and Mario took the canoe to San Pedro to see what was keeping her.

Meanwhile, Jerry showed us exercises to enhance our chi, or life-energy. One has to squat, with the back very straight, knees straight out front—much more difficult than it sounds. With Rudy and Moises, with Steve and Jerry, we debated questions like: what percentage of the time do you think an ant is crawling on you? Our estimates ranged from 100 percent (Jerry) to 10 percent (Steve).

At two-thirty, Moises returned, without Ilda. With a nervous smile, he announced softly: "Some bad luck today." We expected to hear that Mario's mother had confused the date, or had some urgent errand. But no: Mario's three-year-old son, who had been playing so tenderly with the woolly monkey in San Pedro just days before, who had given us the gorgeous smile in return for a handful of candies, had, this morning, fallen into the river and drowned.

He had fallen off the raft docked just outside the house where he had been playing, and was swept away by the current.

Mario, Moises told us, was out in his canoe right now, working with the men of the village in a search party to try to recover the body. Some bodies of drowned people are never found; it is said the bufeo steals them away to the Encante. Actually, the dolphins may eat corpses, for their diet is varied. At high water, chances are better that bodies can be recovered, Moises told us; during this time of plenty, it is less likely that the corpses will be scavenged.

The moment Moises stopped speaking, the rain swept down with renewed force. A woman rain, we thought, that could cry all day.

Steve and I sat stunned. Dianne went outside and cried, then came back and stared vacantly while smoking a cigarette. I sat stupidly repeating, "I can't believe it. I can't believe it." We did not know what to do with the grief, or with the horror, or with the guilt. We had reveled in the danger of the Amazon, thinking we were remote from it. We had observed it like a work of art, like a drama on a stage, not thinking the river, the mother of this place, could swallow one of us whole.

A few minutes later, Moises sat down and in his soft, dreamy voice, announced he had a story for us. Its name, he said, was "Cuento del Delfin y el Yacuruna." Like a father calming frightened children, he began:

"I remember when I was younger, there was only one village every two or three miles, even near Iquitos," he said. "The tributaries were more quiet. Many different animals lived in the area. But the motors in the Amazon scared the animals. And I think this is the reason many of the phantasms have disappeared." He began to draw, and a face appeared on the piece of paper.

Moises' voice is very low, and he often draws as he talks—often maps of the waterways, to show us exactly where something happened. His words came as softly as the lead strokes of his pencil, the picture and the story taking shape at once.

"This guy here," he said, pointing to his drawing, "he sees the phantasm.

"My grandmother lived in a village in Brazil, which is now a big town. Only two families lived in this town. The nights were quiet. She heard big crocodiles in the night, and dolphins in the river." The nights were more silent then, and darker. The family had no flashlights. For lamp oil, they burned manatee fat in a big bucket.

One day, he explained, when his grandmother was about fourteen years old, her father went to Iquitos to sell bush meat in the market— a week-and-a-half-long trip by canoe. She and her brother were alone in the house, with a canoe, a shotgun, and two dogs.

Their fourth night alone was a moonless one. She and her brother sat on the front of the house by the wide, rain-swollen river. The manatee oil burned in the corner. She looked at the river and watched it move. A dolphin gasped.

And then, perhaps a mile downriver, they saw a great soft light shining from beneath the water—shining like a diamond. They asked each other: what could it be? They had never seen light like that. Watching, transfixed, they saw it was a great boat, bigger than a house, coming toward them slowly, almost magisterially, and incredibly, making no sound.

The magnificent boat came closer. Finally, it was close enough for her to see inside: It was packed with people, and the sounds of their laughter and music drifted to the children on shore. Men were dressed in wide hats, black shoes, white pants, and there was a beautiful girl dressed like a princess. in the wheelhouse of the boat, she saw a big man reclining like a king. His teeth were pure gold, and the diamond-light, she saw, was coming from his mouth.

The two dogs began to bark, and the young girl who would become Moises' grandmother grew scared. "Take the gun!" she shouted to her brother. He fired three shots.

The boat began to sink slowly back down into the water. But the diamond-light strangely rose. Within ten minutes, the boat had vanished—but in its place, pink dolphins leapt and blew.

The next night, Moises' grandmother and her brother went to stay with the other family in the village. But on their way, dolphins surrounded their canoe, as if they were trying to convey some message.

The message, Moises explained, came to his grandmother in a dream. The Yacuruna said to her, "Why were you scared when you saw my boat? I am a rich man. The beautiful girl you saw is my wife, the princess. I have many employees in the boat. The people in the white clothes you saw, they are dolphins. I have a big city in the water, with towers and a palace. I want to give you diamonds and gold, if you will come to live with me."

When her father came home, she told him about the boat, the light, and the dream. But he didn't believe it—not until later, when he went fishing in a canal near the mouth of the big lake.

He was looking for tiger catfish, which are best caught at night, and had brought along his cigarettes and his harpoon and long lines with big hooks. In the middle of the night, he felt something big pull on the line, and he pulled hard, but it wouldn't give. It kept pulling, so hard that his lamp fell into the water. Finally, he felt his canoe might go underwater, too, so he hurriedly tied it to a tree. Later he returned with his son, and the creature on the line again pulled so hard that the canoe seemed to be fighting huge waves. "Something is trying to catch me!" said the father. And the son said, "I know. I saw his boat."

After that, the father fell ill. The son had to fetch a shaman from Tabatinga in Brazil—the best shamans used to live there, Moises explained. A learned shaman was found, and he sought the answer in a trance. In his dream, he saw the Yacuruna, and spoke with him, and once the trance was done, the shaman revealed what he had learned. "You are a good man," the shaman told the father, "and the Yacuruna wants your daughter to live with him." The shaman blew tobacco smoke on him and sucked on his stomach, and the illness was gone. But the Yacuruna was still there, and he is there still. There was nothing the family could do but move to another town. They moved to a village called Malupa.

"But what if your grandmother had gone to live with the Yacuruna and the dolphins underwater?" I wanted to know. "What is it like there?"

"The shamans say life in the water is the same as here, but better," Moises said. A shaman in Iquitos had told him, for instance, that underwater there are more hospitals. There are epidemics here—malaria, cholera—but not in the Encante. People live longer there; one month underwater is the same as a year here. But even in the Encante, there are dangers. The shaman told Moises the story of a young man who went to live beneath the water.

One time, at the mouth of the Napo River, a young man's boat disappeared, and his family was devastated. But just a little while later, the young man appeared to his mother in a dream. "All is well," he told his mother. "I am married to a beautiful girl who is a princess. I live underwater, in a beautiful city. It is good here," he said, "but tell my sister not to wash her clothes in the river, or the dolphins may come to steal her away to the Encante."

For twenty years, he lived happily beneath the water. But one day, he told his wife, the princess, that he would like to visit his mother and sister on the land. His wife told him, "Until you return to me, I will give you a little rock, and it is your life. Please don't lose it." So the young man came to visit his mother and sister. As the mother was taking water from the river, she saw her son coming toward her in his canoe. They hugged and cried.

He kept the stone in his pocket, and when he swam in the river he could touch his wife. But one night the village held a celebration, with masato and liquor, and he lost the stone. The following morning, his mother found him dead in his hammock. His hair had turned white, like an old man's.

The story ended, and we sat together in the lamplight, thinking of death. Then suddenly, a terrified scream erupted from the direction of the cold-water showers—a woman's voice, Graciella or Gladys. Without thinking to grab my flashlight, I ran toward the voice. About halfway there, I realized I was running in the dark toward something that made a person who lives here scream. Gladys had collapsed near the sink and was crying hysterically. *"Onde fica perigo?"* ("Where is the danger?") I asked, forgetting that Gladys speaks Spanish, not Portuguese. *"Serpiente,"* she said between sobs, and then for some reason I demanded in Bengali, *"Shap kothai?"* ("Where is the snake?") and in English, "Did it bite you?"

A contingent of other staff as well as Dianne and Steve appeared in the dark, and in a second, with his lightning hand, Steve had caught the snake, pinning its head gently but firmly between his right thumb and forefinger. it was a three-foot yellow tree boa, whose triangular head gave it the look of a viper, but it was harmless. Steve handed it to me and let it wrap its lovely length around my arm, like a caress. I felt immense gratitude toward this snake: I was grateful that it had not bitten Gladys, that it was not poisonous, that I could touch it without fear. At that moment, I fervently loved that snake, for I could admire its beauty without fearing its cruelty. Unlike the Amazon that had swallowed Mario's son, I could adore it wholly, and feel no guilt for loving it.

We released the snake by the front steps leading to the dock, where we expected it would reappear on a fishing pole or in our boat the next morning.

After dinner, Moises had an announcement: the little boy's body had been found, and there would be a gathering at the house that night. We were all invited.

Dianne felt we shouldn't go. She and her husband, Pepper, knew what it was like to lose a son. At the time, she hadn't wanted to see anybody. She had hated having to smile at the well-wishers, who would say things like "I know how you feel," when they actually had no idea, and counsel, "Time heals all wounds," when nothing ever heals such heartbreak, not really. What would Mario's family want with a bunch of rich tourists gawking at their dead son? She felt we should butt out.

But perhaps, I worried, Mario's family would be offended if we didn't go. I asked Moises what he thought we should do. The family, he said in his soft voice, would consider it an honor if we attended.

The front of the house was jammed with canoes when we arrived that night. Ours was the only boat with a motor. Five men were sitting outside, smoking, atop an overturned canoe. The grandfather, Juan, whom we had met here just three days ago, greeted us with a smile and a handshake and *"Buenas noches."* We stood silently outside for a few minutes, then mounted the steps to the stilt house and joined the crowd inside.

About fifty people were there. In the flickering lamplight, we could see men playing casino, gambling for cigarettes, in a corner behind the mosquito net. Women lined one wall, sitting on wooden benches and rocking children in two hammocks while piles of other children slept like puppies at their feet. It seemed like a party, except the peccary-hide drum was still in the rafters, stilled, and no one was dancing. But no one was crying, either. In fact, people were laughing and telling stories. Everyone, including the few children who were still awake, was drinking masato, the beer made from manioc root, which the women chew and spit out to ferment in a jar, or, for a really big party, in a dugout canoe. The grandfather, Juan, offered cigarettes to everybody with a kind smile, exactly like a hostess passing canapés at a party.

In the midst of it all, Mario's son lay dead on a table, his little body wrapped in white cloth decorated with red plastic flowers, a crucifix at his head and two candles burning at his feet. Mucus bubbled from his nose periodically, and his older sister, perhaps five, unceremoniously wiped it with a handkerchief, a motion she had completed hundreds of times before. She had done this for him while he was alive; why should she not do so now that he was dead?

Soon Mario appeared, wearing a towel around his neck, joined by a friend wearing a T-shirt that proclaimed DO THE WILD THING. "We're so sorry, Mario," we said in English, reaching for his hand. Mario smiled at all of us, his great, gold-glinting smile. He was glad we had come.

Then Mario turned to his son on the table. Together with his friend, Mario slid out a tape measure alongside the little boy's body, running from head to foot. Minutes later, we heard a handsaw at work. They were making the coffin.

We sat down on benches and looked around the room. Almost every woman of fertile age was visibly pregnant, including one gray-haired, stooped grandmother who wore her pregnancy like a basket too heavy to carry. Imagine having to bear a child at her age, I said. "I would shoot myself," said Dianne. Yet the abortion vine is growing everywhere, I observed. The crucifix at the head of the child's bier, though, probably put an end to much of that.

I wondered how these pregnant women felt, here at the wake of their friends' child? My friends at home would have felt guilty, I knew, thinking the great ripe fruits of their bellies an affront to the bereaved parents. I remembered how one friend of mine, who had just given birth to a healthy son, had grown shy around a woman friend whose baby girl had been born with a slight deformity; another friend, newly pregnant, would not discuss her pregnancy with a girlfriend who was barren. Both felt guilty for their own fortune. But this is not the way of the people here. Death is no freak in the Amazon, but a companion with whom one walks daily—not without fear, not without mourning, but with composure and grace.

Most of the people in this house would stay the night with the family. Some would sleep, and some would play cards and smoke and drink masato and tell stories. They offered their presence like a gift, to stay beside the family to prove they aren't alone. They don't defy death, but they defy loneliness.

Like people confronting death everywhere, everyone brought food:

Food equals life. One person brought a rooster. And just before we left, we saw Mario carrying it by the feet, a tin pot in his other hand, in the direction of the kitchen. Then we heard it scream.

from The Custom of the Sea
by Neil Hanson

Captain Tom Dudley and three crewmen in 1884 tried to sail the 50-foot racing yacht Mignonette *from England to Australia. A forty-foot wave swamped the ship 1,000 miles off Africa. The crew cast off in a 13-foot skiff. Supplies: two cans of turnips. Neil Hanson here describes the men's subsequent behavior, grounds for one of Victorian England's greatest scandals.*

I n the immediate traumatic stress of a shipwreck, the body is flooded with adrenalin. Heart rate and blood pressure increase, the surface blood vessels constrict, minimizing heat loss and feeding more blood to the muscles, and the liver releases more sugar.

Without the necessary experience, knowledge and strength of will, however, much of this energy can be misdirected and shipwreck survivors often make catastrophic mistakes during this brief initial period of intense activity.

As the adrenalin ebbs and realization of the enormity of their predicament dawns, men respond in different ways. Some become dazed and disorganized, incapable of action or decision, and await the end with dumb passivity. Others react with strength and resolution, but over time, the physical effects of thirst and starvation aggravate the psychological impact of being adrift on the ocean and the mental and emotional stability of even the strongest man begins to falter.

Keeping to a routine, formulating plans to improve the chances of rescue, and keeping up morale by prayer, meditation, conversation or song, enhance the prospects of survival. Those who survive for days and weeks in an open boat do so on strength of will more than any physical characteristics, but ultimately even the strongest-willed person will be tempted to evade reality through dreams, fantasies or simply torpor. Dehydration, malnutrition, sleep deprivation, and the effects of sunburn and exposure will eventually lead to delirium and hallucinations.

Some will be driven to the extreme of self-destruction: suicide. Others will adopt the other extreme of self-preservation: the practice of cannibalism.

In the fading light they rowed through the slick of debris from the wreck. They found the chronometer and sextant as they were tossed on the swell and they also rescued the wooden base of the water-breaker, but the barrel itself had disappeared and the other four tins of provisions had been swept away. The only other items they managed to salvage were the wooden grating from the head sheets, which had floated off as the yacht sank, and a handful of sodden oakum.

Brooks pulled the oakum from the waves and used it to make a rough plug for the hole in the dinghy's side, slowing the rush of water into the boat. 'The seas were mountainous high and at times it was dreadful. We had formed a hole in our boat but we had managed to stop the great rush and had got her free when a great sea came in and filled her tip to the thwarts, but we again managed to get her free and we all of us offered up prayers to be brought through our present danger.'

They baled with everything to hand, using the two halves of the chronometer box as well as the baler, but the level in the boat still rose higher as each wave flooded in faster than they could throw water over the side.

Tom shouted to Brooks. 'We must head her into the sea or she'll founder.'

Half drowned by the waves crashing over them, the others kept baling, while Tom worked with frantic haste. He lashed together the breaker stand, the wooden grating and all the boards that could be spared from the boat and then threw them over the bow. The rope tightened with a snap and the dead weight of the makeshift sea-anchor began to drag the dinghy head-to-sea.

Each giant wave still seemed certain to bury the frail boat under tons of water, but each time the bow rose to meet the wave towering above them and followed it down into the trough. There was barely a moment's respite before the next wave was upon them.

Despite their fatigue, they were driven by the adrenalin of fear and maintained the frantic pace with the baler until the water level inside the boat at last began to fall. Nothing more could be done until daybreak and the men were too tired and dispirited to speak.

Tom stared into the darkness. He began to think of their situation: no water and only two one-pound tins as their stock of provisions, it was just becoming dark, the seas were mountainously high at times. He thought about his family back at home, and he was filled with dread.

Each man baled for an hour, then took a turn on watch, while the others, still soaked to the skin, snatched what rest they could.

The dinghy was still pitching on a steep swell when around eleven at night, as near as Tom could judge from the moon, he was jolted from a fitful doze by a thud against the underside of the boat. It was followed by a grinding noise and the dinghy lurched to one side. For a moment he thought they had run aground but there was no sound of breaking waves, no phosphorescent surf-line to be seen on the black sea.

Tom peered over the side and sensed as much as saw a swirl in the water ahead of them. A great shark, almost as long as the dinghy itself, sped back towards them, knocking its tail against the frail boat.

Tom saw a glint of moonlight on its grey, leathery hide as it broke surface. There was another crash as the shark thrashed its tall against the side of the boat. Waking from their daze, the other men gripped the gunwales and turned their frightened faces towards him.

The shark moved a short distance away, but then appeared to swim to and fro, as if keeping station ten or fifteen yards from the starboard side of the dinghy. Tom felt a surge of fear as it turned and surfaced again. He grabbed one of the oars and slapped the flat of the blade down on the sea. Even in the midst of the gale, the crack was like a musket shot and the splash of white foam caused the shark to veer away. There was a swirl of water and it disappeared.

Tom felt his heart pounding as he scanned the waves, but the seconds passed without any sign of its return. Then Brooks gave a cry. It had broken surface on the other side of the boat. Tom saw the glistening hide knifing through the water towards them, and scrambled across the dinghy, sending the gunwale dipping level with the water.

He stood half upright, swaying with the rhythm of the boat, and held the oar high above his head. As the shark closed on the dinghy, Tom brought the oar down on its head with all the strength he could muster. He was forced to his knees as the boat rocked wildly. There was a splash of white water and the shark dived beneath the boat and disappeared.

It returned several more times over the next hour, but each time Tom drove it away by battering it with the oar. At last they settled into an uneasy rest, praying for the dawn.

By first light, the worst of the storm had passed, though the towering seas were still heavier than Tom had ever known. He told Stephens, the tallest member of the crew, to haul himself upright to look for a sail and scan the sea for a sight of the missing water-breaker. It was a thin hope: the sea and wind could have driven it miles from them during the night, and after searching the ocean all around them he shook his head in despair.

Tom looked along the length of the dinghy. It was barely thirteen feet long, four feet wide and just twenty inches deep. Richard's pale, frightened face stared back at him, searching his expression for some glimmer of hope. There was little that Tom could offer. Stephens looked outwardly calm but Tom could see a muscle in his cheek tugging in an insistent nervous tic. Only Brooks's lined face remained stolid and expressionless, staring back at his captain, awaiting his orders.

'We can decide nothing until we know our position,' Tom said.

'Stephens, set to with the sextant. Brooks and Parker, bale while I plug this hole a little better.'

He took out his clasp knife and cut a few inches from the bottom of the legs of his trousers. As he pulled the sodden oakum out of the hole, water once more began to gush into the boat. It slowed to a trickle as he began to pack the hole with the black cloth. It took him almost an hour to secure it to his satisfaction, then he sat back on his haunches and motioned Stephens to join him in the bow, away from the others.

'Where are we?' He kept his voice low, not wishing to further alarm the boy, who had no real sense of how far from land they were and how desperate was their plight.

Ordinary seamen like Parker and Brooks had no knowledge whatsoever of navigation, particularly the complex process of establishing longitude. Few seamen had the education or interest in it and fewer still had the necessary funds, for ships' officers had to purchase their own navigation equipment. The expense of sextants and chronometers meant that sometimes even officers responsible for the navigation of their ships didn't carry them, and one expert witness to the 1836 Select Committee investigating the causes of shipwrecks admitted 'very many' instances of ships being three or four hundred miles from their estimated position.

It was also the deliberate policy of ship-owners and officers to keep their crews in ignorance. The one means by which a ship's captain ensured that his men could not rise up in mutiny against an often tyrannical rule was that only he and his senior officers had the necessary skill to navigate the ship safely back to port. The mysteries of navigation were therefore strictly controlled; it was an offence punishable by flogging for an ordinary seaman to attempt to keep his own log or take his own sightings.

Once they were out of sight of land, neither Brooks nor Richard had the slightest idea of where they were or which way to steer. Without Tom and Stephens to navigate, they would find land only by accident, not design.

'By dead reckoning we were twenty-seven degrees, ten minutes south and nine degrees, fifty minutes west when the ship sank,' Stephens said.

'Where is our nearest land?'

The mate shrugged. 'We could not be much worse placed. We are almost midway between St Helena seven hundred miles to the north and Tristan da Cunha perhaps seven hundred and fifty miles to the south-west, and even further from the coast of Africa.'

'The Cape?'

'South-east perhaps fifteen hundred miles, but we are still in the south-east trades at these latitudes. Whatever sail we manage to rig, we will not make ground to windward.'

'South America, then?'

'But that is more than two thousand miles.'

Tom thought for a moment, then turned to face the others. 'We are already well to the west of the steamship route to the Cape. We'll sail before the wind and make what speed we can towards the route of the barques and clippers. God willing, a ship will find us soon.'

'Or we may strike land,' Richard said, with a nervous, hopeful look.

Tom merely nodded.

Brooks remained silent. Although he knew nothing of latitude and longitude, he had been at sea long enough to realize the vastness of the ocean on which they were adrift.

Tom thought carefully before he spoke again. Ordinary seamen may have been ignorant of navigation, but they knew enough of maritime law to be aware that, when a ship sank, the captain's authority went down with it. From now on he could lead only by example. If they chose to disobey or unite against him, there was nothing he could do.

He cleared his throat. 'Our situation is poor. We have no water and little food, and we must conserve what we have.' He glanced at Brooks. 'What is in those tins?'

'Turnips.'

It was not the answer he had hoped for, but he held his expression unchanged. 'We shall not open them yet.' He paused, but no one argued with him. 'We will divide the day into four watches and take turns baling and steering.'

Brooks shook his head. 'The boy can bale but he does not have the skill to steer the boat. He is too young.'

Tom nodded. 'He will take his turn only when sea conditions allow. I'll take the first watch, Brooks the second, Stephens the third. We must also keep the boat trimmed. The boy and I will take berths in the stern, the other two forward. We will have to keep her head-to-wind, but if we rig a sail, we can make some progress sternways.'

Brooks interrupted him again. 'We have no sail.'

'Then we must fashion one out of our shirts.'

Brooks glanced at Stephens, and after a moment's hesitation, he shook his head. Richard gazed uncertainly from one to another.

'You would defy me?' Tom said.

'Are we to risk our death of cold or sunstroke to move a little faster before the wind, when we have not the least idea where we are heading?' Stephens said.

Tom checked, surprised at opposition from that quarter. 'We have our oilskins.'

'And we will suffer heatstroke if we wear them,' Stephens said.

'But we must make for South America.'

'We will all be dead long before we reach it.'

Tom saw Richard's frightened, hopeless look as he digested Stephens's words.

'But it is the only way,' Tom said. 'A ship may cross our path.'

Stephens nodded. 'It may, but we are far from the shipping lanes and it is no more and no less likely to do so here than at any other place on this ocean.'

Tom ignored him for the moment and looked towards the others. 'Will you not do as I ask?'

Neither of them replied.

Tom turned away to hide the anger on his face. He began pulling at the bottom boards of the dinghy. 'Then we must at least raise these.'

Brooks hesitated, then helped him to free the boards. They wedged them upright in the stern.

As Tom looked round he saw Richard kneeling against the side of the dinghy, urinating into the sea. 'Stop!'

Startled, the boy paused in mid-flow.

'We cannot survive without water,' Tom said. 'You know as well as I that drinking sea-water will send us mad. We have no fresh water, all that we have is our own.'

It took a moment for Richard to grasp his meaning. 'No. I will not do that. Are we dogs or men?'

'We are men who may die of thirst if a ship does not find us soon. Richard, if you are to survive, you must drink it.'

Richard hesitated, then reached for the wooden baler.

Tom shook his head. 'It is contaminated with sea-water. Use this.' He passed him the metal case from the chronometer. Richard urinated into the case, but stared at it for a long time before he put it to his lips. He swallowed a mouthful but then gagged and vomited over the side.

Tom reached out and rested a hand on his shoulder. 'You must make yourself drink it, or you will not survive.'

'I cannot, sir,' he said, but after a few deep breaths, he again raised the case to his lips. He drained it in one gulp, shuddered and wiped the back of his hand furiously across his mouth.

Tom held the gaze of each of them in turn. 'We must do what we have to do to survive. And survive we will.' He paused. 'Now, it is Sunday morning. Let us say a prayer together that the Lord will see fit to save us and restore us to our families.'

They bowed their heads and joined him in prayer, the murmur of their voices lost in the immense void of sea and sky.

Tom took the first watch. Despite the confident face he had tried to present to his crew, he had little genuine hope of survival. While the others closed their eyes in semblance of sleep, he unfolded the certificate wedged inside the back of the chronometer case, their sole piece of paper. He fumbled in his pocket for a stub of pencil and began scribbling a farewell note to his wife on the back of it.

July 6th 1884. To my dear wife—Phil Dudley, Myrtle Road, Sutton, in Surrey. *Mignonette* foundered yesterday. Weather knocked side in. We had five minutes to get in boat without

food or water. You and our children were in my thoughts
to the end. God bless and keep you. Your loving husband, Tom.

He folded the letter tightly and placed it in his inside pocket, then
leaned on the oar as he stared, unseeing, at the endless ocean swell.

Stephens had been watching him. He asked Tom for his knife and
scratched an even more terse note of farewell to his wife in the var-
nished surface of the sextant case, then added the boat's estimated
position. The scratching of the knife blade against the wood was the
only sound other than the scrape of the baler and the slap of waves
against the hull.

They drifted all that day without sight of a sail. In the evening, Tom
made a fresh attempt to get them to give up their shirts. 'The wind is
with us. We must make headway to westward into the track of the
sailing ships.'

Once more Brooks shook his head. 'We will be burned by the sun,
half frozen at night, as a sail is as likely to capsize us as to send us westward. I say no.'

Tom looked at the others. 'And are you with him or me in this?'

They both averted their eyes.

The next day dawned without sight of a sail. The sight and sound of
the waves lapping at the boat was a constant reminder of their thirst.
Tom's throat felt tight and sore and his lips were swollen and cracked.
Early in the morning he told Brooks to open the first tin of turnips. He
took out his knife and drove it into the top of the tin, using the
wooden baler as a hammer. He worked the knife around the top and
peeled back the lid. 'Five pieces. Divide one piece between two and give
us each a little of the fluid. We shall ration the rest to last us until
tomorrow night.'

The taste of the turnip was intensely sweet, and it seemed so cool as
it slipped down Tom's parched throat. He felt saliva start to his mouth,
but the bare mouthful of fluid gave only fleeting relief.

Stephens managed to take a rough altitude of the sun at noon and guessing the declination, fixed their latitude at roughly twenty-four degrees, fifty minutes south, almost on the line of the Tropic of Capricorn. The winds remained strong, driving them north-west, closer and closer to the equator.

The burning heat gave them no respite. Richard leaned over the side to splash his face, the boat lurched and suddenly he was in the sea. Tom could not say whether he had jumped or fallen. The thought of sharks chilled his blood, but he did not hesitate; neither Brooks nor Stephens could swim.

He tore off his shirt and threw himself into the sea. When he broke surface there was at first no sign of the boy, but as he was carried upwards on the swell he saw an upraised arm and Richard's face, with his mouth gaping open. Then the sea closed over him again.

Tom thrashed the water with his arms, driving himself towards the boy. The sea was empty, but for the boat. Then, through the grey-green water, he saw the pale shape of an upturned face and dark hair floating on the surface like seaweed.

He dived below the waves and grabbed Richard as he began to sink again. He kicked for the dim light of the surface above them as the dead weight of the boy and their waterlogged clothing threatened to drag them both down.

Kicking again, he clawed at the water with his free hand towards the surface, seemingly an eternity away. There was a roaring in his ears and stabbing pains in his chest. The stale air in his lungs bubbled up to the surface.

He held his breath until he could do so no longer, then took a convulsive, instinctive breath. Water filled his mouth and throat. Then he felt the slap of a wave against his face.

Coughing and choking, he drew air into his lungs and heard the boy gag and retch alongside him. His arms began to flail again. Tom cursed him. 'Be still. You'll drown us both. Be still.'

Still supporting the boy with one arm, he began to battle the swell towards the boat. Already exhausted, his stroke was feeble and ragged, and at each wave-crest the dinghy seemed as distant as ever. He felt his strength ebbing and drowsiness began to overcome him. Reaching the boat no longer seemed so important. He was tired; he would pause and rest for a few minutes, then swim on.

His head slipped beneath the waves. He choked and spat water, then struck out for the boat again. He heard a splash and a swirl of water, and froze, bracing himself for the impact as a shark tore him apart. Instead he heard another splash and through the spray he saw the black outline of an oar.

He grasped for it, missed, flung himself forward and caught it. He hauled himself along, hand over hand until he reached the side of the dinghy. Richard seemed barely aware of his surroundings, but Tom dragged him round to face the dinghy. 'Take hold of the gunwale.' He shook the boy. 'Take hold of the gunwale. Both hands.'

A moment later he felt the burden lift from his arm as Richard took his own weight for the first time. Tom clung to the side of the dinghy, too weary for the moment to do more. 'Keep watch for sharks,' he said.

They hung there for several minutes. Fearing a capsize, Tom worked his way round to the far side of the dinghy and hung from the gunwale as a counter-balance, while the others tried to haul the boy back into the boat. The dinghy rocked, then settled, as he slumped on to the bottom boards. Aided by Brooks and Stephens, Tom dragged himself over the gunwale with agonizing slowness, then curled up next to the boy, too weary to speak or move again.

The next day was a black day. Hunger was a constant dull, nagging pain, but thirst threatened to overwhelm them. Splashing their faces, necks and arms and wetting their hair seemed to help, but it offered little more than momentary relief.

Tom's throat was parched and his tongue sore and swollen, and the sea-water he had inadvertently swallowed made his thirst even more extreme. He rinsed out his mouth and gargled to ease his thirst and encouraged the others to do the same, but he watched carefully as they did so, giving constant warnings of the dangers of swallowing any. The temptation to lean over the gunwale, scoop up some sea-water and drink it down was overpowering, but with the blind certainty of every seaman, he knew the terrifying consequences.

There was ample anecdotal evidence to support Tom's belief. The tales told by the survivors of shipwrecks and passed on in ships' forecastles and during the long hours of the night watches all had the same conclusion: shipwrecked sailors who drank sea-water experienced delirium, insanity and death.

> The sailor then started to drink sea-water and soon became delirious. On one occasion he told me he was going for a walk and went over the side. After a struggle I managed to drag him back into the boat . . . I struggled with him throughout the night of the eleventh day. By the morning I, too, was becoming weak and delirious and could not restrain the sailor any longer. He went overboard some time on the twelfth day.

> Six of the survivors [were] taking occasional drinks of salt water. I warned them they would die a terrible death if they persisted. They obeyed me for a day or two but I soon found them again taking surreptitious drinks of sea-water. As they drank more and more they rapidly became delirious, imagining they could see rivers of water and snow . . . Three of them jumped overboard shortly after drinking the salt water.

> The poor man's face was a ghastly sight. His eyes protruded straight out of their sockets, while his lips were drawn back over his teeth in a bestial smile. His lips and teeth were covered with a thick white froth. His whole body shook periodically with great convulsions. Suddenly, as three or four men were trying to hold him down, the man . . . threw them off and leapt for the side of the boat.

The dangers of drinking sea-water were accepted without question until the early 1950s, when a Frenchman, Dr Alain Bombard, claimed that a castaway who drank small quantities of sea-water from the beginning of his ordeal, rather than waiting until thirst overwhelmed him, could survive. To prove his theory, he set out to cross the North Atlantic in an inflatable boat, *L'Hérétique*, carrying no supplies of fresh water with him. 'I had no rainwater for the first twenty-three days . . . During the whole of that period I proved conclusively that I could quench my thirst from fish and that the sea itself provided the liquid necessary to health . . . I drank seawater for fourteen days in all and fish juice for forty-three days. I had conquered the menace of thirst at sea.'

Dr Bombard's triumphalist conclusion was not entirely accurate. The metabolism of fish allows them to excrete the salt from the food and seawater they absorb. The fluids Dr Bombard extracted from the fish he caught were enough to dilute the small quantities of sea-water he drank. Had he drunk it on its own, he would not have survived.

Other mariners, including Thor Heyerdahl aboard *Kon Tiki* and Sir Francis Chichester on *Gypsy Moth IV*, also drank small amounts of sea-water without ill effect, and other experiments have shown that mixing it with fresh water in a ratio not exceeding five to one is not harmful, but any higher proportion can be fatal.

The old seaman's superstition that drinking sea-water sends you mad and kills you is absolutely correct. It does so because it dehydrates the body. Sea-water is a concentrated solution of sodium chloride and other salts, and has a higher specific gravity than fresh water. Through a process of osmosis—the tendency of solvents to diffuse through a porous partition, the stomach wall, into a more concentrated solution—water from the rest of the body is drawn into the stomach in an effort to dilute the sea-water.

The body's response to this dehydration is thirst, stimulating the urge to drink, but if that drink is also sea-water, the downward spiral continues. The sufferer gulps down more and more in a vain effort to slake this raging thirst, but each mouthful only exacerbates the problem. As they become progressively more dehydrated, the cells of the body contract, and shrinkage of the brain cells causes the delusions and insanity. The opposite effect occurs if a child swallows large quantities of chlorinated water after falling into a swimming-pool. It has a lower specific gravity than fresh water and passes through the stomach wall into the body, swelling the brain cells and causing fits in the child.

Although Tom Dudley was unaware of the fact and urged his men to drink their own urine, the urea contained in it has a similar, if lesser dehydrating effect. Despite Dr Bombard's experiment, unless there is also a sufficient supply of fresh water to dilute it, drinking sea-water or urine will hasten dehydration and death.

When they shared out the next ration of turnip, Tom held his piece in his mouth as long as he could, but most of the moisture had already evaporated from the tin and within a few minutes it felt as rough and dry as pumice. It was all he could do to chew and swallow it.

A lassitude had crept over them all. Their throats were so tight and sore that they barely spoke, staring into the green water, each alone with his thoughts. Towards dusk they ate the last of the first tin of turnips and shared the dribble of viscous, almost congealed fluid in the bottom of the tin. It was a relief when nightfall shrouded the others from Tom's sight.

Early the next morning, 9 July, Brooks saw a dark shape on the surface, just off their bow. For a moment terror gripped him, certain that the shark had returned to the attack. Then he recognized the shape of the creature and roused the others with a shout. 'A turtle! To the oars before it dives.'

The turtle was sleeping on the surface, no more than twenty yards off the port side of the boat. A few strokes of the oars brought them within range. Tom gripped the back of Stephens's shirt as he hung over the side of the boat, his fingers scrabbling for grip on the turtle's flippers as it struggled to break free.

Stephens lost his hold on the front flipper and threw himself further forward, his head dipping below the surface as he grabbed for it again. Then he straightened up, coughing and gasping, but clinging to the turtle. He dragged it over the side and dropped it on to the bottom boards, where it lay helpless on its back, its flippers waving.

Tom pulled out his knife. 'We must drink the blood,' he said. 'It will do us more good than the meat.'

He picked up the empty tin of turnips, then set it aside and reached for the chronometer case. Stephens held the turtle still as Tom slipped the case under its head and severed its neck with a single slash of his knife. Its struggles in its death throes sent blood pulsing into the metal bowl.

Craning his neck to watch Tom, Brooks had allowed the dinghy to drift beam-on to the waves. The next one broke over the gunwale, flooding the bottom of the boat and filling the chronometer case with sea-water. The men stared at it aghast.

Richard leaned forward. 'It is only a little water, surely we can drink it still?'

Tom hesitated for a second, then threw it over the side. 'It is conta-minated with sea-water. It will send us mad.'

Stephens stared at the red stain merging with the green water, then rounded on Brooks. 'If you had minded your work, we, not the fishes, would have been drinking that.'

Brooks clenched his fists and half rose to face him. 'You mind your words or you'll be the one feeding the fishes.'

Tom was again stooping over the turtle, catching the last few drops of blood as they dripped from its neck. He did not raise his eyes, but his voice cut through their shouts. 'You'll both sit down. Fighting amongst ourselves will only hasten our end.' He held out the case. 'There's little enough. Each man must take only his fair share.'

He handed it first to the boy, then passed it to Stephens and Brooks, and took the last and smallest share himself. There was barely a mouthful of the congealing blood remaining. It was warm, sweet and sickly and hard to force down but he felt a little strength returning almost as soon as he had swallowed it.

Richard baled out the dinghy, then Tom set down the chronometer case in the bottom of the boat and began to butcher the turtle. He severed the tough flippers and laid them in a row on one of the cross-members, then tore the turtle from its shell.

He removed the head and entrails and threw them over the side, but he dropped the heart and liver into the metal case and cut them in quarters. All four men fell on them ravenously, despite the fishy stench. Almost at once, Tom felt stronger.

He cut the turtle's flesh into strips and Stephens hung them around the boat to dry. There were only a few pounds of meat, but they were so overjoyed at their good fortune that, in the euphoria of the moment, they ate the rest of the second tin of turnips as well, savouring the sensation and the sweetness.

For over a week the gales continued. They were driven stern-first by a south-easterly gale—the trade winds that had failed them on the *Mignonette*—unable to turn and run before the wind for fear of being swamped. Even with the sea-anchor out, the bow of the dinghy constantly sheered off a few degrees either side of the wind. One man worked a steering oar at the stern, fighting to hold the dinghy head-on to each rising wave, but they broke constantly over the bows. At times they were a few seconds from foundering as the water level inside the boat rose to within inches of the gunwales. Everyone joined in frantic baling of the boat with anything that came to hand—the chronometer case, an empty tin or the wooden box that housed the sextant—until the water level began to drop again. Finally, on 13 July, the storm at last blew itself out, the seas slackened and they slumped into an exhausted sleep.

Each dawn Tom dragged himself up to search the horizon for a sail. Although he knew there was no land within hundreds of miles he could not stop himself from scanning the sky for the greenish tint of light reflected from the shallow water of a lagoon, or a telltale cloud formation—a patch of fixed cumulus in a clear sky or a thin line of the cloud—that indicated an island or a coastline nearby. There were no such signs on that day or on any of the succeeding days, only the endless march of the waves to the horizon.

At each passing squall or cloud they held out their oilskin capes to catch the rainwater. They put them on back to front, and held out their arms, as Stephens later said, 'waiting with burning throats and stomachs, and praying to the Almighty for water until the squall had passed. If we caught a little, how thankful we were.'

Many squalls seemed almost to mock them. On several occasions rain pocked the surface of the sea within sight of the dinghy, yet not a drop fell on them. The first of any rain that did fall had to be cast away, used only to clean the salt from their oilskins, and few squalls yielded more than a mouthful of drinkable water. Often even that would be spoiled by waves breaking over the boat before they could drink, but one storm give them each about a pint.

As he drank it down, forcing himself to sip it and roll each mouthful around his mouth before swallowing it, Tom felt saliva in his mouth and the constriction of his throat ease for the first time in days.

It was to be the last rain for four days, however, and soon they were again suffering in the savage heat. They could talk for no more than a few seconds before their hoarse whispers turned into hacking coughs.

Tom cut off a bone button from his oilskins and placed it in his mouth, hoping it would ease his thirst like a pebble in the desert. It seemed to soften a little in his mouth and there was a faint taste on his tongue. As he sucked it over the next few hours the button grew smaller and eventually dissolved completely. He cut off another and another over the succeeding days, until they had all been used.

Every couple of hours they rinsed their mouths and gargled with sea-water. Late one burning afternoon, Tom thought he saw the boy swallowing a mouthful. 'Lad, we are all driven mad with thirst, but you must not drink that.'

The boy's sallow cheeks flushed. 'Surely it will do no harm if we just drink a little of it.'

'Regard it as the poison that will kill you.'

The heat troubled them as much as their thirst. Their exposed flesh was burned an angry red, pocked with white blisters, and the rubbing of their salt-encrusted flannel shirts was agonizing to their skin.

To cool themselves, Stephens suggested soaking their flannel shirts, wringing them out and putting them on again. He and Brooks tried the experiment, but they soaked them again too close to dusk and shivered uncontrollably in their wet clothes during the night.

On the following days they all stripped naked and took turns to hang from the gunwale and dip themselves once or twice in the water. They did it one at a time, for only a few seconds, while the others remained in the boat on watch, for every time they bathed in this way, sharks would soon circle the boat, as if able to sense the naked bodies in the water.

The cool water on their skins refreshed them and even slaked their thirst a little, but as the days went by, they became too weak even to undress themselves. They could only ladle a little water over their heads and the effort required even for that task left them exhausted.

As Tom took his turn on watch, he looked with horror on the bodies of his crew. Their ribs and hip-bones were already showing through their wasting flesh. There were angry, ulcerating sores on their elbows, knees and feet, their lips were cracked and their tongues blackened and swollen.

They had continued to live on the turtle-flesh for a week, even though some of the fat became putrid in the fierce heat. Tom cut out the worst parts and threw them overboard, but they devoured the rest and when the flesh was finished, they chewed the bones and leathery skin.

They ate the last rancid scraps of it on the evening of 17 July. When he had finished chewing on his piece, Tom looked at the others. 'If no boat comes soon, we shall have to draw lots.'

Richard darted him a nervous look, too scared to meet his eye. Neither of the others showed any surprise at the subject Tom had raised. There was a long silence. 'We would be better to die together,' Brooks said. After a moment, Stephens nodded.

'So let it be,' Tom said, 'but it is hard for four to die when perhaps one might save the rest.'

'A boat will come,' Brooks said.

'So it may, but if one does not, or if it passes us by . . . '

The boy gave him a frightened look. 'Why would a ship pass us by?'

'If they see four mouths to feed,' Brooks said, 'they may not stop.'

Richard turned towards Tom. 'Surely no Christian men would leave us to die for want of a scrap of their bread and water.'

Tom saw the plea in the boy's eyes, but knowing the truth of Brooks's words, he could only nod his head. 'If the seas are high or the wind strong, they may fear wrecking themselves if they come to our aid.'

Brooks interrupted him. 'But we have all heard tales enough of ships that have sailed by a wreck though the water was as flat and calm as the Itchen on a summer's day. Some look away and pretend they have not heard, though the poor wretches plead, cry, rail and curse against them. Others, more brazen . . . .' His voice trailed away as Richard buried his face in his hands and began to sob, a terrible dry, rasping sound. No one moved to console him, each man too wrapped in his own dark thoughts.

As the boy's hoarse sobs still echoed through the boat, Stephens rounded on Brooks. 'What use was there in upsetting the boy with your foolish talk?'

'I spoke no more than the truth.'

They began a senseless, bitter argument. Fists clenched, they glared at each other and might have fought had Tom not interposed himself and cursed them both to silence.

Brooks retreated to his sanctuary in the bow. He lay down and wormed his way under the scrap of canvas covering it, hiding his head like a child burrowing under his bedsheets, and spoke no more to anyone that day.

'We were now in our worst straits,' Stephens later said. 'We used to sit and look at each other gradually wasting away, hunger and thirst in each face. The nights were the worst time. We used to dread them very much; they seemed never to end. We were so weak and cramped that we could hardly move. If we did get any sleep our dreams would be of eating and drinking.'

That night a rain squall passed over them and they caught some more water. Tom's hands were shaking so much that he spilled much of it as he tried to transfer some from his oilskin to the chronometer case, hoping to save it for a later moment.

There was no rain on the next day or the next, Sunday, 20 July, when Tom at last prevailed on them to give up their shirts. Stephens and the boy seemed past caring, lying listless in the bottom of the boat. Brooks began to argue again, then shrugged. 'What does it matter? We're doomed anyway. We'll die of sunstroke or thirst, but die we shall.' He took off his shirt and handed it to Tom.

Tom let Richard keep his shirt, but lashed the other three together, two above and one below, to form a triangular sail. They used an oar for a mast and split one of the boards for a yardarm. Tom hammered the back of his knife with the baler to open a crack in the wood, then forced it apart with the edge of the chronometer case until the board split along its length.

The shrouds and stays were fashioned out of the heart and outer strands of the boat's painter. With the makeshift sail rigged, the stern seats lashed up and a strong south-easterly blowing, they found the boat would run sternways before the wind, as long as there was not too much of a swell, and they made two or three knots.

Tom still had the burning determination within him to survive, but he could tell from the faces of the others that the faint hope of rescue to which they had clung was now extinguished.

The sting of salt on their skin added to the pain of their sunburn and together with the salt-water boils from which they were all suffering made even the slightest pressure unbearable. As they crawled about the cramped dinghy, taking their turns to steer and bale, it was impossible not to brush against each other, but the pain it caused was so agonizing that Stephens screamed aloud whenever he was touched.

When he asked to borrow Tom's knife and began scratching a further message in the lid of the sextant case, Tom knew that Stephens had given up his last hope of survival. Stephens scrawled his estimate of their position over the previous few days and then added:

To whoever picks this up Sunday July 20th PM We Thomas

Dudley, Edwin Stephens, Edmund Brooks and Richard Parker, the crew of the Yacht *Mignonette* which foundered on Saturday the 5th. of July, have been in our little dingy 15 days. We have neither food or water and are greatly reduced. We suppose our Latitude to be 25° South our Longitude 28° W May the Lord have mercy upon us Please forward this to Southampton.

That night the wind dropped and in the calmer conditions Richard took the night watch. Tom and Brooks were asleep but Stephens was only dozing when he heard an unfamiliar sound and opened his eyes. Richard was leaning over the side, scooping up sea-water in one of the empty tins. He drank some of it then looked round. He started as he saw the mate watching him.

Stephens put his finger to his lips, then worked his way back to the stern. He bent close to the boy's ear and whispered, 'How does it taste, Dick?'

'Not so bad.'

Stephens glanced behind him, then took the tin and swallowed a mouthful. He coughed and spluttered, then spat out the remainder. 'It burns my throat like fire. It's madness, Dick, you should not do that again.'

'Then what would you have me do—die of thirst instead?'

Stephens crawled back to his berth and huddled down in the bottom of the boat, but just before he closed his eyes, he again saw Richard lower the tin into the water.

Tom was woken by the sound of the boy retching and vomiting over the side. Brooks grabbed the steering oar and Richard fell back and lay on the bottom of the dinghy, gasping for breath.

Tom put his hand on the boy's forehead. It was burning hot. 'What ails you, boy?'

'I—I drank sea-water.'

'How much did you drink?'

'I don't know, perhaps three pints.'

'Then you're worse than a fool,' Brooks said.

Richard began to cry. No tears came from his matted eyes but his chest heaved with dry sobs. 'I had to drink something.'

Brooks hesitated, then put a hand on his shoulder. 'Cheer up, Dicky, it will all come right.'

He shook his head. 'We shall all die.'

They left him where he lay and over the next few hours his condition worsened. He began to suffer from violent diarrhoea and several times Tom and Brooks had to help him to squat over the gunwale as his body was shaken by spasms. Then he crawled back into the bottom of the boat and lay bent double from the pains in his stomach.

That night he became delirious, shouting and ranting, and he began slipping in and out of consciousness. Each time he woke, he said the same thing, 'I want a ship to get on board.'

The ship was all they ever heard him speak about. Whatever the frictions between them from time to time, the three others all shared an affection for the boy and did their best to lift his spirits, but he seemed barely to recognize them or hear their cracked voices. In one of his rare intervals of lucidity, he tried to drink some of his urine but was unable to do so, gagging and choking on it instead. He slumped down again.

There was a question in Tom's eyes as he glanced at the others, but neither man would meet his gaze. 'Something must be done,' he said.

Brooks looked up. 'Let us not talk of that further. Another ship will come.'

Tom shook his head and looked away. He pressed his fingers into the swollen flesh of his legs. The impressed marks turned white and remained visible for a long time after he released his grip. As he stared at them he felt something loose in his mouth. One of his teeth had dropped out. He spat it into his hand and threw it into the sea. He tested each of his other teeth with his fingers. All of them were loose in their sockets, barely held by his soft, pulpy gums.

Despite the positive face he took care to present to his crew, he was now beginning to despair. He took out the note he had begun writing to Philippa the morning after the shipwreck and scrawled a few more lines with the stub of his pencil.

9th picked up turtle. 21st July we have been here 17 days and have no food. We are all four living hoping to get passing ship if not dear we must soon die. Mr Thomson will put everything right if you go to him and I am sorry dear I ever started such a trip but I was doing it for our best. Thought so at the time. You know dear I should so much like to be spared you would find I should lead a Christian life for the remainder of my days. If ever this note reaches your hands dear you know the last of your Tom and loving husband. I am sorry things are gone against us thus far but hope to meet you and all our dear children in heaven. Do love them for my sake dear bless them and you all. I love you all dearly you know but it is God's will if I am to part from you but have hopes of being saved. We were about 1300 miles from Cape Town when the affair happened. So goodbye and God bless you all and may He provide for you all. Your loving husband, Tom Dudley.

There was no rain again that day. They lay sprawled in the boat without speaking, neither awake nor asleep, their minds drifting. Tom was astonished at the breadth and depth of his recall. Long-forgotten events, some great, some small, returned to him with crystal clarity. He heard the voices of childhood in his head and saw the village children scrambling over the fields, marshes and saltings. He saw Philippa at the piano in their first house in Oreston and heard every note of the songs she sang.

When he fell asleep, he was tortured by the same constant recurring dreams—soft rainfall speckling the surface of the Blackwater, morning mist hanging over Woodrolfe Creek, the cool shade of the trees in the sunlit meadows where he and Philippa used to walk, and the lemonade, cold from the cellar, that she would bring to him as he sat in the garden at Sutton and the children played in the grass around his feet.

Then he would jerk awake, dragged back to the present by his thirst and the pains in his body. To move was agony, but to remain still for long was an impossibility, as the rough boards dug into him and his salt-encrusted clothes chafed at his sores.

Even the effort of swallowing his urine tortured him. It was thick, yellow and stained with blood, and his throat seemed so dry and constricted that he could barely force it down without choking. It gave him no relief from his thirst.

By the following morning the men's mouths had become so parched and their tongues so swollen, they could hardly speak at all. Richard still lay in the bottom of the boat drifting between consciousness and oblivion.

Tom looked down at him, then glanced at the others. 'Better for one to die than for all of us.' Even to speak was torture, the words seeming to tear at his dry, cracked throat. 'I am willing to take my chance with the rest, but we must draw lots.'

'No. We shall see a ship tomorrow,' Stephens said.

'And if we do not?'

No one replied.

The day passed without rain and when a shower did come just after midnight, it barely troubled their upturned mouths or dampened their capes.

Although he hardly slept at all, Tom's mind drifted constantly. Mirages began to appear to him. He saw lush Islands and snow-capped mountains rising sheer from the sea, and a bank of haze lying on the water became the chalk cliffs of Kent. Sailing ships bore down on the dinghy and he was pulling himself upright, heart pounding with joy, when the vision faded again, leaving only the endless wastes of empty ocean.

Then he saw his father standing on the end of a jetty, beckoning to him. He felt drawn to the side of the dinghy and had to fight the urge to slip over the side into the water. He shook his head and shouted, 'No, I cannot do it,' in his cracked voice. The others barely stirred as he slumped down again.

Whenever he did lapse into unconsciousness, he dreamed of walking out of the dinghy across the sea to a beach or a waiting boat.

Once he woke to find that his legs were already over the gunwale, his feet trailing in the water. The discovery barely shocked him; sometimes he saw himself slipping downwards as the green waters closed over him, and dreamed that he was already dead.

The next morning dawned hot and leaden once more. Tom leaned forward and laid his hand on the boy's forehead. It was still burning hot and his breathing was shallow and erratic. 'Dick? Do you hear me, boy?' he said, his voice a cracked whisper.

There was no reply.

Tom sat back on his haunches and looked at the others. 'You both know what must be done.'

'Better for us all to die than for that,' Brooks said.

'Even when the death of one might save the lives of the rest? You are a bachelor, but Stephens and I are family men. It is not just our own lives, we have the fate of others to consider. Would you have us see our children cast into destitution, even the workhouse, when we have the means at hand to save ourselves and keep them from that fate?'

'I, too, have a—' Brooks began, then fell silent. 'At least wait for him to die,' he said. 'Let us not have the boy's murder on our consciences.'

'But if we wait for him to die, his blood will congeal in his veins. We must kill him if we are to drink the blood. And it must be done, it may save three lives.'

Brooks again shook his head. He lay down in the bow and hid his head under the canvas.

Stephens did not speak, but Tom read a different message in his eyes.

That night Brooks had the watch from midnight. While he steered, Tom and Stephens sat in the bow, talking in whispers.

'What's to be done?' Tom said. 'I believe the boy is dying. Brooks is a bachelor—or says he is—but you have a wife and five children, and I have a wife and three children. Human flesh has been eaten before.'

Stephens hesitated. 'See what daylight brings forth.'

'But if sunrise brings no rain and no sign of a sail?'

Stephens stared out over the dark water, then muttered, 'God forgive me,' and nodded his assent.

Soon after dawn Tom and Stephens hauled themselves up in turn on the improvised rigging and searched the horizon for a sail. There was none in sight under the cloudless sky. Richard still lay in the bottom of the boat, with hiss head on the starboard side and his feet on the port side, his arm across his face. He was rapidly sinking into unconsciousness.

'We shall have to draw lots,' Stephens said. 'It is the custom of the sea.'

Richard lay comatose in the bottom of the dinghy and gave no sign that he had heard Stephens's words. Brooks remained silent and Tom did not wait for a reply from him. He pulled out his knife and whittled four thin slivers of wood from the gunwale of the dinghy. He trimmed three to equal length and cut the other one a half-inch shorter.

'We'll have to draw Dick's lot for him,' Stephens said.

The three men exchanged looks between themselves. Tom laid the pieces of wood across his palm, the ends protruding beyond his index finger. The shortest lot was on the right. Palm open, he showed them to Stephens and Brooks. Then, without changing their positions, he closed his hand over the bottom ends of the slivers and held them out.

Brooks licked his blackened lips and, as Stephens hesitated, he reached past him and took the left-hand lot. Stephens took the next. Tom was about to complete the ritual by taking the next when he paused, looked the others in the eye and then threw the remaining slivers into the sea.

'Why go through this charade?' he said. 'What is to be gained when one lies dying anyway? We all know what must be done. Let us be honest men about it, at least.'

No further word was exchanged, but Stephens looked down at the boy and nodded. Both then turned towards Brooks. He hesitated, then bowed his head.

'Who is to do it?'

'I cannot,' Brooks said.

Stephens shook his head. 'Nor I.'

'Then I shall have to,' Tom said.

He stared at Brooks. 'You had better go forward and have a rest. Stephens, take over the watch.'

Stephens took the steering oar, while Brooks moved towards the bow and lay down, once more hiding his face under the canvas sheet.

Shading his eyes against the glare of the burning sun, Tom took hold of the shrouds and pulled himself up to search the horizon all around them for any trace of a ship. Nothing broke the glassy surface of the sea.

He remained motionless for a moment, offering a prayer for the boy's soul, and asking forgiveness of his Maker. Then he placed the chronometer case next to Richard's head, took out his knife and opened the blade. The sunlight glinted from the blue steel.

He glanced towards Stephens. 'Hold the boy's legs if he struggles.'

Richard had appeared to be unconscious but his eyes flickered open at the words. His pupils had lost almost all their pigment and were the colour of skimmed milk. Tom doubted whether he could even still see.

'What—me, sir?' he said.

Tom made no reply. He placed the knife against the boy's neck. Trying to close his mind to what he was about to do, he began reciting under his breath the instructions in *The Steward's Handbook* that he had been forced to learn years before on his first voyage as cook-steward. '"Proceed immediately to bleed the beast. This is done by cutting up the gullet and severing the arteries and veins on each side of the neck, near to the head. The blood will now flow out quite freely."'

He took a handful of the boy's hair in his left hand, holding his head still against the boards, then plunged the knife into his neck. He jerked the blade sideways, severing an artery and slicing into the windpipe, then dropped the knife and held the metal bowl against Richard's neck.

The boy did not even cry out, but as blood began to pump from the wound in a slow, palsied beat, his arms flailed and a terrible, wet sucking sound came from his torn windpipe. His white eyes stared sightlessly up at Tom.

He tried to shut his ears to the sound of the boy's death throes, but they echoed in his mind long after the noises had at last ceased and the twitching body lay still. Only a dribble of blood still flowed from the wound.

The blood he had collected in the chronometer case was thick and viscous and already beginning to congeal. They began to drink it in turn. Brooks scrambled from under his canvas cover. 'Give me a drop of that,' he said, and they shared it with him.

As soon as they had finished the blood, Tom and Stephens stripped the clothes from the boy's body. Tom then pushed the knife into the stomach just below the breastbone and forced it downwards, opening a deep slit in Richard's belly. Even strengthened a little by the blood, he was so weak and slow that the cut seemed to take minutes to complete.

He paused, his breath coming in hoarse gasps. '"Now make a slit in the stomach and run the knife right up to the tail. Remove the fat from round the intestines and then pull out the intestines, paunch, and liver. Cut the gall bladder off the liver right away. Turn the kidney fat over and remove the kidneys. Now cut through the diaphragm, commonly called the skirt, which separates the organs within the chest from the intestines, and remove the lungs, heart, and thorax."'

He reached into the still warm chest cavity and pulled out the heart and liver. He put them in the chronometer case and cut them up. The three men ate them ravenously, squabbling over the pieces like dogs.

When they had eaten the last scrap, Tom raised his gaze from the bloodstained bowl and stared at the others. Their faces were smeared with blood and their eyes were wild. He shuddered, knowing that his own visage was no different, but he could already feel strength flowing back into his body. '"When this has all been done, get some warm water and wash out the carcass, and any blood that may be on it must be washed off."'

He leaned over the gunwale and rinsed the blood from his face, then sent Brooks aft to steer the boat while Stephens helped him to butcher the body. Not wanting to see the dead boy's face in front of him as he worked, Tom first cut off the head and threw it overboard. His fingers slippery with blood, he worked as fast as he could, hacking off strips of flesh, which Stephens washed in the sea and laid across the cross-beams to dry.

At first Tom used the wooden cross-member as a butcher's block, but fearing that he might further damage the boat's thin planking as he hacked and sawed at the body with his knife, he did the heavier cutting—parting the joints and severing the tendons—against the brass crutches of the oars. It took three hours to complete the grisly task.

The larger bones, and Richard's feet, genitals and intestines, were also thrown overboard. They looked on in horror as, astern of the boat, sharks thrashed the water into a pink froth, fighting over the bloody fragments. One was bitten in the head by a larger shark as they fought over some part of the body. In an instant, every one of the pack of sharks circling the remains had turned on the wounded creature. It was ripped apart in little more than a minute.

Even when the blood and entrails had been consumed or dissipated by the waves, sharks continued to track the dinghy. A fin showed above the water from time to time and there was a grinding thud as one broke surface right alongside the dinghy, sending it crabbing sideways. Tom tried to drive it off by hitting it with an oar, but already weak and further exhausted by his struggle to butcher the carcass, he barely had the strength to raise it above his head.

Brooks took over, and though he did not manage to hit the shark, the noise of the oar banging on the water was enough to scare it off. From time to time they glimpsed the sharks astern of the dinghy, and even when unseen, all of them continued to fear their presence.

from Godforsaken Sea

by Derek Lundy

Sailors entering France's Vendée Globe race know they'll encounter storms—the route takes them on a solo voyage from France's Bay of Biscay, around Antarctica through the Southern Ocean, and back to France. Still, participants in the 1996-to-97 race were surprised by the ferocity of the weather in the Southern Ocean. Derek Lundy describes that weather's impact on several of the hardest-hit racers.

The difficulties in this race weren't long in coming. So far, there had been withdrawals, collisions, knockdowns—the normal quota of trouble in any Vendée Globe or BOC. Only ten boats remained officially in the running. But at Christmas, seven and a half weeks after the race began, its rough yet familiar tenor suddenly shifted. The catastrophic events of the ensuing two weeks changed the race so completely that it seemed to become a mutated version of itself, a new species, recognizable in form but exhibiting novel and frightening behavior. The Vendée Globe fleet staggered as the EPIRBs began to go off, one after the other.

Remember December 25—Dinelli's boat capsizing in the force 11 winds and big rollers of the unexpected, close-isobar depression. His mast smashing a hole in the boat's deck, and *Algimouss* filling with water, the boat rolling sluggishly upright again, Dinelli lashing himself to his awash deck, beginning his wait, his life a toss-up.

Now the fragile line of succor between sailors in the Southern Ocean would stretch to the limit. Would it hold?

Dinelli's EPIRB signals were picked up quickly by satellite, his personal signal identified and relayed to race headquarters. Philippe Jeantot moved fast to try to cobble together a rescue. Patrick de Radiguès, only sixty miles away from Dinelli's position, was the closest sailor and, most important, he was upwind. Even in these extreme conditions, he stood a good chance of being able to guide *Afibel*, his fast-running boat, downwind toward Dinelli. But de Radiguès was incommunicado. The electrical problems that had plagued him throughout the race meant that neither his radio nor his fax was working. Jeantot tried to raise him for two or three hours, without success.

The only other possibility was Pete Goss.

Goss was close enough to Dinelli—about 160 miles downwind of him—to have experienced the rapid onset and development of the same storm. Christmas Day had started out genuinely blessed—bright and sunny, with a pleasant twenty-knot northerly wind. But Goss knew it wouldn't last. It was unusual enough to have sunshine and light winds in the first place. And he too had heard Chabaud's warning about the moderate low-pressure system she was sailing through, which would overtake him and Dinelli before the day was out. Goss had a feeling about this one, however, a sense that it was going to be worse than Chabaud had suggested. It was an intuition of impending disaster, he said later.

And no wonder. The barometric pressure dropped forty-six millibars in twenty-four hours, most of that in the last twelve hours of the day. That was a very steep drop, and no sailor could have doubted that something big and menacing was in the works. Weatherfaxes and high-seas weather forecasts were all very well, with their neat, colored satellite pictures and detailed predictions, but they were unreliable in the Southern Ocean. Weatherfax information was a matter of supply and demand. No one went there; why waste resources on forecasting its weather? Both the pictures and the forecasts covered vast sea areas. The sailor could never be sure what would actually happen at any given moment in any particular square mile of sea. The barometer, that old harbinger of weather change, could sometimes tell you more than modern instruments about what was ready to drop on your head.

At sea with low and falling glass,/Soundly sleeps the careless ass.

A diving mercury wouldn't, by itself, identify the center of the low or tell you what else was on the way. But it was certainly a predictor of generalized misery, and its likely intensity. You knew that shit was about to happen, and right on top of you. A fast-falling glass was like the slow scream of a shell coming in on the soldier's position. Pain was inevitable.

Goss's premonitions were right. Because of *Aqua Quorum's* location in relation to the dense low's center, the wind went round to the southwest almost right away. And it rose like an elevator— forty, fifty, up to about sixty knots in three hours, as the tightly packed mass of the low swept over him. Conditions got so bad so quickly that he spent almost all that time continuously reducing the boat's sail area, just keeping on top of it. And then the boat was screaming and surfing at twenty-eight knots, under bare poles—no sail up, driven by wind pressure on the mast and rigging alone.

As the storm grew, things quickly became dangerous for Goss. The race receded into the background as he found himself in survival conditions, trying to cope with the increasingly dangerous seas. It was a classic development of Southern Ocean low-pressure-system waves. The northerly wave set, created by the storm as it first approached, was crossed by the southwesterly seas that ensued after the quick wind change, resulting in truly vicious breakers. He was knocked down three times and started to sustain damage. "It was bloody hairy, really. I nearly pitchpoled a couple of times, and a lot of water got in everywhere."

In the middle of this mayhem, his computer beeped, and he noticed that a Mayday had been registered somewhere, but he was too busy to check the position. He didn't recognize it as Dinelli's emergency beacon. Because the Frenchman had been a late entry, Goss didn't register the name of Dinelli's boat—he was used to dealing with the other skippers using only their first names. The distress signal could have come from anywhere off the Australian coast. It just didn't occur to him that it could be one of his fellow racers. When he had a few seconds' breather, he began to look for a chart in the scrambled mess of his cabin so that he could see where the Mayday was originating. Just then, his computer beeped again. It was Jeantot telling him that the Mayday was Dinelli.

"I asked Pete what was his condition," said Jeantot. "Because I knew he was sailing under bare poles and that conditions were very, very bad. And I asked him, Do you think it's possible for you to head back and help Dinelli?"

Goss fixed back immediately to tell Jeantot that he had problems, that he'd been knocked down, that things were a bit dicey. He wanted more information. What about de Radiguès? he asked Jeantot. Goss knew the Belgian's position and that he was only three hours upwind of Dinelli. And he knew that trying to go upwind 160 miles in the storm would be very dangerous. He might not survive.

But right after he had sent the fax, he thought, Well, I've got to go back anyway. No matter what information Jeantot responded with.

"People have often asked about the decision to go back," he said.

"But it was easy. It's just what you do when someone's in trouble. I suppose it was a decision made by tradition of the sea. Having made it, and thinking about it, I had to come to terms with the consequences of it. You know, you sit down for thirty seconds and think about your family and everything. But at the end of the day, for me, it's a simple process: you either stand by your morals and principles, or you don't."

Goss was responding to the unwritten law of the sea, the sailor's prime directive: that aid must be rendered to anyone at sea who asks for help. Even if it cost a lot of money—supertankers or big freighters, for example, steaming days out of their way and incurring hundreds of thousands of dollars in extra operating costs, or delivery-delay penalties, to search for a single sailor in trouble on a small yacht. Even if it put the helper's own life in some jeopardy.

According to Jeantot, Goss then simply told him, "I have no choice. I'll do it."

Goss crawled out into *Aqua Quorum*'s cockpit and, in hurricane-force winds of seventy knots or so, in the enormous and confused seas, he hoisted a tiny storm jib. He needed some sail up in order to have any chance of beating back upwind. It took him a long time to get the sail up. It was only possible at all because, with his boat's speed, the apparent wind strength was only about fifty knots (Beaufort force 10, a full storm). Goss couldn't distinguish sea from air because of airborne spray and spume. The boat's motion was extremely dangerous—violent, quick, unpredictable. And the fear, which only an insane person would not feel, permeated everything. Sailing his boat to windward in this storm could subject it to stress that no designer would ever build into a hull, let alone into the more vulnerable mast and its supporting standing rigging. It was a real possibility—in fact, it might be more accurate to say that it was probable—that *Aqua Quorum* would not survive the punishment Goss was about to inflict on it.

The time had come. If any man has a moment in his life in which everything is in the balance, where death is as likely, or more likely, an outcome as life, Goss was entering such a moment now. It would be a prolonged moment, two days or more to get back to Dinelli's position—if he got back at all.

He put the helm over and turned his boat into the wind and waves. The apparent wind immediately increased by the twenty-five-knot speed the boat had been traveling downwind, and Goss felt the full force of the hurricane he was turning into. It knocked *Aqua Quorum* down right away and pinned it there, flat on the water, the mast top across the waves, the guardrails under the surface. Goss thought, Shit, can we do anything in this at all?

For a minute or so, willing though he was to risk his life, it looked as if the wind just wouldn't let him. He might not be able to move the boat toward Dinelli.

Then, in a slight lull, the mast came up very slowly and grudgingly out of the water, and the boat began to move to windward. Goss found that he could sail at five or six knots about eighty degrees off the wind. Remember what this is like: the five- or six-story buildings, some even higher; the toppling crests, two stories or so high, with their tons of avalanching water moving at thirty miles an hour; the wind lulling in the troughs of the waves as the sea to windward blocks it, the boat losing speed and steerageway; the long, steep-angled climb to the wave top, the wind increasing in force as the boat climbs until, on the crest, the full force of wind accelerates the boat down the fifty-foot slope of the wave into the next trough.

Goss couldn't open his eyes to windward and it was difficult to breathe. The noise was unrelenting and deafening, at a decibel level approaching that of a nearby jet engine. In gusts, the wind blew well into the range of hurricane force, and *Aqua Quorum* and her skipper endured the full strength of every knot of it.

As his boat made its slow, concussive progress, climbing one mountainous wave after another, Goss kept wondering if it would hold together. No boat, and no specialized Vendée Globe design in particular, could be counted on to withstand the shocking loads this violent motion was inflicting on its components. Other boats had begun to come apart in much less severe conditions than this.

In fact, not even *Aqua Quorum's* designer was sure the boat would remain intact. When Adrian Thompson and his associates heard what Goss was up to, they were very apprehensive. "To be honest," said Thompson, "we were sitting in the design office in a state of extreme nervousness and stress."

None of the hull-load calculations had been the result of exact science. As their boat confronted the Southern Ocean in its stormy spate, they could only hope they had been on the right side of the line when they drew up their specifications. This was the most extreme test imaginable, but, they hoped, not a test to destruction.

With his ingrained soldier's approach to danger, Goss broke his rescue mission into a series of distinct phases. Phase one was to survive the storm. Rescue phases would follow. It was a very grim night. He was knocked down every half hour; there was lots of damage, gear everywhere. At one point, he was hurled across the cabin and landed hard on the elbow that had become infected early in the race. It had been bothering him ever since, in spite of his self-treatment with antibiotics. The punishment it took that night began a chain of complications that would later test Goss in a different way. In the meantime, he was being thrown around so much that he had to climb into his bunk and tie himself down.

Luckily, the next day, the worst of the low passed over. It was a shorter than usual shellacking because, for once, the boat was heading against the storm's track rather than running with it, and the system passed over quickly in the opposite direction. The wind dropped to forty-five knots. It seemed like a calm day to Goss; it was amazing what you could get used to, he thought. He began to repair damage to his mainsail and other gear. His aft watertight compartment was full of water, and he bailed it out.

Goss had no idea whether the French sailor was still alive. But he was sure that Dinelli's "clock was ticking" and that it was just time that would save his life. Goss received hourly satellite weather information from Météo France via Jeantot, who spent a sleepless day and night himself. Another low-pressure system was on the way.

By nightfall, Goss finally heard from the Australian air force. It had been notified of Dinelli's distress signal, standard procedure, and one of its planes, operating at the very limit of its useful range, had homed in on Dinelli's EPIRB signals and found him. He was alive, the Australians told Goss, and had managed to get into one of the two life rafts they'd dropped to him just before his boat sank.

● ● ●

He hadn't felt afraid, Dinelli said, as he had stood on frozen feet in great pain, tethered to the deck of his sinking boat, ice-cold waves breaking over him.

"I think that this is in no way heroic. I think that when man faces an extreme situation, if he becomes afraid, he loses all his capacities. I stayed this way for thirty-six hours without eating or drinking. At the end, my eyes were burnt by the sun, the salt, the wind. My feet were freezing; I could not feel them anymore."

He hoped that the Australians or de Radiguès, or perhaps Goss, would get to him before he sank. But he knew it would be close. The Australian plane located him an hour before dark. Ten minutes after he tumbled into the life raft, his boat sank.

"I knew I only had one hour left before dark, and if the airplane had not shown up, it was finished. I would be dead. Death was one hour away. I knew the limits."

Dinelli was too cold. He knew he couldn't survive until a ship got to him. Everyone involved in the rescue knew that, too. No ship was dispatched. Goss was Dinelli's only hope—his ferry away from death.

It took Goss the rest of that day and until midnight the next night to get to the general area of Dinelli's Mayday. He was, after all, still beating to windward into the teeth of a strong gale (force 9 on the Beaufort scale), with big seas left over from the storm system. He searched for Dinelli's life raft for the rest of the night, but the Mayday position fix kept jumping, a quarter mile or so every two hours. True to its wild form, the Southern Ocean flung the predicted front across the area, and in the deteriorating conditions, a quarter mile might as well have been a hundred miles. Visibility was bad, with heavy rain. Goss would cover an area as best he could, then a different position would come through. So he'd search that area, and then another. With growing desperation, Goss hunted through the valleys and crests of the big seas for the tiny, low-lying, eight-foot-diameter raft.

Goss would not have found Dinelli's raft on his own. At one point, he probably passed within a few hundred yards of it without seeing anything. He could look around him briefly when his boat was on the crest of a wave, but the rest of the time, he could see only the walls of water hemming him in. He was exhausted; he hadn't slept for more than two days, he was battered and bruised, and he was drained of nervous energy by the beat through the storm. He also hadn't eaten anything, or had much to drink. In the thirty hours it took him to get back close to Dinelli, he lost an estimated seven or eight pounds in weight.

The next morning, the Australian air force plane came back out. From its vantage point, it found Dinelli's tiny raft and dropped smoke flares to mark his location. Goss couldn't see even those in the driving spray and big waves. Finally, the plane flew over Dinelli and, as it did so, turned on its landing lights. Goss saw them and got a compass bearing. He was about three miles away from the raft. He thought there was a good chance that Dinelli was badly injured or had died during the night from exposure and hypothermia. He worried it would be Dinelli's corpse that he would have to drag out of the raft. He wondered what he would tell the French sailor's family. Then the Australian plane radioed him with news: Dinelli had waved to them. He was still alive.

When Dinelli first saw Goss's boat, he thought it must be de Radiguès; he thought it very unlikely that Goss could make it back to be his rescuer. The pickup went like clockwork; it was clinical, Goss said. He beat to windward of the raft, then turned downwind and ran toward it. Two boat-lengths away, he rounded up into the wind again. He backed his little storm jib and drifted down beside the raft, the boat rolling violently but creating a slightly calmer lee for the raft, smoothing the transfer. Stricken though he was, Dinelli came aboard *Aqua Quorum* with professional panache. He handed up his emergency beacons to Goss so they wouldn't keep transmitting Maydays. Then, to Goss's astonishment, and in a quintessential Gallic gesture, Dinelli handed him a bottle of champagne. He'd managed to hang on to it through everything, in a pocket of his survival suit. Goss hauled him aboard.

Dinelli's coolness masked his desperate condition.

"I got him onto the boat," Goss said, "and we were rolling violently and I thought, All right, I'll leave him there, he's fine, and put the storm jib about, and get the boat going downwind, and I can come back to him."

But when Goss let go of Dinelli, the French sailor fell flat on his face, almost breaking his nose. He was as stiff as a board and could barely move by himself. Then Goss realized how far gone Dinelli was. He rolled him over onto his back. "And all you could see was his eyes," Goss said. "And it was just ... the emotion in the pair of eyes was just amazing, really. He was trying to say 'Thank you, thank you'; he couldn't really talk. He was very cold."

And the two men hugged each other.

As he was telling me this, Goss paused for a few seconds, staring out *Aqua Quorum*'s hatch at the tarred and barnacled Southampton dock nearby. Six months afterward, the emotion of the moment of rescue—when he returned Dinelli's life to him—was still strong.

Goss dragged Dinelli to the shelter of his cockpit spray hood and propped him on a little seat. He got the jib trimmed and turned the boat downwind under autopilot. Dinelli was so stiff that Goss had trouble bending his arms and legs to angle him in through the small companionway hatch and into the cabin. He stripped off Dinelli's sodden survival suit and got him into his own thermal suit and then into his sleeping bag. He radioed the Australian plane and asked them to tell Dinelli's family that he would survive and that he could handle the situation—not that there was a lot they could do anyway.

"Raphaël is on board," Goss told them. "He is very cold and happy. He has no injuries. I have just given him a cup of tea. I have all his ARGOS on board. Cheers."

In an exchange of national stereotypes, Goss replied to Dinelli's gift of champagne with his now-famous English cup of tea. It was a cyclist's bottle, to be precise—warm, very sugary tea that Dinelli could suck up through the nipple on the bottle. It was important to get his core body temperature up again.

"And then, I was absolutely knackered," said Goss. "Oh, completely shagged, and I thought, Great, I need an hour's sleep, and I'll get back to it." But Dinelli was high on the adrenaline rush of his own, unexpected survival. He wouldn't shut up.

"He was bloody rabbiting away," said Goss.

"Poor Pete," Dinelli said. "He had to look after me during the day, and then I kept him up all night talking."

Goss couldn't speak French. But Dinelli had a sort of pidgin English and, because he was very bright, his language improved quickly. The two men drew pictures and went through charades. By the end of their ten-day sail to Hobart, Tasmania, where Goss would drop Dinelli off, they were having deep conversations.

Dinelli couldn't feel his hands or feet, and long strips of skin began to peel off the frostbitten limbs. For five days, he was a helpless invalid. Goss had to lift him onto the toilet bucket and hold him there and feed him every four hours; he gave him muscle relaxants and pain medication. By the time they arrived in Hobart, Dinelli was, shakily, back on his feet. He would make a complete recovery. . . .

Four days into the new year, the string of Vendée Globe boats stretched out to more than five thousand miles. Day by day, Auguin had increased his lead over Roufs, and he was now sixteen hundred miles ahead of the Canadian and just nine hundred miles from the Horn, his "gate to the exit from hell." He'd had it with the cold, the wind, the stress. Then something strange happened to the weather. Auguin and the next four boats—Roufs, Thiercelin, Laurent, and de Broc—found themselves in an unusual weather system, two thousand miles across, with light wind, frequent squalls, and snow. In the changeable conditions, the sailors had to constantly reef the sails, then shake out the reefs, trim the sheets, and adjust the course. Auguin had an hour's sleep in twenty-four. Laurent complained that Météo France had predicted a day of light winds, but the calmer conditions had unaccountably stretch'ed out to three days. It was a break from gales and big waves, but it wasn't getting them out of the Southern Ocean, and more of the usual lows were on the way—boats farther back were getting them. As Knox-Johnston had said, waiting for it was almost as bad as getting it. For once, the Southern Ocean weather wasn't more or less uniform for the whole fleet. Dumont, for example, three thousand miles back, was going through an average forty-knot gale with heavier squalls. Nothing special. Chabaud, four thousand miles behind Auguin, was in the middle of sixty-knot wind.

At the back of the fleet, Bullimore and Dubois, sailing within forty miles of each other, had a strong northwest gale on their hands. More ominously, however, the weather forecast for their area seemed to be picking up the early signs of what meteorologists call a "bomb"—a very fast-developing and intense low—which would soon overtake them. They could expect a high-latitude depression, typical in its structure, but with more explosive winds than usual and a very abrupt wind shift from west to southwest as the center tracked by. This wasn't just another depression. This was trouble.

And indeed, the rescue of Dinelli quickly became merely the opening act in the Vendée Globe Christmas drama. Goss was still sailing the lucky survivor to Hobart when the beacons went off again.

Bullimore's boat flipped when its keel suddenly broke off. Not even a preliminary broach. *Exide Challenger* just rolled over as it surfed down a wave, Bullimore rolling with it. No mug of tea left, but finishing his cigarette, thinking out what to do next. Then the window smashed by the boom, the boat instantly flooding, the cabin contents sucked out into the sea. Bullimore diving down and through the companionway hatch to try to cut away his life raft. The hatch slamming shut, chop-

ping off his finger. Floating one of his ARGOS beacons out the broken
window through the swirling wreckage of rigging and spars, up to what
he hoped was the surface. Climbing up onto his little shelf, half in, half
out of the freezing water. Waiting for whatever might happen: most
likely death.

Almost simultaneously, the dismasted Dubois righted, rolling
over again and staying that way. After two hours, climbing out
through the transom hatch, unable to reach his 406 EPIRB, and setting off two of his ARGOS beacons, lashing them to his body the way
mountain climbers do, scrambling up the steep, slick slope of the
hull to cling to one of the twin rudders. Getting washed off into the
sea. Somehow managing to clamber back onto the hull again,
exposed to the full force of bitterly cold waves and subzero windchill. Waiting, like Bullimore.

Jeantot and the regional search-and-rescue operational center in Brit-
tany—CROSS in the French acronym—passed along to the Australians
the job of responding to the distress calls. These Maydays, like Dinelli's,
were their bailiwick. This time, no other racers were within striking distance of either Bullimore or Dubois. Running at the rear of the Vendée
Globe fleet because of their forced port calls, they were particularly isolated. The closest sailor was Chabaud, more than twelve hundred miles
downwind to the east. It was impossible for her to get back. Only the
Australians had any chance of rescuing the two men, assuming they
were still alive. The Australian maritime rescue coordination center in
Canberra asked the air force and navy to help. An air force P-3 Orion
long-distance search-and-rescue plane was dispatched right away, followed the next day by a frigate, the *Adelaide*.

Even this fast warship would take four days to reach the wounded
boats—assuming that the weather would allow it to negotiate its
Southern Ocean passage at top cruising speed. Assuming, too, that it
didn't run into trouble itself in the strong winds and big waves. Like
most modern warships, it was a lightly built aluminum vessel, and its

three-eighths-inch-thick hull had finite wave-impact resistance. Large amounts of ice had been reported around fifty-two degrees south, not far from the yachts' positions. The *Adelaide* was as vulnerable to ice damage as the Vendée Globe boats were. It wasn't designed to surf on Southern Ocean combers either—no one had complete confidence in its handling abilities in heavy southern weather. It would need to be refueled as well to have any chance of getting to the ARGOS positions at top speed, maneuvering there, and getting back again. A naval tanker was authorized to sail from Fremantle and to rendezvous with the *Adelaide* on its way back to port.

Bullimore and Dubois had been sailing at fifty-one degrees latitude. They were considerably closer to Antarctica than Australia. No one had conducted a rescue this far from land before, and this was as dicey an operation as you could get—a quick thrust through stormy seas toward Antarctica in a race against the next big low already showing up on the weather charts.

As for the planes, the Orions could fly out that far and back if they stayed no more than three hours at the scene, if the fuel calculations were correct and if there were no unforeseen head winds or mechanical problems. The usual operational requirement that the planes land with at least enough fuel for forty-five minutes flying was waived. They would be allowed to reduce their grace period to just fifteen minutes. This is a very fine margin. The operation would risk the planes and the ship, and would put their men in jeopardy, too.

Following standard procedure, the rescue center put out a call for commercial ships in the area. A tanker responded, the only vessel in that remote sea. The *Sanko Phoenix* was more than seven hundred miles from the Mayday positions—half the distance to Fremantle, where the *Adelaide* was coming from. But the heavily loaded ship could do only eleven knots and, even if the weather didn't deteriorate further, would take at least two and a half days to reach the search area. The ninety-thousand-ton ship's diversion toward the two ten-ton yachts and back to its course again afterward would cost its owners close to $100,000.

But the unwritten law of the sea is compelling. The tanker's master responded to the Australian request right away and turned toward the ARGOS positions.

The first Orion to fly out on the morning of January 5 was lucky.

Flying three hundred feet above the five-story waves in a raging seventy-knot wind, it found Dubois's boat in spite of the stale position information from the old polar-orbiting ARGOS satellites. The plane's crew could make out Dubois, still perched on the bottom of his boat, its keel intact, with one arm around a rudder, frantically waving. As it turned out, apprehensions about the righting ability of the Vendée Globe designs hadn't been misplaced. In spite of its keel's weight, Dubois's boat had remained upside down for half a day and seemed comfortably stable.

The Orion managed to drop two life rafts into the water close to Dubois. Under the circumstances—with storm-force wind and seas, allowing for the plane's airspeed and the boat's drift—this was a difficult job. Judging the long, flying parabolic curve of the rafts from the plane's belly to the water's surface was purely a matter of innate hominid hand-eye expertise—like the long forward pass or the looping three-pointer into the basket. Low on fuel, the Orion immediately had to climb away from the Frenchman and head back. As the plane disappeared, Dubois, frozen and desperate, launched himself from his boat into the sea to swim the hundred yards to the rafts, like an untethered astronaut stepping away from his ship into the void of space. It was the swim of his life. As he tried to climb into one of the rafts, a wave flipped it over. He was too far from his boat to be able to swim back to it. Once again, he thought he was about to die. He felt the peculiar sadness and regret of the young, dying too soon. But he didn't panic. Eventually, he managed to drag himself into the damaged and slowly deflating life raft, where he lay in a pool of water enduring the bitter cold.

An hour later, a second Orion arrived, homing in on the signal from a buoy dropped by the first plane. This Orion dropped another raft almost on top of Dubois. He was finally able to crawl into a functioning life raft with some emergency food and water stowed inside, sheltered from the minus thirty Celsius windchill, mostly out of the freezing water—though temporarily, as it happened. Within an hour, the raft was capsized by a wave and Dubois was thrown back into the sea. With the gale still blowing between force 9 and 10, up to fifty-five knots, he somehow got it turned right side up again and climbed back in.

The Orion turned to search for Bullimore's boat. It was close to nightfall and no more planes would come out until the next day. Visibility was a half mile or so, the ceiling less than three hundred feet, the wind still blowing at fifty to sixty knots. With position information from the ARGOS satellites coming in slowly, the crew reverted to a standard visual-search pattern. Against all odds— everyone's luck was flowing freely on this rescue operation—the plane found *Exide Challenger*, upside down, low in the water, without its keel, surrounded by bits and pieces of its rigging and masts, no signs of life on board. It was impossible to tell whether Bullimore was dead or alive inside the white, fragile-looking, overturned hull, or if he'd drifted away in his life raft. At the end of its on-site fuel limit, the Orion could do nothing else. In the Southern Ocean dusk, the storm still howling, it turned back toward land.

Bullimore was still alive. He was cold, nine-fingered, with no idea if his ARGOS beacons had worked or if a rescue was under way. The world would know he was in some sort of a jam because his ARGOS transponder would have stopped beeping his position when he capsized. But if his emergency signals hadn't been received, Jeantot might not start a search for some time. He might ascribe the loss of signal to electrical problems, or to a malfunction that Bullimore was unaware of. If his emergency beacons hadn't worked, if there was no recent position, what rescuers would ever find him in this wilderness? Add his name to the list of disappearances without explanation. But in the faint daytime glow of light through the swirling waves—not enough to see much of anything by, but encouraging nevertheless—and in the absolute blackness of the Southern Ocean night, he was going to hang on.

"Tough as old bootlaces," he said. "A bit unusual; things don't rattle me." Still going through the pluses and minuses of his various survival plans. At fifty-seven years old, far from finished.

The waves poured in and out of the cabin: "It was like a washing machine from hell." In places, when he stood up, the water reached his neck. Occasionally it washed right over his head. The cold made his eyeballs hurt. Waves continued to break up the inside of the cabin—the chart table, his food, the instruments, the sextant, pieces of his berth, all sucked out through the hole of the big broken cabin window. The water swirling in and out set up a kind of siphon effect, which pumped air in and out of the boat with each roll or pitch. "The wind was like a bloody blizzard in the boat."

On top of everything else, Bullimore had to deal with the effects of windchill inside his shattered cabin.

He found and ate a salty-tasting chocolate bar. Only a few ounces of fresh water survived the rollover, but he salvaged his hand desalinating pump. One thousand strokes made one cup of drinkable water. He pumped away for hours with the end of the hose in his mouth, sucking out the precious water drop by drop.

His life raft was still intact but was tied down on the floor of the inverted cockpit. He dove down into the frigid water a dozen times to try to free it. For hours after each dive, his head ached with the cold. He wanted to drag the raft into the cabin and prepare it for launching from there. He thought he could push it out through the cabin window on a line, then follow the line himself, up to the surface, where he could inflate the raft. Because there was no guarantee that *Exide Challenger* would stay afloat, getting the raft ready in case it didn't was one of his survival plans. But it wouldn't budge: the raft was too buoyant for him to manhandle down and through the companionway hatch.

Finally, in the austral summer morning of January 9, four and a half days after his capsize, the *Adelaide* reached Bullimore's boat. He was lying on his shelf, by now frostbitten, hypothermic, almost in shock, but alive. He heard a chugging noise and then a loud banging on the hull. It was the warship's inflatable. One of the crewmen was hitting the resonant carbon fiber with the blunt side of an axe. They thought they would have to chop a hole in the hull to get at Bullimore, alive or dead. If he was there at all; if he hadn't drifted away in his life raft.

"By then, I'm down in the water, aren't I. I'm down like a rocket. I've got my ear against the side of the hull."

Bullimore wanted to be sure there was someone there before he tried to dive down through his hatch and up to the surface. If he was hallucinating and there wasn't anyone there, he wouldn't be able to get back into the boat again. He would be swimming alone in the Southern Ocean with nowhere to go. Then he was sure he heard people talking in English. He shouted that he was there, took a deep breath, and dove down through the hatch into the cockpit, mustering all his strength against the bulk and buoyancy of his survival suit and the drag of his seaboots to dive down even farther below the coamings, through the lifelines, then finally, up through the rat's nest of lines and pieces of mast and boat, his lungs barely holding, arms and legs tangling and then untangling in the web of wreckage.

Then: *Pop!* He was on the surface. Sitting right in front of him was the *Adelaide*. He had never, as the saying goes, seen anything so beautiful in his life. He felt a surge of relief; the tension drained away immediately. Then he felt euphoria, elation, joy. He realized how surprised he was that he would live.

The inflatable was on the other side of his boat from where he surfaced, its crew deliberating about how to chop a hole in the tough hull material. At first they didn't see Bullimore desperately treading water. Then, over the top of the overturned hull, they spotted him. A navy diver got to him first, wrapping his arms around him, lips against his ear: "I've got you; you'll be okay."

In the inflatable, the crewmen wrapped him in a foil heat blanket and hugged him. His head was cradled in a lap. He waved the stub of his severed finger at them, worried that someone might try to grab his hand.

"You'll be all right, mate. You'll be all right!"

Bullimore heard the Australian accents, so much like his own, on the far side of the earth from England. An inheritance of the British empire of the sea. They lifted the whole inflatable out of the sea and onto the ship's deck with tackles, rather than trying to get Bullimore up a ladder. On deck, to Bullimore's astonishment, Dubois stepped forward, grabbed his hand, and shook it. Bullimore, of course, knew nothing about the Frenchman's ordeal. The *Adelaide*'s Seahawk helicopter had finally been able to fly when the wind dropped to below forty knots. It had picked Dubois out of his life raft a few hours earlier.

The weather forecast predicted another imminent depression: a large system lying to the southwest, the whole mess moving fast toward them at forty knots. They were lucky to have found the sailors so quickly: the *Adelaide* did not have enough fuel to ride out a storm and then conduct a sea search and rescue. Within hours, the northwest wind had risen to storm force once again; the seas, still big, began to build higher. By evening, when the front passed by, the wind, following its custom, would back to the west and then the southwest and blow even harder. As the warship turned north for port, the abandoned Vendée Globe boats drifted away on the wild Southern Ocean rollers.

A brave man struggling with adversity is a spectacle for the gods. Seneca, the philosopher of Stoicism, was talking about how people react to the unavoidable, unsought misfortune and suffering that life brings. Every man a Job. The gods supposedly watch our passive endurance with their usual lofty and detached curiosity. But what about the adversity that humans bring upon themselves? When we put our own necks in the wringer? Every man or woman a hero, looking for adventure, seeking out risk and mastering it. Surely that interests the gods as well, provokes in them admiration for our boldness and ingenuity. If we succeed, doesn't that mean that we are blessed?

If there are no gods, or if they don't care what we do, then we can make a secular conclusion. The four men who had been part of the Vendée Globe Christmas miracles—Dinelli, Goss, Dubois, Bullimore—had responded well to the challenge of their lives. The profound risks involved in sailing the Southern Ocean could not have been more vividly demonstrated. But they had come through all right; they'd kept their nerve and survived.

Into the Jaws of Destiny
by Bill Belleville

Sharks more than any other creatures remind us that we can be food. Writer and scuba diver Bill Belleville (born 1946) is as scared of them as the rest of us are. He set out in 1998 to confront his fear by diving into a shark-infested Caribbean reef—along with a full chum bucket.

Monday

I have stopped telling my friends I'm going diving with sharks. Their reactions have been less than encouraging.

"Isn't that, ah, fairly dangerous?" asks one, a marketing VP. "You'll be inside a cage, right?" asks another, an editor. Lastly, from a left-brained attorney: "Sounds like a death wish to me."

My tack has been to smile inscrutably and explain that sharks are generally shy, that a cage won't be necessary—and, indeed, I am more likely to be attacked and bitten by a domestic pig than a shark. *Jaws* did this to us, I remind them, portraying every sleek, dorsal-finned creature as a demonic eating machine with a pea-sized brain. In fact, I say, *Snouts* would be a far more realistic danger.

No one laughs.

To reassure myself, I call up a more reasonable and informed friend, Dr. John McCosker at the California Academy of Sciences. McCosker, a renowned ichthyologist, has co-authored a book, *Great White Shark,* on the most dangerous of the breed. He sets me straight.

"Sharks have a lot more to fear from us than we do from them," explains McCosker. Worldwide, they are over-fished for fins, meat and sport. Out of 368 species, only four—the great white, bull, tiger and oceanic whitetip—have been involved in unprovoked attacks, and then only on the rarest of occasions.

Worldwide, says McCosker, there are an average of 100 attacks on humans yearly—with about 30 fatal. But most of those are on swimmers or waders in shallow water, and most are cases of bite-and-run in which the human was mistaken for a more tasty seal or sea turtle.

McCosker also tells me it was probably a great white—instead of a whale—that swallowed Jonah. "The good news is, he was spit back up."

I lodge all this comforting information safely inside my brain.

Outside my brain, in that little place in my mammalian stomach that secretly replays the theme to *Jaws* every time I imagine a mouth full of sharp teeth coming at me, things are still a bit unsteady.

I admit it: I do have an underlying, visceral reaction to this whole idea. Maybe it comes from the prospect of entering the ocean and getting bumped a couple of notches down the food chain by another species that's faster, stronger and, on occasion, even more merciless than humans. Downsizing may be brutal, but it has nothing on a shark attack.

More to the point, I'm also a genetic victim of the fight-or-flight syndrome. We battle fear in great explosions of adrenaline, or we run. That was a useful reaction when we lived in caves or hid back in the tall grasses. But now that we are civilized, a more rational response is required. If I could deal with my most dramatic fear of all—the prospect of being eaten—I could learn to cope with most anything.

I pack my scuba diving gear, toss in some clothes and head for Fort Lauderdale, Fla. There I will hop aboard something called Island Express for a flight to the southernmost edge of the Bahamas and my rendezvous with aquatic, dorsal-finned destiny.

Wednesday

The twin-propped Cessna 402 from Island Express Airlines taxis to a stop on the runway at the international airport at Long Island in the Bahamas. The off-white plane, apparently in the midst of re-painting, has been spot-sprayed in bursts of green, as if a kid with an aerosol can went on a rampage. It didn't fly yesterday because of mechanic problems.

The runway is a narrow, rutted strip of asphalt thick with black tire skid marks—including a few that our own earring-studded pilot just left. The airport is a two-room wood and stucco hut split in half by a patio. A wind sock flies at the edge of the runway, not far from the turquoise sea. I'm clearly in a Jimmy Buffett song.

A large, black-skinned man comes out to greet me and picks up my gear as it's offloaded from the plane. Like other Bahamians, he speaks in a lilting patois, a blend of African and old English flavored by 300 years of island living. He piles my two bags onto a wood bench marked "Customs." I hand him my passport and he smiles, *no mon*. He is a taxi driver.

Off we go to a local German-run resort, my shark-diving base for the next few days. While there are over 150 such dives worldwide, this Long Island lodge is the granddaddy of them all—and that is a big part of why I am here. If you're going to swim with the sharks, you might as well do it with someone who has experience.

The place exudes an efficiency not always found in the wider Caribbean—must be the Germans. Over the 3,000-acre estate, there are enough rooms for only 120 people. It is a place of seclusion, a retreat the upwardly mobile use to emotionally decompress from hectic, fast-paced, mainland lives. It is *uber Margueritaville.*

Here, everyone chills out in different ways. Some rent cars and drive around the 76-mile-long island, past the ruins of colonial cotton plantations and villages like "Burnt Ground" and "Glenton's," maybe dropping in at a native restaurant for a meal of fresh spiny lobster. Others learn to scuba dive. If so inclined, a few swim with the sharks.

Shark-wise, the results have been good: In over 1,000 dives in 20 years, there have been no skirmishes between sharks and divers. Shark attacks must be messy, emotional affairs; I figure the Germans simply have no time for them.

My room is one of four in a spacious, ranch-style stucco and wood house, perched on the edge of the limestone island next to the frothing green surf. A sign outside shows a cartoon dolphin leaping over the words "Haus Delphin." The air here is clean, flavored with the scent of tropical blossoms and the sea. The U.S. is not all that far from here, but it is light years away in ambience. There is no room key, no telephone or television. It is me and my regulator and the turquoise sea. It's hard to be buttoned-down in an environment like this.

I unpack my gear and reflect on tomorrow's dive. Going underwater is like visiting another planet, one where you have to carry your entire life support system on your back. I've found that the experience has the strange effect of sweeping the emotional slate clean, leaving you to pursue new challenges with a fresh perspective.

And if my diving adventures—in the Caribbean, the Bahamas and on Australia's Great Barrier Reef—have buoyed my psyche, they have also made me more attuned to the complex world beneath the waves. The sea, that great vast unknown, has become a lot less so for me.

Still, a piece of this puzzle is missing: Sharks, skittish and cautious in the wild, have eluded me. Underwater, I have only caught fleeting glimpses of them as they dashed away in a blur of tail and fin. With scant firsthand knowledge of them, my subliminal human fear grew out of proportion to the danger they represented.

Now, I would finally have the chance to meet the fear head-on, to look it right in the beady little eyeballs. The ones set back on either side of the head—right above the mouth that seems ready to Cuisinart everything in its path.

Thursday

It is 9 a.m. sharp, and a flatbed truck with two benches full of smiling American and German tourists is beeping its horn at my door. It has come to take me to the sharks. I climb aboard with my gear, comforted that so many others have also chosen to overcome their shark anxieties with me today.

We drive down a dirt road paralleling the sea, past coconut palms and papayas, flowering bougainvillea and a rubber tree the size of a small house. When we reach the marina on the leeward shore of the island, everyone but me and a sturdy blonde German woman piles off the truck and onto an immense 65-foot boat. Off they go, headed for a series of deserted local beaches, giddy with their snorkeling gear and coolers of cold Kalik, the Bahamian beer.

The two of us climb aboard a smaller 31-foot inboard cruiser. I turn to the German woman, whose name is Helga. "Looks like just you and me and the sharks," I say, adding a casual, nonchalant smile.

"No," she corrects me. "Just you. I ride on the boat and look at them from where it is safe." Gulp.

Bahamians Omar Daley and Christopher Carroll Smith—"Call me Smitty"—are our boat captains and underwater guides. After sojourns in Nassau, both men have returned to their remote native island. Omar is a quiet man with an athletic build, and Smitty's lean and congenial, if a bit wired.

A dark rain cloud moves across the horizon and our boat tries to outrun it as we head for "Shark Reef." Smitty, in his Reebok cap and workout jacket and khaki shorts, is upbeat. "'Dis is my island, mon. I know the rain and the sunshine. We will have no problem."

Soon, we are over the shallow, 35-feet-deep site. "Here, you have the fish and the coral and the sponges," says Smitty. "Every-ting we need for the beau-tif-i-cation of the reef." Then, as an afterthought, "and here, especially, we have the sharks."

Smitty gives me the shark-wrangling history of Long Island. Years ago, a French documentary team arrived here to film sharks. But, since sharks are pelagic—strong, streamlined swimmers who generally hunt in deeper, open waters with only brief forays into the shallows—finding a subject willing to terrorize the picturesque coral reef wasn't easy. And, except for the rare unprovoked attacks, wild sharks generally avoid humans. Indeed, the exhalation of scuba bubbles may even spook them.

So, locals obliged the French filmmakers by spearing bloody fish on the reef—a guaranteed Pavlovian dinner bell. Other photographers in search of dramatic images heard of the Long Island sharks and the shark-baiting continued. Adventurous divers later joined in on the action. And today there is a simple formula: Divers descend to the bottom, a chum bucket is dropped into the water overhead and the fun begins.

Candidly, the notion of baiting any wild animal to get it to do something it wouldn't ordinarily do generally doesn't sit well with me. I don't like to see animals encouraged to perform, just because we want them to. Alligators fed in Florida's urban lakes lose their fear of humans and learn to associate them with food—swimmers, fishermen and poodles find a spot on the menu. But here, I figure the sharks have been at it long enough to have developed a routine. Whatever happened to get the ball rolling in these parts predates my appearance by a couple of decades.

Finally, Smitty says out loud what I have been thinking since I first packed my dive gear. "Yea, mon, it is a fear for most people. Seeing these big animals with teeth like they want to make dinner out of you. But it is not just about the sharks; it is about facing up to fear. You do it and later, when you see a shark, you don't have the fear." Surely, self-help authors have written entire books elaborating on Smitty's gunwale-side manner.

I slip into my wet suit, hoist on my scuba tank and weight belt and sit down on the stern of the boat. My feet dangle in the water as I put on my fins. I look into the clear sea below and immediately see great, brown-gray shapes moving in slow circles under me. They have been lured here by the sound of our motor and swash of our hull. It seems the show has already started.

Omar settles down beside me in his scuba gear. I can't help but notice he is carrying a large metal pole in his hand. "Ah, Omar," I ask, as casual as possible, "if this dive is so safe, why are you carrying that big stick?"

"My CYA stick, mon," explains Omar. "Cover your ass." Then he puts his regulator into his mouth and slips under the sea, into the phalanx of circling fins.

Like a true believer, I wordlessly follow, ablaze with newfound trust. This will work, I tell myself, because Omar has done this many times before and he is not even mildly scared.

Then again, he has the stick.

Underwater, I count seven or eight Caribbean reef sharks circling me like giant, steel-gray torpedoes. I concentrate on trying to move slowly and deliberately, like I would ordinarily do if I were here on the reef without sharks. I check my air pressure gauge, neutralize my buoyancy and—reminding myself this is perfectly natural—settle down on the sandy bottom not far from a towering mound of Technicolor corals.

As soon as I'm on the bottom, a lone seven-foot shark swims straight towards me, his mouth in a perpetual grimace, looking like Peter Falk's Columbo on a bad hunch. For a split second, my senses freeze—along with my sphincter muscle. I want to run but I can't, and for the most fleeting of moments, I have a sort of out-of-body experience, as if I am watching myself watch the shark.

Remembering the old adage of not showing fear to a mad dog, I stay my ground. At a distance of three feet, the shark turns abruptly, as if someone has pulled an invisible chain. This happens several more times, before the sharks tire of it and resume swimming in circles just above.

And then I figure if I am going to really swim with the sharks, I need to get off my butt and head up to their level. I do so, rising ever slowly upward. The circling sharks swim just a wee bit wider to avoid bumping me.

Some scientists suspect that sharks, with their heightened sense of smell, can even detect adrenaline. I think of the little twits with backward baseball caps who weave in and out of traffic back in Florida with NO FEAR decals on the back of their jacked-up pickups. A Caribbean reef tip shark would peel that decal in a nanosecond.

More than anything I've ever done, there is a be-here-now element to this experience that commands my senses. Whatever shards of anxiety remain from my top-side life—career, mortgage, deadlines—vanish.

Breathing, something I take for granted back on the surface, becomes a conscious, auditory event. In comes the good air in a long, relaxed suck; out goes the bad in a series of gently exploding exhaust bubbles. Around me, the bubbles become domes of mercury and drift up to the surface. To control myself, I control my breathing, turning it into a Zen-like exercise. As I do, the environment seems to absorb me. I become one with it.

And then something magical happens. I see the sharks more clearly. Gill slits, eyes and mouths come into focus. The grace of their swimming awes me. I watch how little they twist their body to make a turn, how small the energy investment is compared to my awkward surface-mammal gyrations. Instead of mindless eating machines, they become elegant, smooth-skinned beasts: giant, underwater panthers. I begin to admire them.

As I do, my fear dissolves with my exhaust bubbles. I settle back down to the bottom on my knees, next to Omar and his stick. He gives a signal to Smitty, who is watching the action from back on the boat.

Down into the water comes a PVC can full of fish heads and guts. New sharks I have not seen before dash to the bucket from somewhere just beyond my range of vision. There must be 30 of them in the water now, and they are fired up. The bucket is theirs.

The sharks attack the chum, slashing and biting at it. The bucket drops to the bottom in slow motion, sharks slamming into it from every which way. As it settles onto the sand, the commotion they kick up creates a storm of dust. The storm grows, spreading towards me, sharks veering in and out of it with fire in their eyes.

When the edge of the storm is only a couple of yards away, I back away gingerly, careful not to thrash about as I do.

As quickly as the frenzy started, it is over. The chum bucket, now scored with teeth marks, is empty, lying next to me on the sand.

My air is starting to run low. I carefully ascend, moving deliberately. Midway up, I pause and raise a tiny plastic underwater camera to snap photos of the remaining sharks.

As I do, I listen closely to my gut for sounds of alarm. But I hear none.

There is only the rhythm of my steady exhaust now, and it is more comforting than it has ever been.

Among the Man-Eaters
by Philip Caputo

Novelist and journalist Philip Caputo (born 1941) is best known for A Rumor of War, *a memoir of his experience as a Marine in Vietnam. He traveled in early 2000 to Kenya's Tsavo National Park to learn more about the region's lions—infamous for their appetite for human flesh.*

There are few words as disturbing as "man-eater." Instantly, it dissolves hundreds of thousands of years of human progress and carries us back to our humble beginnings, where we were puny hominids, slouching across the African savanna, huddling in fireless caves, waiting for death to rush us from out of the long grass. The thought of being devoured offends our sense of human dignity, subverts our cherished belief that we are higher beings, "the paragon of animals," to borrow a line from *Hamlet.* The man-eater's actions say to us, "I don't care if you're the President of the United States, the Queen of England, the inventor of the microchip, or just an ordinary Joe or Jill; you're no paragon in *my* book, but the same as a zebra or gazelle—a source of protein. In fact, I'd rather hunt you, because you're so slow and feeble."

We didn't know if the big male lion in front of us had ever tasted human flesh. He did inhabit a region of Kenya that had given birth to the two most infamous man-eating lions in history, and that still harbors lions with a proclivity to hunt man: Only two years ago, a cattle herder had been killed and devoured by a lion not far from where this male now lay looking at us with eyes that glowed like brass in firelight. He must have gone 400 pounds, and he was ugly in the way certain prizefighters are ugly—not a photogenic, Oscar De La Hoya sort of lion, but a Jake LaMotta lion, with only a scruff of a mane, his face and hide scarred from the thorny country he lived in, or from battles with rival lions, or from the kicks of the zebra and buffalo he killed for food. He was only 25 feet away, but we were safe—provided we stayed in our Land Rover. Panting in the late afternoon heat, his gaze impassive, he rested in the shade of a tall bush beside the carcass of a young Cape buffalo killed the night before. Around him, well fed and yawning, five lionesses lazed in the short yellow grass. Two cubs licked and nibbled the buffalo's hindquarters, the ragged strips of meat in the hollowed-out cavity showing bright red under the black skin. Nothing else remained of the animal except the horned head, the front hooves, and a few scattered bones.

Photographer Rob Howard and I were taking pictures from the roof, using it to support our bulky 300-millimeter lenses. Inside, my wife, Leslie, observed through binoculars, while our guides, Iain Allan and Clive Ward, kept an eye on things.

I ran out of film and dropped through the roof hatch to fetch another roll from my camera bag. Rob stood up, trying for another angle. Immediately, the drowsy, indifferent expression went out of the male's eyes; they focused on Rob with absolute concentration. Rob's camera continued to whir and click, and I wondered if he noticed that he'd disturbed the lion. Now, with its stare still fixed on him, it grunted, first out of one side of its mouth, then the other, gathered its forepaws into itself, and raised its haunches. The long, black-tufted tail switched in the grass.

"Say, Rob, might be a good idea to sit down again," Iain advised in an undertone. "Move slowly, though."

He had barely finished this instruction when the lion made a noise like a man clearing his throat, only a good deal louder, and lunged across half the distance between us and him, swatting the air with one paw before he stopped. Rob tumbled through the roof hatch, almost landing on top of me in a clatter of camera equipment, a flailing of arms and legs.

"Jesus Christ!" he said, obviously impressed. The big male had settled down again, although his tail continued to sweep back and forth.

"The short, happy life of Rob Howard," I wisecracked. "It's embarrassing to see a man lose his nerve like that." A bit of bravado.

We were going to spend only part of this safari in a vehicle. For the rest, we would try to track and photograph lions on foot. How would my own nerve hold up then? Perhaps Rob was wondering the same thing about himself. He asked Iain if the lion could have jumped on the roof.

"Could have, but he wouldn't have," Iain replied, a smile cracking across his rough, ruddy face. "That was just a demonstration, to let you know the rules. Of course, you had no way of knowing that."

There was a lot we didn't know about these Tsavo lions—practically everything—and we had come to Kenya to begin filling in the gaps in our knowledge. After hiring Iain, whose safari company, Tropical Ice, is one of the most experienced in the country, we journeyed by Land Rover from Nairobi to the eastern section of Tsavo National Park—the largest in Kenya, with an area of 8,034 square miles (the size of Massachusetts). Here, some 200 miles southeast of Nairobi, you can get at least a taste of the wide-open wilds that Isak Dinesen described in *Out of Africa* and that aviator/adventurer Beryl Markham explored by air. It is the Africa that's all but vanished from the rest of Kenya's national parks and game reserves, which have become vast outdoor zoos, except that the animals are free while the visitors are caged in minivans.

Iain loves Tsavo—the dense palm and saltbush forests of the river valleys, the endless red and khaki plains. "Africa without any fat on it," he called it. "It's raw and primitive and it doesn't tolerate fools or forgive mistakes."

But Tsavo also has a dark history that's centuries old. Its name means "Place of Slaughter" in a local language—a reference to inter-tribal massacres committed by Masai warriors in the distant past. Ivory traders told spooky tales about men who vanished from their midst when their caravans stopped at the Tsavo River for water and rest. The traders blamed the mysterious disappearances on evil spirits.

The region's forbidding reputation spread worldwide in 1898, when two lions literally stopped the British Empire in its tracks by killing and eating an estimated 140 people, most of them workers building a rail-road bridge over the Tsavo River, in what was then called the East Africa Protectorate. The predators' reign of terror lasted nine months, until they were hunted down and shot by the British Army engineer in charge of the project, John H. Patterson. Working as a team, the lions sneaked into the camps at night, snatched men from their tents, and consumed them. Patterson, who'd had considerable experience hunting tigers in India, devised ingenious traps and ruses to bring the animals to bay. But they outwitted him time and again, proving so crafty that the workmen—mostly contract laborers imported from India—came to believe the ancient legends about body-snatching demons, adding their own anti-imperial spin to the myth. The lions, they said, were the incarnate spirits of African chieftains angered by the building of a railroad through their ancestral lands. The workers would lie in their tents, listening to the beasts roar in the darkness. When the roars stopped, the men would call out to each other, "Beware, brothers, the devil is coming!"

In 1907, Patterson, by then a lieutenant colonel, published a book about the ordeal, *The Man-Eaters of Tsavo*, which is widely regarded as the greatest saga in the annals of big-game hunting. Still in print, it has inspired two feature films, *Bwana Devil* in 1952 and *The Ghost and the Darkness* in 1996, with Val Kilmer portraying Patterson.

While lecturing in the United States, 17 years after the book's publi-cation, Patterson sold the lions' skins and skulls to the Field Museum of Natural History in Chicago. A taxidermist turned the hides into life-like mounts and they were put on exhibit, where they have been ever since, a source of grim fascination to countless visitors. I saw them when I was in high school, and though I can't remember any other exhibit I looked at that day, I've never forgotten those two lions, poised on a replica of sandstone, one crouched, the other standing with right paw slightly raised, both looking intently in the same direction. They had no manes, and the absence of the adornment that gives postcard lions such a majestic appearance made them look sinister. It was as if nature had dispensed with distracting ornamentation to show the beasts in their essence—stripped-down assemblies of muscle and teeth and claws, whose sole purpose was to kill. But it was their eyes that impressed me most. They were glass facsimiles, yet they possessed a fixed, attentive, concentrated expression that must have been in the living eyes when they spotted human prey, decades before, on the plains of Africa.

Patterson's account of their raids reads like a gothic novel. Here's how he describes his discovery of the remains of his Sikh crew leader, Ungan Singh, who had been seized by one of the lions the previous night: "The ground all round was covered with blood and morsels of flesh and bones, but the head had been left intact, save for the holes made by the lion's tusks. It was the most gruesome sight I had ever seen."

Singh was one of the lions' early victims, and his ghastly death sent Patterson in avenging pursuit. He didn't know what he was in for, but he found out soon enough. The construction camps were scattered up and down the railroad right-of-way: The lions would strike at a particular camp one night and Patterson would stake it out the next, waiting with his .303 rifle—but the cats always seemed to know where he was, and would attack elsewhere.

The workmen, meanwhile, surrounded their camps with high *bomas*, or protective fences, made from thorny *Commiphora* shrubs. For a while, the attacks stopped. One night a few workers figured it was safe to sleep outside their tent but inside the boma—a bad decision. One of the lions forced its way through the fence and, ignoring the stones and firebrands that the workers threw, grabbed a man and dragged him through the thorns. It was joined by its partner, and the two savored their meal within earshot of the man's friends.

Perhaps Patterson's worst memory was of the night when he was in his boma and both lions carried their most recent kill close to him. It was too dark to aim and fire. He sat there, listening to the crunching of bones and to what he described as a contented "purring"—sounds that he could not get out of his head for days.

Patterson finally got the upper hand in December 1898. He lashed a partly eaten donkey carcass to a tree stump as bait, built a shooting platform for his protection, and waited. When the lion crept in, it ignored the bait and instead began to circle Patterson's rickety perch. Patterson blazed away into the brush; the lion's snarls grew weaker and weaker, and finally ceased. The next day, the first man-eater's body was recovered. It measured nine feet, eight inches from nose to tail tip, and was so heavy it required eight men to carry it back to camp.

To dispatch its partner, Patterson tied three live goats to a length of railroad track, then hid in a shanty nearby. The lion came just before dawn, killed one of the goats, and began to carry it away—along with the other two goats and the 250-pound rail. Patterson fired, missing the lion but killing one of the goats. The lion escaped.

The dogged Patterson stalked it for the next two weeks, and finally managed to wound it. He and his gun bearer followed the bloody spoor for a quarter mile until at last they spotted their quarry. Patterson took careful aim and fired. The lion charged. A second shot bowled it over, but it rose and charged again. Patterson fired a third time without effect. He then joined his terrified gun bearer in a nearby tree, from which he finally dropped the lion with a fourth slug. When he climbed down, he was stunned to see the lion jump up and charge him again. He pumped two more rounds into it—one in its chest, another in its head—and the huge cat went down for good. The reign of terror was over.

Throughout history, the beast with a taste for human flesh has been regarded as an aberration, even as an outlaw. Patterson's book often refers to the lions in terms commonly applied to criminals or psychopaths. Even the more objective scientific literature tends to explain man-eating as the exception that proves the rule: Humans are not normally on the predator's grocery list. Lions are generally believed to turn to eating humans only when injuries or old age prevent them from pursuing their usual prey.

It's true that old, sick, or wounded lions have been responsible for most attacks on people. However, a team of researchers from Chicago's Field Museum headed by Dr. Bruce Patterson (no relation to the colonel) has come up with—well, it would be an exaggeration to say "evidence"—tantalizing *hints* that there may be some lions with a more or less genetic predisposition to prey on humans, even when strong and healthy enough to bring down a zebra or a buffalo. The explanation for this behavior would then subtly but significantly shift from the pathological to the Darwinian: Conditions in a lion's environment, as much as changes in its physiology, can drive it to hunt people—and there's nothing aberrant or "criminal" about it.

Still, such a beast poses a mystery, and the key to that mystery may be found in the lions of Tsavo, which truly are a different breed of cat from the glorious, regal lions of, say, the Serengeti. Most Tsavo males are maneless, and larger than the Serengeti male, which measures 36 inches at the shoulder and weighs between 385 and 410 pounds. Tsavo lions are up to a foot taller and can tip the scales at about 460 to 520 pounds, giving you a cat the size of a small grizzly. They are also distinguished by their behavior. On the plains, the adult male's role is to mate and protect the pride, leaving the hunting to females. In Tsavo, where scarcity of game makes prides smaller, males share in the hunting, and may even do most of it.

"There's no doubt in my mind that Tsavo lions are different," Iain told us on the drive from Nairobi. "They're total opportunists, killing machines that will attack and eat even little African hares. They're also more cunning than pride lions, often killing from ambush instead of stalk-and-spring. There's something sinister about them."

Iain is not a big-cat biologist, but 28 years of leading walking and driving safaris in Kenya and Tanzania have given him the kind of direct experience that compensates for any lack of scientific training. And he's never had an experience more direct, or more terrifying, than the one he had on a Tsavo safari last July.

It was early in the afternoon, the time when he usually checks in with his Nairobi office by satellite phone. He ambled down to the wide, sandy banks of the Galana River, where reception was better than it was in his tree-shrouded tent camp. As he chatted with his secretary, he observed a bushbuck poke its way through a saltbush thicket some distance downriver, then begin to drink. Suddenly, the animal raised its head and froze; an instant later, a lioness sprang from the saltbush still farther downriver, and the bushbuck bolted in Iain's direction, the lioness in pursuit. When she was about 50 yards from Iain, without breaking stride the lioness veered off and headed straight for him, bursts of sand flying behind her as she ran. In a microsecond that seemed like minutes, Iain realized that he needn't worry about her teeth and claws; he was going to be killed by the impact of 300 pounds of sinew and muscle smashing into him at 25 miles an hour. When she was only 20 feet from where he stood, she veered again, kicked sand all over him, and vanished.

Iain suspects that the lioness charged him because she was confused, annoyed, or curious. "That," he said, "is the closest I've ever come to getting killed."

If he had been, he would have joined a long roster of Tsavo lion victims, the most recent being that cattle herder, taken in July 1998. Are the lions of Tsavo predisposed to prey on people? Do they represent a subspecies of lion? Why are they maneless? Why are they larger than average? Can they tell us anything new about the king of beasts? Those are the questions that prompted us to go to Tsavo.

On our first day, after settling into Iain's tent camp on the Voi (Goshi) River, we drove down a red laterite road to the Aruba Dam. There is a small lake behind the dam, where Samuel Andanje, a young researcher with the Kenya Wildlife Service, directed us to the scarfaced male and his harem of five females. They were part of a pride of 23 lions, said Andanje, who spends his nights locating the animals by their roars and his days tracking them in a Land Rover.

Shortly after the male had sent Rob tumbling back into our truck, the females, with the cubs in tow, moved off toward the lake to drink. They made a fine sight in the golden afternoon fight, walking slowly through the dun-colored grass with movements that suggested water flowing. Scarface remained behind to eat his fill of the buffalo before the jackals and hyenas got to it.

As the sun lowered, we heard a series of throaty grunts from the male lion, which Clive said were a call to the females and cubs to return. Clive Ward is 56 years old, tall and spare, with the face of an ascetic and a clipped way of speaking that sometimes leaves the words trapped in his mouth. Like the 52-year-old Iain, he has guided safaris for years, and is an alpinist by avocation. He and Iain have led countless parties of trekkers up Mount Kilimanjaro and Mount Kenya, and have scaled many of the world's major peaks together. Over the years, they have developed a relationship that seems to combine war-buddy comradeship with the easy familiarity of an old married couple; they bicker now and then, and needle each other, but beneath the bickering and needling, you sense an abiding bond knit on sheer rock faces and icy crags and long, hot tramps through the African bush.

As the lions padded silently through the grass, we left—it was growing dark—and came upon a lone lioness, lying at the junction of the road and the two-track that led to camp. She didn't move as the Land Rover passed within six feet of her. She seemed to regard the intersection as hers, and, of course, it was.

The big storks roosting in the branches of trees along the Voi riverbed looked ominous in the twilight. Up ahead and across the river, waterless now in the dry season, the glow of kerosene lamps and a campfire made a more cheerful sight.

Iain believes that you don't need to practice being miserable: His safaris hark back to the stylish roughing-it of a bygone age—commodious wall tents with cots, a large, communal mess tent, outdoor showers, portable privies in canvas enclosures, laundry service, and a six-man staff to do the cooking and camp chores. On an open fire, Kahiu, the cook, whips up meals equal to anything served in Nairobi restaurants, and you wash them down with South African and Italian wines, making you feel pretty *pukka sahib.*

After dinner, we sat around the campfire on folding chairs, and once, when the wind turned, we heard lions roaring in the distance. The sound inspired Iain to offer a sequel to the tale of his encounter with the charging lioness.

"After she disappeared, I had the feeling that she'd come into camp, so I ran back and told my clients to get in their tents and zip them up, and warned the staff that a lion was in camp. Well, they looked at me as if to say that the old boy had had too much sun, and when I didn't see the lioness for a while, I figured they were right. I was about to tell my clients that they could come on out when I turned around and saw eight Africans running like hell for our pickup, with the lioness running among them—not after them, but *right in the middle of them.* The men leaped up to the truck bed in one bound. I think that old girl was very confused: She'd started off chasing a bushbuck, ended up in a camp fall of people, tents, vehicles—things she'd never seen—and must have wondered, 'How did I get into this mess?' She ran out, but stopped at the edge of camp and stayed there all day. Just sat there, like the lioness we saw a little while ago."

"What good did zipping up tent flaps do?" I asked. "She could have shredded that thin canvas if she wanted to."

"Lions don't recognize a closed tent as anything; they can't be bothered," Iain explained. "Just last August, in Zimbabwe, a young Englishman, the nephew of an earl, was on a camping safari. He went into his tent and fell asleep without closing the flaps. Sometime during the night, a lioness got close to his tent. He woke up and ran out, scared as hell, right into a mob of other lions. Lions like things that run, same as any cat. When they got through with him, I don't think there was anything left."

This was not a bedtime story to tell in lion country. When Leslie and I went to our tent, we not only secured the flaps, we zipped up the covers to the mesh ventilation windows—and could barely breathe the stifling air. I wasn't encouraged by Iain's assurance that lions couldn't be bothered with tents. Hadn't the man-eaters of Tsavo barged into the tents of the construction crews? But maybe the workmen hadn't closed the flaps, I thought. My sole armament was a K-bar, the ten-inch trench knife issued to me when I was in the Marine Corps in Vietnam. It was resting in its sheath on the night table next to my cot, but it seemed to me that the best thing I could do with it in the event of a lion attack would be to fall on it and save the lion the trouble.

"Jambo!" a staff member called from outside our tent: hello in Swahili. "Jambo," we answered, and got dressed by lantern light. After breakfast, and with dawn erasing the last morning stars, we rolled out to the Aruba Dam to look for Scarface and his family.

They were not where we had left them. We drove along slowly, looking for pugmarks in the soft, rust-colored earth, until we heard a deep bass groan that ended in a chesty cough. It was so loud we thought the lion was only 50 yards away. We set off in the direction of the sound, bouncing over a prairie of short, dry grass tinted pale gold by the early morning sun, Clive, Rob, and I standing with our heads poking out of the roof hatches.

"Ah, there he is," said Iain, at the wheel.

"Him all right," Clive seconded.

I spend a lot of time in the woods, and am not bad at spotting game, but I had no idea what they were talking about.

"It's the ears, you look for the ears sticking above the grass when you're looking for a lion," Iain said, driving on. And then I saw them—two triangles that could have been mistaken for knots in a stump if they hadn't moved. We were 20 or 30 yards away when he stood up, with a movement fluid and unhurried, and I thought, Christ, if you were on foot, you would trip over him before you knew he was there, and that would be the last thing you would ever know in this world. Ugly-handsome Scarface went down a game trail at the leonine version of a stroll, then up over a rise and down toward a marsh, its green swath spread between the tawny ridges. We stayed with him all the way, keeping a respectful distance. He was one big boy, and if he was a man-eater, this is what he would do after he killed you: flay off your skin with his tongue, which is covered with small spines that give it the texture of coarse-grained sandpaper and are used to bring nutritious blood to the surface; next, he would bite into your abdomen or groin, open you up, and scoop out your entrails and internal organs and consume them, because they are rich in protein, your liver especially; then he would savor your meatiest parts, thighs and buttocks, followed by your arms, shoulders, and calves. The bones would be left for the hyenas, which have stronger jaws. Vultures and jackals would take care of your head and whatever scraps of flesh remained, so that, a few hours after your sudden death, it would be as though you had never existed. There is a terrible thoroughness to the mechanics of death in Africa, and we are not exempt.

Scarface led us right to his harem, and then, after posing on a knoll, he moved off into the marsh, the lionesses and cubs following soon after.

"That's that for now," said Iain. "Have to come back in the late afternoon. Let's look up Sam and try to find the rest of this pride."

Sam Andanje led us to a remote stretch of the Voi, and we followed his Land Rover through *Commiphora* scrub. I mentioned the bomas that Patterson's laborers had constructed, and how the lions had found ways through them, with the canniness of trained guerrillas infiltrating an enemy's barbed wire. Four-footed killers with above-average IQs.

"I don't doubt but that the lions had the whole thing totally wired," Iain remarked. "The difference between people and animals is that we can see the big picture, and figure out how to survive in any environment, but within their area of specialization, most animals are as smart as we are, maybe smarter." He paused, chewing over a further thought. "Take a look at this country. It's sparse and harsh—there aren't any huge herds of wildebeest, like the kind you get in the Masai Mara or the Serengeti. Tsavo lions have to take what they can get, whatever comes along. I'm convinced that they have territories they know as well as you know your backyard, with their ambush places all staked out. They're clever. They know where to be and when."

We found no lions, and by 10:30, the quest was hopeless. It was nearly 100°F, and the cats were laid up, deep within the thickets. In the late afternoon, we returned to the marsh near the Aruba Dam. There, Scarface's harem lolled with the cubs on the slope overlooking the marsh, where a solitary bull elephant grazed. Iain parked about 30 yards from the lions, and we began observing and photographing.

Later, as the sun dropped below the Taita Hills and a sundowner began to blow, the lions stirred. A small herd of Grant's gazelles daintily walked down into the marsh to graze, and the biggest lioness, the dominant female, raised her head and fastened her gaze on them.

"She's looking for a slight limp in one of the gazelles," Iain observed. "Any sign of weakness—but gazelle isn't a lion's favored prey. They're so fast, and there isn't much meat on them, so it's hardly worth the effort. Lions are lazy hunters." Gesturing to the marsh, he returned to the theme of feline intelligence. "A lot of thought went into choosing this position, above the swamp and with most of its prey upwind, so they can see or scent almost anything that comes along. It's perfect buffalo country. The sun's lowering, they're rested, and the lions will be getting hungry soon."

On our fourth morning in Tsavo, Iain's staff struck the tents, in preparation for moving to his "walking safari" campsite at a place called Durusikale, on the Galana River. If you want to experience the Africa of Isak Dinesen, then you have to do it on shank's mare.

Roused at 4:30 a.m. by another "Jambo," we breakfasted under the Southern Cross, and then drove northward, down a road paralleling a riverbed called the Hatulo Bisani, where we had seen a large herd of Cape buffalo the day before. It was Iain's theory that a lion pride might be trailing them. During the long rains of November, the Hatulo Bisani would be a torrent; now, with a mere trickle flowing between wide swaths of bright green sedge, it resembled a river of grass.

We found fresh pugmarks in the road, followed them for a while, then lost them when they angled off into the scrub. A short distance ahead, the buffalo, maybe 600 of them, grazed in the riverbed, their gray-black bodies looking like boulders.

We sat there eyeball to eyeball with one of the biggest, strongest, fiercest animals in Africa—an animal that helps to explain why Tsavo lions are so big, and why they're likely to turn man-eater. Cape buffalo are among the most numerous of Tsavo's herd animals and lions pray on them. Lions elsewhere do so only when deprived of easier game, and even then only in large bands; no average-size lion will take down a 1,500-pound Cape buffalo alone. In other words, the lions of Tsavo are big because the dense, brushy country compels them to hunt in small groups. Still, no matter how hefty a lion gets, hunting buffalo is a risky business. Recently, Andanje found a lion stomped to death by a buffalo. More frequently, the cats suffer broken bones and puncture wounds; they then turn to easier prey, like livestock—and the people who tend it.

Tom Gnoske and Dr. Julian Kerbis Peterhans, members of the research team from the Field Museum, have discovered an interesting twist to such behavior: A lion that becomes a man-eater because it's injured doesn't go back to its traditional prey even after it recovers. Eating people, Gnoske says, "is an easy way to make a living."

Intriguingly, one of the Tsavo man-eaters Patterson killed had a severely broken canine tooth with an exposed root. The tooth was well worn and polished, and the entire skull had undergone "cranial remodeling" in response to the trauma, indicating that the injury was an old one. It's in the record that at least one man-eater had been prowling about Tsavo before Patterson and his bridge-building gangs arrived in March 1898. A railroad surveyor, R.O. Preston, lost several members of his crew to a man-eater near the Tsavo River early in 1897. When Preston and his men searched for remains, they found the skulls and bones of individuals who had been killed earlier still. There is no proof that an injury was the lion's "motive" for turning man-eater, but it's a plausible explanation. He might have been kicked in the jaw by a buffalo and lost a tooth; he stuck to preying on humans after the injury healed, having found out how safe and convenient it was. The arrival of the railroad workers, packed into tent camps, would have been manna from leonine heaven.

But what about his partner, who was in prime health? The Field Museum researchers speculate that an epidemic of rinderpest disease may have played a role in the lion's change of eating habits. In the early 1890s, the disease all but wiped out buffalo and domestic cattle. With its usual prey eliminated, the starving lion had to look to villages and construction camps for its meals.

Another, more disquieting, explanation lies elsewhere—with the elephants of Tsavo.

We turned off the Hatulo Bisani road and started down the Galana river road toward the campsite, some 25 miles downstream. Partway there, we stopped to climb one of the Sobo rocks, a series of sandstone outcrops, to scan with our binoculars for game. The Galana, fed by melting snows on Mount Kilimanjaro, showed a brassy brown as it slid slowly between galleries of saltbush and doum palm toward its distant meeting with the Indian Ocean. Beyond the river, the scorched plains rose and fell, seemingly without end. And on a far-off ridge, we saw one of Africa's primitive, elemental sights—a procession of elephants, raising dust as they migrated to the river to drink and cool themselves in the midday heat.

Forgetting our lion quest for the moment, we returned to the Land Rover and cut cross-country toward the herd, drawing close enough to count the animals—about 60 altogether, the calves trotting alongside their mothers, a huge matriarch out front, other old females guarding the flanks and rear, tusks flashing in the harsh sunlight.

Iain and Clive are elephant enthusiasts. When they saw the herd shambling toward the Galana, they drove off to a spot on the river where we had a good chance of observing the animals at close hand. We picnicked in the shade of a tamarind tree, with a broad, sandy beach in front of us. Twenty minutes later, the elephants arrived, moving within a hundred yards of where we sat. They came on down with a gliding, stiff-legged gait. The marvelous thing was how silent they were, passing through the saltbush with barely a rustle. It seemed to us that we were beholding Tsavo's wild soul made flesh.

With cat-burglar creeps, we positioned ourselves on the shore, watching and photographing for almost an hour. The animals' trunks curved into their mouths or bent back to spray their heads with water. An incredible organ, the elephant's trunk: It contains 40,000 separate muscles and tendons, and serves the elephant as a hand that feeds, a nose, a drinking straw, a built-in shower, and a weapon, all in one.

Tsavo elephants have all the reason in the world to fear and hate people. Slaughtering them for their ivory is a very old story, going back to ancient times. And the caravans that once passed through Tsavo laden with tusks may hold another explanation for the man-eating tendencies of Tsavo lions.

Dr. Chapurukha Kusimba, an anthropological archaeologist, grew up in Kenya hearing the story of the man-eaters and Patterson's epic hunt. Now an associate curator of African anthropology at the Field Museum, he began working with the Tsavo lion research team in 1994. Studying the traditional caravan routes from the interior to the coast, Kusimba learned that the caravans carried slaves as well as ivory. The Tsavo River was an important stop, where traders refreshed themselves and restocked their water supplies before moving on. However, historical texts suggest that they disposed of unnecessary cargo first: Captives too sick or weak to travel farther were abandoned there to die.

With so many corpses around, predators in the vicinity would have had an abundance of people to feed on. From there, it wouldn't have been a big step for the cats to go after living people. That may explain the myths about "evil spirits"—the men who mysteriously disappeared from the caravans' campsites had been seized not by devils but by lions. The slave and ivory caravans had passed through Tsavo for centuries—and that leads us to the truly disturbing aspect of the theory. *Panthera leo* is a social animal, capable of adopting "cultural traditions" that are passed on from generation to generation. If a lioness is hunting people, her young will grow to regard them as a normal part of their diet, and pass that knowledge on to their own young. The upshot is that Patterson's man-eaters may have done what they did not because they were handicapped by injuries, or even because their traditional prey had been wiped out, but simply because they came from a man-eating lineage so long that an appetite for human flesh was ingrained in them. Stalking and devouring the "paragon of animals" wasn't the exception, but their rule.

That's just a theory, but if you're in a tent in lion country it's the kind to make you wake up at two in the morning and hear the pad of a lion's paws in every rustle outside; to mistake your wife's breathing for a lion's; to picture him creeping up on the thin canvas that separates you from him; and to know that he isn't there out of curiosity or because he smelled the food in the cook's tent or because he winded a zebra herd beyond camp and is only passing by, but because he's scented *you* and *you* are what he's after; the kind of supposition to make you imagine the horror of what it's like to feel him bite down on your ankle or shoulder with his strong jaws and then drag you out and run off with you, wonderful, indispensable you, apple of your mother's eye, and you screaming and scratching and kicking and punching, all to no avail, until he releases his grip to free his jaws to crush your windpipe, and the last sensation you have is of his hot breath in your face.

Such were my waking nightmares that night. And yet, only that afternoon, I had been as captivated by a lion as Joy Adamson had been by Elsa. We had left camp on a game drive, and rounded a bend in the road a few miles downriver, and suddenly she was there, walking purposefully ahead of us. There was nothing beautiful about her: Old scratches and cuts marred her skin like sewn rips in a threadbare sofa, and her ribs showed, though not in a way to suggest starvation so much as a spare toughness. If the sleek pride lions of the Serengeti are the haute bourgeoisie of the leonine world, Tsavo lions are the proletariat, blue-collar cats that have to work hard for a meager living. I recalled Iain's description of Tsavo as a land intolerant of fools and unforgiving of mistakes. This lioness blended right into such a landscape; she looked neither tolerant nor forgiving, but very focused. We trailed her, but she was never alarmed. Now and then, she threw a glance at us, just to check on our distance or our behavior. If we edged too close, she simply angled away, maintaining a space of perhaps 15 yards. A lady with a mission, she went on through the intermittent salt-bush with the steady, unflagging pace of a veteran foot soldier.

After she covered some two miles, the lioness began to call with low grunts. We figured she was trying to locate her pride, but if they answered, we did not hear them. Another quarter of a mile, and she stopped and called more loudly—a sound that seemed to come from her belly instead of her throat, part moan, part cough. *Wa-uggh, Wa-uggh.* In a moment, two cubs bounded from a saltbush thicket a hundred yards away. They leaped on their mother, licking face and flanks, and she licked theirs.

With her cubs following, the lioness retraced her steps, and we again followed. The wary cubs often stopped to stare or hiss at us. Iain speculated that she had stashed the cubs in the saltbush to go scouting. Now she was leading the cubs back to the pride.

It would be good if she led us to the pride; our four-day foot safari was to begin the next morning, and knowing where the pride was would give us an objective. I love walking in the wild, but I love walking with a purpose even more. The lioness pressed on with her journey, and then she and the cubs pulled one of the vanishing acts that seem to be a Tsavo lion specialty. We looked for ten minutes; then, as suddenly as they'd disappeared, they reappeared, wading across the river. They stopped on a sandbar in midstream. There the cubs gamboled for a while, one mounting its forepaws on its mother's hindquarters and allowing her to pull it along as she looked for a spot to complete the crossing.

"All we need now is background music from *Born Free*," Iain remarked, but I thought of Santiago's dream in *The Old Man and the Sea*, his dream of lions on the beach.

The lioness plunged into the river and swam the channel, the cubs paddling after her. The three climbed the bank and were swallowed by the saltbush. We were sorry to see the lioness go; for all her scruffy appearance, we had grown fond of her and her self-possessed air. Still, she looked awfully lean, and I said that I would have felt better about her prospects if I had seen her and the cubs reunited with their pride.

"Don't worry about her," Iain commented. "She's in complete command of her situation."

I'm not sure how, in the span of a few hours, I went from feeling sorry for a real lion to being in abject terror of an imaginary one. At two in the morning, the rational brain doesn't function as well as it does at two in the afternoon, and you start thinking with the older brain, that cesspit of primeval dreads. Or maybe my heebie-jeebies were a reaction to another of Iain's bedtime stories, told over another of Kahiu's superb dinners: grilled eggplant, pumpkin soup, and bread pudding with hot cream.

A Texas couple and their two sons were on safari with Tropical Ice. One midnight, Iain was awakened by the parents' screams: "Iain! They're here! They're coming in!" He tumbled out of bed, unzipped his tent flap, and saw a lioness walk past him. Worse, he could hear other lions in the underbrush near camp—and the crunching of bones. Iain shouted to his clients to get on the floors of their tents and cover themselves with their mattresses. More lions appeared, playfully batting at the couple's tent, as if to tease the frightened occupants. Iain, who was trapped in his own tent, yelled to his two armed Masai guards, who had managed to sleep through the commotion. As they approached the thicket in which Iain had heard the hideous crunching noise, they were greeted by growls. The Masai did not live up to their reputation as fearless lion hunters; they fled in panic. It turned out that the lions were guarding their kill, which wasn't a person, but a warthog. Iain attempted to drive them off by clapping his hands—a sound that normally frightens lions, because no other animal makes it. It had no effect on these lions, who eventually just sauntered away.

The next day, as Iain brought the pickup around, he saw what he termed "a horrifying sight." A lioness was strolling alongside the woman's tent, which was open at one end. As calmly as he could, Iain told her to come out, but not to run, and get in the car. She had no sooner jumped in and shut the door than the lioness rounded the corner and walked into the tent. Had the woman still been inside, the lioness would have killed her. "Maybe not eaten her," Iain added, reassuringly, "but definitely killed her, because she would have tried to run."

Dangers imagined are always worse than dangers confronted. I was in good spirits the next morning, and actually looking forward to facing a lion on foot, if for no other reason than to conquer my fear. To protect us, Iain had contracted two Kenya Wildlife Service rangers, Adan and Hassan, who were armed with semiautomatic assault rifles. Dressed in jaunty berets, camouflage uniforms, and combat boots, they looked more like commandos than park rangers. Only safaris with special permission from the park's senior warden are allowed into the vast area north of the Galana; the guards are strongly recommended.

I hoped that Adan and Hassan would not imitate the behavior of the Masai in Iain's story. If they did, we didn't have much else in the way of self-defense: my trusty K-bar; Iain's Gurkha kris, a souvenir from a trek in the Himalaya; and Clive's Masai short sword, called a *simi*. African lore is full of stories about strong men who have killed lions with knives, but lions weren't the only dangerous game we might encounter. The saltbush forests easily conceal elephants, Cape buffalo, and the hippopotamus, which kills more people in Africa than any other mammal. Since Tropical Ice started running safaris in 1978, Iain's guards have rarely had to fire over the heads of elephants, and have never shot a lion, but they have had to kill six hippos, which are very stubborn and very aggressive.

With Hassan on point and Adan as rearguard, we waded the warm Galana to the north side, Iain instructing us to stay close together so that we would sound not like seven average-size things but like one big thing—an elephant—to deter crocodiles. We saw one of the reptiles, a nine- or ten-footer, 15 minutes after we'd forded. We continued upriver toward the Sobo rocks, and ran into a dozen hippos, entirely submerged except for the tops of their dark heads and their piggish, protruding eyes. They tolerated our photographing them for a while, but when we crept closer, one big bull lunged from the water with astonishing speed, his cavernous mouth open and threatening. A warning, which we heeded by moving on.

The morning was overcast and breezy, but by ten o'clock the air was hot and searing—reminiscent of Arizona in July. We had the whole immense wild to ourselves, because most tourists are unwilling to walk miles in triple-digit temperatures, and too timid to confront wild creatures on foot. What a difference, to observe game animals on their own terms. To photograph them, we had to read the wind as a hunter does, practicing stealth and watching for the slightest motion. We stalked up close to a band of Cape buffalo and a small elephant herd, and the experience was far more satisfying than driving up to them. Sweating, exercising caution and bush-craft, we earned the right to bag them on film.

We were on the last mile of the trek when we found pugmarks in the sand, leading straight along the shore toward a grove of doum palms some 300 yards away. They were deep and well-defined—that is, recent. Iain and I fell into a discussion as to just how recent. Clive, looking ahead with unaided eye, said they were very recent, because two lions were laid up under the palms. Clive pointed, and Iain and I raised our binoculars.

"It's a log," I said. "A big palm log."

Iain concurred.

"I am telling you, lions," Clive insisted peevishly. "Two bloody lions. One's maned, too."

Then Adan said, "Lions, 100 percent," but he spoke too loudly. The log lifted its head.

My binoculars framed an atypical Tsavo lion, a Metro-Goldwyn-Mayer emblem with a golden mane, lying in the shade with his companion and gazing straight back at us. With the palms overhead, the scene looked biblical.

The easterly wind favored us. We began a stalk, heading up over the embankment to approach the lions from above, Rob and I with our cameras ready, Adan with his rifle at low port, prepared to shoot if necessary. Hassan's was braced on his shoulder, the muzzle pointing backward at the rest of us. Iain pushed the rifle barrel aside. Hassan shifted the gun to the crook of his arm, holding it upside down as if he were cradling a baby, and sauntered along like a man strolling in Hyde Park, instead of in Tsavo with two big lions just ahead. A less than reassuring guard. I decided to grab his rifle if I had to.

We filed along a game trail between the saltbush and the riverbank, closing the distance. The idea was to capture an image of lions up close—while on foot. All right, what was the difference between a picture taken from a car and one taken on foot? I don't know, only that there seemed to be a difference. Listen to the ancient Roman Stoic Epictetus: "Reflect that the chief source of all evils to man, and of baseness and cowardice, is not death, but the fear of death." Still true, I'd say. The real point of life is to be brave; it is to master fear of death, which is the genesis of all fears. And one of the exercises by which you can steel yourself to that fear is to confront something that could break your neck with one swipe of its paw.

I don't wish to exaggerate the emotions of the moment. None of us was trembling. Instead, we were apprehensive, in the old sense of the word. We apprehended, in a state of heightened awareness—alert to every sound and movement. Coming abreast of the palm grove, Iain walked in a crouch, and we followed suit, trailing him and Hassan over the lip of the embankment to look down into the pool of shade beneath the trees. I raised my camera.

The lions were gone. They must have fled at the sound of our voices, though we never saw them move. Their tracks disappeared into the brush. It was as though they had dematerialized.

Two hours into the next day's trek, we found evidence of an old lion kill: the skull and horns of a big Cape buffalo, resting in the grass beside a lugga, or dry streambed. Iain and Clive poked around, studying the area like homicide detectives.

"Probably an old bull, alone," said Iain. "The lions were down in the lugga, behind that big bush, three of them. They sprang at the buffalo from the side, just as he was about to come down the bank."

But that was all the evidence we saw of lions that morning. By eleven o'clock, with my shirt soaked through with sweat and my eyeballs feeling sunburned, we crossed back to the south side of the Galana, where we were picked up in a Land Cruiser—and were told that we need not have walked ten miles to find lions; they had found us. Soon after we left, four males had appeared on the north side of the river, almost directly across from camp. By now they had moved off.

I took a nap after lunch, took some notes, then sat shirtless and shoeless in my camp, my baked brain a perfect tabula rasa. Iain appeared, walking fast over the Bermuda grass. Gesturing, he told us in a whisper to follow him, and to be quiet. The four lions had returned.

With cameras and binoculars, we ran on tiptoe. Across the river, between 200 and 300 yards downstream, two of the four were crouched on the bank, drinking. Their hides so perfectly matched the sand and beige rock that they seemed made of the same stuff. I put the binoculars on them. They lacked manes, and I would have thought they were females, but their size suggested otherwise. Thirst slaked, one turned and padded up the bank, and it was clear that he was a male. He disappeared into a clump of doum palm; the second drank a while longer, then joined his friend. A moment later, the first lion emerged to walk slowly into the saltbush behind the palms, the other following shortly afterward, and then a third.

"See how relaxed they are?" said Iain, softly. "They're not acting as if they're aware we're here. If they are, and they're this casual about it, we may have some major problems tonight."

Just as I got out of my seat to fetch my field notes from my tent, the fourth lion showed up. He caught my movement and stopped, turning his head to face in our direction. Carefully raising my binoculars, I eased back down, and had the unsettling impression that I was staring into the lion's face, and he into mine, from a distance of, say, ten yards. Crouched low, the joints of his bent forelegs forming triangles, his shoulders a mound of muscle, sinew, and tendons, he was so still that he could have been a carving. Like the others, he had no mane.

No one knows the reason for this characteristic. It is thought by some that it evolved in Tsavo males because a mane is a liability in such thick thornbush country. Another theory is that pride lions on the plains sport manes as symbols of power and health to attract females and warn off rival males. A mane would be useless for those purposes in Tsavo, where vision is often limited to a few yards. However, bald male lions do occur throughout sub-Saharan Africa, though they tend to be found most frequently in harsh scrub-bush habitats similar to Tsavo's. What's really intriguing is that some experts in leonine behavior believe they have identified a historical trend in man-eating, which can be traced geographically to such environments. If they are correct, it could mean that maneless lions are more likely to prey on humans.

You can ask Wayne Hosek about that. Hosek, a 56-year-old California estate planner and hunter, was born in Chicago; he had also seen the Tsavo man-eaters in his school days, and had become mesmerized by Patterson's saga. Many years later, in 1991, he was on a shooting safari near Zambia's Luangwa National Parks, a region of dense bush. People in the town of Mfuwe, near where Hosek was hunting with a professional guide and trackers, told him that they had been terrorized by a huge lion that had killed and eaten six of their neighbors. They thought it was a female, because it had no mane. Local hunters had shot six lionesses, believing each was the one responsible, but the attacks continued. The villagers pleaded with Hosek to rid them of the menace. For the next week, he and his guide virtually relived Patterson's experiences. Tracks told them that the lion wasn't just big, it was enormous. But it also was canny, outsmarting them time after time. It always seemed to know where they were and how to avoid them. As Hosek describes it, the experience ceased to be a sport and became a kind of war. Finally, concealed in a ground blind, Hosek killed the lion with one shot, from a range of 70 yards. The lion indeed was without a mane, but it was a male—and huge. Four feet at the shoulder and ten feet, six inches from its nose to the tip of its tail, it weighed 500 pounds—the biggest man-eating lion on record.

The nature of the environment, the size of the lion, the absence of a mane—Hosek's trophy fit in with the theories. I reflected on that, gazing at the big fellow across the river. He crept down to the edge of the bank, lowered his head, and drank, pausing to look at us again. He then leisurely climbed back up and lay down in the shade. If he was concerned about us, he didn't show it.

"What did you mean, if they know we're here and are casual about it that we could be in for problems tonight?" I whispered to Iain.

"They won't attack, but they could come into camp." He didn't say what led him to make such a prediction, and I didn't ask.

That night, as we sat around the campfire, the lions began to roar from across the river. It was deep and resonant, a sound like no other.

The finish line for that day's walk was the starting point for the next. Driving there, we saw two of the lion quartet on a beach, quite a ways off, but they were soon gone. From eight in the morning till noon, we trudged ten miles to Sala Hill, which rises as a perfect pyramid out of the savanna, but we could not find the pride that the four males and the scruffy lioness belonged to.

We made a more concentrated effort the following day, beginning at the spot where we had seen the female and cubs cross the Galana. Distinct pugmarks were printed in the fine sand near a stand of doum palm. The strong sundowner winds in Tsavo scour animal tracks pretty quickly, so the prints must have been made last night or early in the morning. There were more on the sandbar, where the cubs had cavorted with their mother three days earlier, and on the opposite bank. One set of tracks led us into the saltbush, and to a lion's day bed—a patch of flattened grass and dirt—but we lost them farther on, where the earth was like pavement and covered with foot-high yellow grass.

"You can see why that movie called them ghosts," Iain said, referring to The Ghost and the Darkness. "They're always in ambush mode. They stay hidden, come out to hunt and kill, then hide again. They are ghosts."

His commentary was borne out a little farther upriver, when we struck the track of the two males spotted from the truck the previous day. Again we followed it; again we lost it. The lions could have been anywhere or nowhere. As Adan pushed into the saltbush, his rifle at the ready, I mentally compared Tsavo lions not to ghosts, but to the Vietcong: masters of concealment, of hit and run, showing themselves only when they chose. I was beginning to appreciate what Patterson had endured a century ago. It was an adventure for me to track these lions, but I would not have wanted to be charged with the task of finding and killing them.

We continued upriver. Then Adan found another set of prints. "These are very new," whispered Iain, pointing at one. "This is now."

A dry wind blew through the acacias, the palm fronds rattled. I flinched when a sand grouse flushed five feet away. Great predators can make their presence known, even when they aren't seen or heard. When such monarchs are near, your senses quicken, for the simple reason that your life may depend on it. I had experienced that keenness of perception several times in Alaska, coming upon grizzly tracks, and once in Arizona, crossing the fresh prints of a cougar while I was quail hunting, but I'd never experienced it as deeply as in those haunted thickets of Tsavo. There was something else as well. To walk unarmed in the lion's kingdom demands a submission not unlike the submission required of us in the presence of the divine, and it graces those who walk there with the humility that is not humiliation. I was acutely aware of being in a place where I, as a man, did not hold dominion, but had to cede dominion to a thing grander, stronger, and more adept than I.

"I believe that if one of us, right now, tried to walk back to camp alone, we wouldn't make it," Iain said. "The lions would study you, see that you're alone and defenseless, and attack." Suddenly, he stopped, wrinkled his nose, and said, "Smell that?"

I shook my head. My sense of smell was the only one that had not been heightened; I suffer from allergies and my head was stuffed. In fact, one of the things I'm allergic to is cats.

"A kill. There's something dead, rotting in there," said Iain, gesturing at a thicket.

The wind eddied a bit, and I caught it—a little like skunk, a little like week-old garbage.

Adan and Hassan pushed into the saltbush, while we who were unarmed waited in the open. When the two rangers emerged, several minutes later, they reported they had found nothing except hyena and jackal tracks, indicating that the carcass, wherever it was, had been abandoned by the lions and was now the property of scavengers.

The trek ended at the palm grove across from camp, where the four males had laired up. A lot of pugmarks, and some stains in the sand where the lions had urinated, but nothing more.

"Make a perfect movie set, wouldn't it?" Clive whispered. It was two days later, and we had just made our way through the saltbush and entered a grove of old doum palm. The trunks of the high trees were worn smooth where elephants had rubbed up against them, and the lanes between the trees were like shadowy halls, some blocked by flood-wrack from the rainy season—barricades of logs and fronds behind which a dozen lions could have lurked unseen. We expected to hear a low, menacing growl at any moment, an expectation that was not fulfilled until, making a circle, we came out of the trees and reentered the saltbush. The sound wasn't a growl, however—more of a loud grunt or bellow.

What happened next happened all at once. A cloud of dust rose from behind a thicket, Adan whipped around, leveling his rifle, and Iain said, "Get behind me!" to Leslie and me. Just as we did, certain that we were about to be charged by a lion, an elephant appeared, not 20 yards to our right. It was a young female of some two or three tons, shaking her head angrily, her ears flared. She stomped and scuffed the earth, then started toward us. Adan fired a shot over her head to scare her off. She stood her ground and let out a trumpet, her ears flaring again, dust rising from her feet, dust spewing from her hide as she tossed her great head back and forth. Iain yelled to Adan in Swahili. Adan fired again, and for an instant I thought he'd shot her—some trick of light made a puff of dust flying from her shoulder look like the impact of a bullet. In the next instant, as the female ran off, I realized that he'd put the second round over her head.

Iain lit into Adan, all in Swahili, but it was plain that the ranger was getting a royal dressing down. I couldn't understand why.

"Rangers are supposed to know that you don't have to shoot at an elephant to scare it off," Iain explained. "That female was old enough to have seen other elephants shot by poachers. You had to have been here in the eighties to appreciate it. Elephants are traumatized by the sound of gunfire. They're very intelligent animals, and it's not necessary to fire over their heads. A handclap will do it, or just shouting. What we try to do on a foot safari is to observe without disturbing the animals, and move on without them ever being aware that humans are around."

Before heading back to Nairobi, we made a pilgrimage to the "Man-eaters' Den." After Patterson had eliminated the two "brutes," as he called the lions, work resumed on the Tsavo River bridge. While waiting for a shipment of construction materials, he took a break to explore some rocky hills near his camp and to do some recreational hunting. He was in a dry riverbed, pursuing a rhino, when he spotted something that stopped him cold.

"I saw on the other side a fearsome-looking cave which seemed to run back for a considerable distance under the rocky bank," Patterson wrote. "Round the entrance and inside the cavern I was thunderstruck to find a number of human bones with here and there a copper bangle such as the natives wear. Beyond all doubt, the man-eaters' den!"

After taking a photograph, he left his find, and from that day in early 1899 until recently, its location was lost to history. Patterson's characterization of it as a lion's den has aroused controversy and skepticism among naturalists and zoologists for a century: Lions are generally not known to be denning animals (the tale of Daniel in the lion's den notwithstanding).

In 1996, the Field Museum team endeavored to determine who or what had been the cave's true occupants. That year and the next, Kusimba, Kerbis Peterhans, Gnoske, and Andanje made extensive searches southwest of the Tsavo River bridge—the direction Patterson said he'd followed on his excursion. Nothing was found until April 1997, when Gnoske, after rereading Patterson's descriptions and comparing them to the landscape, realized that Patterson's directions had been way off: The "rocky hills" mentioned in the book were not southwest of the bridge, but northwest.

The day after making that determination, Gnoske, Kerbis Peterhans, and Andanje found a cave in a shady riverbed only a mile from the bridge. It perfectly matched the one in Patterson's photograph. After 98 years, the man-eaters' den had been rediscovered.

But was it the man-eaters' den? The next year, the team sifted through the dirt to recover human bones and examine them for teeth marks; if there were any, the researchers could determine if they had been made by lions, hyenas, or leopards. They looked for the copper bangles Patterson had seen, as well as for human teeth to distinguish between Asians and Africans; Asian teeth would be all but incontrovertible proof that the victims had been the Indian railway workers.

The result of that work was surprising, though inconclusive. Kusimba believes that the legendary cave was never a lion's den, nor any sort of den, but in all likelihood a traditional burial cave of the ancient Taita people, who once inhabited the Tsavo region. Gnoske and Kerbis Peterhans, on the other hand, favor a theory that the bones in the cave were, in fact, the remains of lion victims, though they were probably dragged there by hyenas.

Earlier in the trip, when Rob was shooting pictures at park headquarters, Kusimba took him to the cave. Now Rob would show it to us. Iain and Clive, who had never seen the cave, were as eager for a look as Leslie and I. So, with Rob in the lead, the guides became the guided. After thrashing around for a while, we came to a ravine. Rob shouted. And there it was, with a corridor between two big boulders leading beneath an overhang and into a cavern.

"Well, I don't think it looks so fearsome," said Iain, who doesn't have a high opinion of Patterson, considering him to have been an imperial martinet, a so-so hunter, and something of a grandstander.

I agreed that the cool, shady spot was almost idyllic. Then again, we were not trying to build a bridge in the African wilderness and, at the same time, hunt down two clever cats that were using our workforce as a fast-food restaurant. To Patterson, with his memories of his workers' screams, of his crew leader's gruesome remains, of the tense, interminable nights waiting with his rifle, the cave could well have appeared "fearsome." And given the ignorance about lion behavior that prevailed in his time, it was understandable why he may have mistaken a burial cave for a man-eater's den. Imperial martinet or not, he did pretty well with what he had.

That said, I did find Patterson's characterization of his adversaries as brutes and outlaws objectionable. I recalled our second to last morning in Tsavo, as we sat in camp and watched a zebra herd warily come down to the far bank of the Galana to drink. They had been waiting on the ledge above the river for a long time, suffering from what Iain termed "the paradox of survival." The animals were parched, but feared that a lion or crocodile was waiting for them at the river's edge—lions and crocs know that zebras must drink eventually. And so the whole herd stood still, gazing at the river with what seemed to us equal measures of longing and dread, until the desperation of their thirst overcame their fear. Even so, they did not rush down with abandon, but watered in orderly stages. A dozen or so animals would drink, while the others waited their turn and the stallions stood watch. If one group got greedy and took too long, the stallions would let out a series of loud, sharp brays. It was a strange, distressful sound, falling somewhere between a whinny and a bark.

A layman should not anthropomorphize, but to me, the stallions seemed to be saying, "You've had enough, get a move on, we don't have much time." In a way, I identified with them. They were prey; and, out there, so was I. But that recognition did not offend my sense of human dignity. The offense was to my human pride. Nothing wrong with a little pride, except when it becomes excessive. If I had been in Patterson's boots, I would have pursued the lions with as much determination as he—after all, his first responsibility was to finish the bridge and protect his workers' lives—but I don't think I would have regarded the lions as savage brutes violating some law of heaven. If anything, they were only obeying the fundamental law of all creation, which is survival.

To realize that I shared something in common with the wary, anxious zebras was merely to acknowledge my true place in nature where nature is wild—the stage on which the drama of predator and prey is played out.

from The Lost Explorer
by Conrad Anker
and David Roberts

The 1924 disappearance on Everest of George Mallory and Andrew Irvine created mountaineering's greatest mystery: Did they summit? Conrad Anker (born 1964) joined a 1999 expedition to Everest to investigate the question, and discovered Mallory's body. He then joined with David Roberts (born 1943) to write a book about the still-unsolved mystery. Roberts' account of Mallory's last expedition is lucid and illuminating.

Mallory's grim premonition came true: in the end, the 1924 expedition was more like war than mountaineering.

Yet as he sailed from England to India, then as he rode and hiked toward Everest, Britain's finest climber was filled not with foreboding, but with optimism. "I can't see myself coming down defeated," he wrote Ruth from the remote Tibetan village of Shekar Dzong. To his former teammate Tom Longstaff, he predicted, "We're going to sail to the top this time, and God with us—or stamp to the top with our teeth in the wind."

As he had in both 1921 and '22, once more Mallory underestimated Everest. His bravura performance two years before, along with Finch's, had made the summit seem well within his grasp. At times, his certainty about success could approach cocksure arrogance, as during his lecture tour of America, where, envisioning a third expedition, he boasted, "Mount Everest is asking for trouble." Yet at other times, his confidence was laced with threads of doubt, as in a sentence he wrote his sister Mary from shipboard, "Anyway, we've got to get up this time; and if we wait for it and make full preparations, instead of dashing up at the first moment, some of us will reach the summit, I believe."

The 1924 party was even stronger than the 1922 team had been. General Charles Bruce was back as leader, now fifty-eight and in poor health even before the expedition started. But Howard Somervell and Teddy Norton were returning, seasoned by their previous Everest foray. The cool-headed Norton was appointed climbing leader, despite Mallory's greater experience and technical ability. Somervell brought along Bentley Beetham, a young climber of whom much was expected, for in the summer of 1923, the pair had had a season in the Alps few other Englishmen could match, climbing some thirty-five peaks in six weeks.

Noel Odell imported vast funds of exploratory wisdom and alpine expertise, and though he was slow to acclimatize, once he was in shape, he would outperform all his teammates except Norton and Mallory. Odell's Spitsbergen protégé, Sandy Irvine, was an unproven quantity, but quickly showed that his solid athleticism and buoyant spirit could make up for lack of mountaineering experience. Rounding out the party were Geoffrey Bruce, now a mountaineer, thanks to his 1922 campaign; John de Vere Hazard, a fast and experienced climber in the Alps; and photographer-cinematographer John Noel, who would prove staunch in a supporting role.

Mallory thought the team "a really strong lot," and Norton went even further: "I doubt if so strong a party will ever again be got together to climb Mount Everest."

During the journey to the mountain, Mallory badly missed his wife, to whom he wrote often and at great length. The sense of having done her harm, during whatever "difficult time" the couple had gone through the previous autumn, afflicted him. "I fear I don't make you very happy," he wrote from the ship. "Life has too often been a burden to you lately, and it is horrid when we don't get more time and talk together." For Ruth, her husband's absence was a constant ache: "Dearest one, I do hope you are happy and having a good voyage. I am keeping quite cheerful and happy, but I do miss you a lot."

On the approach, General Bruce recurringly felt "seedy" and weak. Unable to keep up with his teammates, he chose a low-altitude detour to get himself to the village of Kampa Dzong two days after the main party. Before he could reach that town, however, he collapsed in a full-blown malarial fever, apparently the flaring up of a long-dormant infection. Bitterly disappointed, he resigned from the expedition and returned to India.

Teddy Norton was made leader of the party, and Mallory climbing leader (which he would have been de facto in any case). Fortunately, the two men got along splendidly, even during the expedition's lowest moments, and made no important decisions without consulting each other.

Mallory's obsession had taken the form of trying to come up with a perfect plan for linked parties to push for the summit. John Noel noted that "he seemed to be ill at ease, always scheming and planning." By April 14, still far from the mountain, he had devised a strategy, which he detailed enthusiastically in a letter to Ruth; then, only three days later, he was seized with what he called a "brain-wave" that presented him a new plan like an epiphany. Essentially it boiled down to putting a pair of parties simultaneously in position to go to the top from different camps. From Camp IV on the North Col, two climbers with fifteen porters would climb to Camp V, build four tent platforms, and descend. Another pair, the first, "gasless" summit party, would occupy Camp V one night, then push on with eight porters, skipping Camp VI, to set up a Camp VII at 27,300 feet—higher than anyone had yet been on earth. At the same time the second summit party, using oxygen, would establish a Camp VI some 800 feet lower than Camp VII. "Then the two parties," wrote Mallory to Ruth, "start next morning and presumably meet on the summit."

The plan looked good on paper, and Norton was won over by it; but of course on Everest the best-laid schemes of men and mountaineers "gang aft a-gley." In the end two parties would indeed try for the summit, one without oxygen, one with, but they would launch four days apart, and by the time the second pair—Mallory and Irvine—set out for the top, the first pair had stumbled down to Camp III. The visionary Camp VII, perched high on an exposed shoulder just below the crest of the northeast ridge, would never be established.

As the team members had sailed for India, a nagging worry plagued their thoughts. The disaster of 1922, when seven porters had died, would still be fresh in the Sherpas' minds: would any volunteers be willing to go back up on the mountain that had proved so deadly? The team was thus overjoyed when they learned through their trading agent that a "number of Sherpas, Bhotias, and hill-men generally" had come in, hoping to be hired.

Yet Mallory and his comrades were right to anticipate the Sherpas' terrors. In 1924 it would take very little to demoralize the porters altogether. A foretaste of their ambivalence came in the behavior of Angtarkay, who had been dug out of the avalanche debris in 1922. "We felt bound to take him on again," wrote General Bruce in the opening chapter of *The Fight for Everest* (which he was proud to pen, despite having given up the expedition), "but he soon broke down, and returned with me." In Bruce's view, the Sherpa had never "really recovered from that terrific experience" of being buried alive in snow.

Mallory's paramount vow was to avoid a recurrence of the 1922 tragedy. As he wrote his sister Mary on May 2, in another passage that resonates with ironic foreshadowing, "No one, climber or porter, is going to get killed if I can help it. That would spoil all."

With some seventy porters, cooks, and "domestic servants" in tow, the expedition rode on ponies through Tibet. An omen of bad fortune, however, awaited them at the Rongbuk Monastery. There they learned that the head lama was ill and could not perform the *puja* on which the porters set such store to keep them safe on the mountain. And there, the climbers beheld a fresh mural painting chillingly memorializing the 1922 accident: in Bentley Beetham's words, it depicted "the party being pitch-forked down the mountain-side by hoofed devils and sent spinning into the colder hell."

Two weeks later, during a lull in the foul May weather that thwarted the expedition, Norton marched the whole team back down to the monastery. Instead of a blessing, however, the head lama offered the Englishmen a malediction. "Your turning back brings pleasure to the demons," he intoned in Tibetan, which an interpreter translated to John Noel. "They have forced you back, and will force you back again."

For all this, as he reached Base Camp, armed with his "brain-wave" scheme, Mallory was still awash in the highest optimism. "I can't tell you how full of hope I am this year," he wrote his sister Mary. "It is all so different from '22, when one was always subconsciously dissatisfied because we had no proper plan of climbing the mountain."

All during the journey to India and the march across Tibet, Mallory had been sizing up Sandy Irvine. From the start, as he wrote Ruth, he found the Oxford undergraduate "sensible and not highly strung," though he could not resist an impish sketch of Irvine as "one to depend on for everything except conversation." Later, during a storm on the mountain, Mallory read poems out loud from his cherished anthology, Robert Bridges's *The Spirit of Man.* Somervell was surprised to learn that Emily Brontë had written poems as well as novels; Odell was stirred by the last lines of Shelley's *Prometheus Unbound,* while "Irvine was rather poetry-shy, but seemed to be favourably impressed by the Epitaph to Gray's 'Elegy.'" (One wonders just how that gloomy meditation in a country churchyard on the anonymous dead resonated with the twenty-two-year-old: "The paths of glory lead but to the grave.")

Norton too was taken with Sandy Irvine's quiet strength. In *The Fight for Everest,* he described his young teammate thus: "Irvine, as befitted a rowing blue, was big and powerful—with fine shoulders and comparatively light legs." Irvine was a little heavier than Mallory, and in superb shape, having rowed two seasons for the Oxford crew that beat Cambridge in 1922 for the first time since 1913. Though not as classically beautiful as Mallory, he was a remarkably handsome young man. A family tradition records that at Oxford, Irvine became a womanizer, conducting an affair with his best friend's stepmother. He had a very fair complexion, whence his nickname; on Everest, Irvine would suffer more than anyone else from sun- and windburn.

Herbert Carr, Irvine's biographer, who knew him at Oxford, thought the youth innately shy. "He had an odd way of laughing," Carr remembered. "It was a silent laugh, visible but not audible, a long low reverberating chuckle which lit up his face with sunny merriment. And as his normal expression was grave, the contrast was all the more striking."

Irvine was born in Birkenhead into genteel circumstances not unlike Mallory's. He attended Shrewsbury public school, then Merton College at Oxford. His academic fortes were chemistry and engineering; in French and Latin, on the other hand, he was woefully weak. Even in adolescence, he was extraordinarily adept at tinkering and inventing. While still at Shrewsbury, he sent the blueprints for two machines of his devising to the War office—an interrupter gear for firing machine guns through propellers, and a gyroscopic airplane stabilizer. Both had already been anticipated by Hiram Maxim (the inventor of the machine gun), but the flabbergasted War Office, according to Herbert Carr, sent him "most warm congratulations . . . with instructions to go on trying."

In Mürren, in Switzerland, at Christmas 1923, Arnold Lunn, who conceived the slalom race, gave Irvine skiing lessons. "He is the only beginner I have ever known," reported Lunn, "who brought off at his first attempt a downhill Telemark." After only three weeks of practice, Irvine entered and won the Strang-Watkins Challenge Cup (a slalom race) against seasoned veterans. He loved the sport, writing Lunn in gratitude, "When I am old, I will look back on Christmas, 1923, as the day when to all intents and purposes I was born. I don't think anybody has ever lived until they have been on ski."

Intensely competitive, on the approach to Everest Irvine found good sport in challenging Mallory to a pony race. The older man was charmed by the self-confident youngster. After several weeks on the East Rongbuk Glacier, Mallory noted that Irvine "has been wonderfully hard-working and brilliantly skilful about the oxygen. Against him is his youth (though it is very much for him, some ways)—hard things seem to hit him a bit harder. . . . However, he'll be an ideal companion, and with as stout a heart as you could wish to find."

Mallory was genuinely dazzled by Irvine's aptitude with the oxygen gear. After the young man had taken the apparatus apart, stripped some four pounds of useless metal from each set, and put the pieces back together, Mallory marveled, "What was provided was full of leaks and faults; and he has practically invented a new instrument." For someone as mechanically inept as Mallory, Irvine's facility was nothing short of miraculous: watching his comrade tinker with the ill-designed equipment, he was like a tone-deaf auditor listening in uncomprehending admiration to the playing of some twenty-two-year-old Mozart.

Ever since 1924, observers have second-guessed Mallory's decision to take Irvine along on the summit push, rather than the far more experienced Odell. Many have wondered whether Irvine's meager skills in the mountains could have contributed to the fatal accident. Walt Unsworth, in his definitive history of Everest, went so far as to speculate whether Mallory "had formed a romantic attachment for the handsome young undergraduate."

One need not reach so far for an explanation. Once Mallory had committed himself to the use of oxygen on his summit attempt, Irvine's expertise became critical. Odell was ostensibly in charge of the oxygen apparatus, but he was a withering skeptic about its benefits. Mallory clearly explained his reasons in a letter to Ruth: not only was Irvine the oxygen expert, but if Mallory paired with Odell, that would leave an all-too-inexperienced duo of Irvine and Geoffrey Bruce as backup.

> And so Irvine will come with me. He will be an extraordinarily stout companion, very capable with the gas and with cooking apparatus. The only doubt is to what extent his lack of mountaineering experience will be a handicap. I hope the ground will be sufficiently easy.

Irvine kept a diary on Everest, making his last entry only the day before setting out with Mallory for the top. The diary was retrieved by Odell and published in 1979. It is a fairly stolid document, written for the most part in the pronoun-less staccato so often favored by the unintrospective: "Spent afternoon repacking Primus stoves, also negotiating to buy pony. . . . Put lightening fasteners on my sleeping bag." Irvine wastes little breath on observing his teammates; a kind of tunnel vision dominates his perspective. Like many another Englishman on his first trip to Asia, he was a bit squeamish. In one Tibetan village, "I was very impressed by the dirtiness of the whole place, and also the smell." In another: "Went this afternoon to see Tibetan Devil dancers—this most weird performance was continuous from 2:00 p.m. to 6:30 p.m., and got rather monotonous towards tea-time."

Somehow during the approach, Irvine received dismaying news from Oxford. "Got wire to say that Cambridge won by 4 1/2 lengths—incredible!" A day later, he had not absorbed the shock: "I still can't get over Oxford being beaten by four and a half lengths—I should like to have details of the race."

Yet the diary captures Irvine's obsessive tinkering, as he records one attempt to fix a piece of equipment after another. The balky oxygen gear became his greatest challenge. A typical passage:

> I spent all afternoon and evening again patching up oxygen apparatus. Out of box No. 2023 I made up two complete instruments (1A and 2A), but without emergency tubes, as all in this box leaked—either the pipe or the brass of the union was porous. Number 3A had a dud flowmeter which I took to pieces—it appeared corroded inside around the bottom bearing. I cleaned this up as well as I could, but it is still sticky at 1 ½ + 3, but works alright if hit every now and then. Number 4A had a blocked reducing valve, so was turned into MkIII pattern.

One can imagine Irvine trying to explain these arcane matters to a puzzled Mallory. Indeed, a kind of unintentional humor emerges from the diary, as Irvine tends to the gear woes of (in Longstaff's pithy characterization from 1922) the "stout hearted baby" who was "quite unfit to be placed in charge of anything, including himself." A sample:

APRIL 11th. . . . I mended Mallory's bed, Beetham's camera, Odell's camera tripod and sealed up a full tin of parrafin. . . .

APRIL 12th. Spent day in camp, did some photography, sorting biscuit boxes and doing a job of work on Mallory's camera, which spun out and took all afternoon.

APRIL 19th. . . . I spent this afternoon mending one of Mallory's ice axes (broken by a coolie). . . .

APRIL 27th. . . . After about an hour Mallory came in with a box of crampons, and I spent till dinner time fitting crampons to Mallory's and my boots, and trying to fix them without having a strap across the toes, which is likely to stop the circulation.

APRIL 28th. . . . Spent most of the afternoon with Beetham's camera, also mending my sleeping bag and Mallory's saddle.

All this compulsive puttering, of course, was of immense practical value to the expedition. Irvine might be "poetry-shy," but he would be irreplaceable high on the mountain when gear malfunctioned.

As the expedition progressed, the bond between Mallory and Irvine grew. After May 7, in Irvine's diary, Mallory is called "George"; the others remain Norton, Somervell, Hazard, and so on. The friendly competitiveness that had dictated a pony race extended onto Everest, where, however, Irvine could never keep up with his older friend, that wizard of motion in the mountains. "When we moved on," Irvine wrote on May 4, "a devil must have got into Mallory, for he ran down all the little bits of downhill and paced all out up the moraine. It was as bad as a boat race trying to keep up with him."

• • •

The party reached base camp beneath the terminus of the Rongbuk Glacier on April 29. At once, the members started sorting out 300 yak-loads of gear to be carried to subsequent camps on the East Rongbuk. Mallory's optimism had reached full bore: he had already decided that May 17, give or take a day or two, would be the summit day; and he predicted to Ruth, "The telegram announcing our success . . . will precede this letter, I suppose; but it will mention no names. How you will hope that I was one of the conquerors!"

Then everything started to go wrong. The weather was fiercely cold and stormy even at the comparatively low altitude of Base Camp. On April 28, "a bitterly cold wind blew, the sky was cloudy, and finally we woke up to find a snowstorm going on. Yesterday was worse, with light snow falling most of the day." The team tried to impose English cheer on their desolate camp, feting their arrival with a five-course meal and several bottles of champagne.

By now, the number of porters and yak herders had swelled to 150. With Gurkha leaders who were veterans from 1922, these natives set out on April 30 without sahibs, singing and joking, to establish Camps I and II. The plan was for half to turn back after dumping their loads at I, with the other half pushing on to II the next day. But on their way back to Base Camp, night caught the porters, and only twenty-two of the seventy-five arrived. They were found the next day unharmed; but their disappearance had launched a devastating series of porter problems that would cripple the expedition in the following weeks.

On May 7, carrying loads to Camp II, the porters ran into such atrocious weather that Mallory ordered them to leave their loads a mile short of camp. Meanwhile another contingent of porters had been trapped at Camp III, at 21,500 feet, "with only one blanket apiece," as Geoffrey Bruce wrote in the expedition book, "and a little uncooked barley to eat, and were now driven out unable to bear it longer, utterly exhausted." When they staggered down to II, they swelled a crowd of porters to twice the number for whom there was tent space. There was no choice but to break open the food and tents intended for higher on the mountain.

At Camp III, Mallory and three teammates endured temperatures as low as -22° F. with high winds. If conditions were this bad low on the mountain, they would be unendurable above the North Col.

Mallory had hoped to establish Camp IV on the North Col by May 9, but that day Odell and Hazard were turned back in a blizzard only three quarters of the way up, dumping their loads in the snow. The men spent a wretched night at III, later described by Bruce:

> The blizzard continued with unabating violence, and snow drifted into our tents covering everything to a depth of an inch or two. The discomfort of that night was acute. At every slightest movement of the body a miniature avalanche of snow would drop inside one's sleeping-bag and melt there into a cold wet patch.

In these conditions, the porters' morale plunged alarmingly. Mallory and his companions did everything they could to exhort the natives to further efforts, but it was a losing battle. No doubt the failure of the men to receive the lama's *puja* at the Rongbuk Monastery contributed to their apathy, as did the frightful weather. Mallory blamed an "Oriental inertia": "They have this Oriental quality that after a certain stage of physical discomfort or mental depression has been reached they simply curl up. Our porters were just curled up in their tents." But he had to admit that the sahibs themselves had also curled up to wait out the storms: they spent "most of the time in the tents—no other place being tolerable."

At last Norton bowed to the inevitable, ordering all the porters and climbers to retreat all thirteen miles back to Base Camp. The column formed, in Bruce's word, "a melancholy procession of snow-blind, sick, and frost-bitten men." Even in retreat, disaster struck, as one porter fell and broke his leg, another developed a blood clot on the brain, and a cobbler had "his feet frost-bitten up to the ankles." The latter two died shortly after, to be buried near Base Camp.

The Englishmen were faring little better, with ailments ranging from hacking coughs to "glacier lassitude." Mallory had weathered intestinal problems so severe it was suspected that he had appendicitis. Beetham was laid low by sciatica so persistent that he would never climb very high on the mountain.

In 1922, the team had reached the North Col by May 13, and Mallory, Somervell, and Norton had launched the first summit attempt only seven days later. During the corresponding week in 1924, the party had failed even to reach the North Col. Instead, they spent six days at Base Camp, licking their wounds. Mallory wrote Ruth, "It has been a very trying time with everything against us."

Not until May 17—the day Mallory had originally plotted for the summit—did the debilitated climbers head back up the mountain. Somervell later judged that the appalling week of waiting out storms at Camp III had "reduced our strength and made us . . . thin and weak and almost invalided, instead of being fit and strong as we had been during the 1922 ascent."

Nonetheless, Mallory rallied his waning optimism, fixing May 28 as his new summit date, and wrote Ruth with dogged hope, "It *is* an effort to pull oneself together and do what is required high up, but it is the power to keep the show going when you don't feel energetic that will enable us to win through if anything does."

At last, on May 20, Mallory, Norton, Odell, and one Sherpa gained the North Col. Mallory took the lead up a steep ice chimney that formed a difficult but safe alternative to the slope that had avalanched in 1922. Norton left a vivid description of that 200-foot lead: "You could positively see his nerves tighten up like fiddle strings. Metaphorically he girt up his loins. . . . Up the wall and chimney he led here, climbing carefully, neatly, and in that beautiful style that was all his own."

The ascent, wrote Mallory, was "a triumph of the old gang." Yet on this expedition where nothing seemed to go right, a further catastrophe struck the four men as they descended.

It began as Mallory decided to head down by the ill-starred 1922 route. Early on, the men hit slopes where they needed the crampons they had left at Camp III. Mallory chopped occasional steps, but following unroped, first Norton slipped, then the Sherpa—both fortunately stopping after short slides. Leading downward, Mallory suddenly plunged ten feet into a hidden crevasse. As during his fall on the Nesthorn in 1909, when, belayed by Geoffrey Winthrop Young, Mallory never let go of his axe, now he showed remarkable self-possession even in mid-plunge. As he wrote Ruth, "I fetched up half-blind and breathless to find myself most precariously supported only by my ice-axe, somehow caught across the crevasse and still held in my right hand—and below was a very unpleasant black hole."

Mallory shouted for help, but his teammates, caught up in their own perils, neither heard him nor knew what had happened. Eventually he "got tired of shouting" and managed to excavate a delicate sideways passage out of the crevasse—only to find himself on the wrong side of it. "I had to cut across a nasty slope of very hard ice and, further down, some mixed unpleasant snow before I was out of the wood." The four men regained Camp III thoroughly exhausted.

Even so, they had finally reached the North Col, the platform from which all summit attempts must be launched, and the weather showed signs of ameliorating. The ice chimney Mallory had so deftly led presented a logistical obstacle to porters getting loads to the Col, but fixed ropes eased the passage, and eventually Irvine wove a rope ladder and hung it on the chimney, turning the pitch into a reasonable scramble for laden men.

Then, just as hope glimmered in Mallory's breast, yet another dire predicament thwarted the team's progress. On May 21, Somervell, Irvine, and Hazard led twelve porters up to the North Col. While Somervell and Irvine descended, Hazard and the porters remained at Camp IV, awaiting the arrival of Bruce and Odell, who planned to use the porters to push on to establish Camp V. But a snowstorm began that evening and continued through the next day, while the temperature again dropped to -22° F. Odell and Bruce never left Camp III. The next day, Hazard decided to descend with the porters.

• • •

Among the expedition members, Hazard was distinctly the odd duck. A loner, he was not well liked by his teammates. As Somervell later wrote, Hazard "built a psychological wall round himself, inside which he lives. Occasionally, he bursts out of this with a 'By Gad, this is fine!' . . . Then the shell closes, to let nothing in."

Now, as he led the porters down the slope made treacherous with new snow, Hazard failed to notice that four of them balked and returned to their tents at Camp IV. When Hazard showed up at III with only eight porters, Mallory was furious. "It is difficult to make out how exactly it happened," he wrote; "but evidently he didn't shepherd his party properly at all."

This was perhaps too harsh a judgment, as the demand that one man be responsible for twelve porters in marginal conditions was a well-nigh impossible one. What the fiasco meant, however, was that four porters, no doubt terrified and possibly suffering frostbite, were stranded above all the sahibs on the mountain.

On May 24, Somervell, Norton, and Mallory headed up to rescue the porters. Norton judged the situation so desperate that, as he later wrote, "I would have taken a bet of two to one against a successful issue to our undertaking." Norton and Somervell were off form, but "Mallory, who on these occasions lived on his nervous energy, kept urging us on." Above the ice chimney, the snow slopes were loaded, ready to avalanche. With the other two belaying from the last safe stance, Somervell led a diagonal traverse, using every bit of the 200 feet of rope the men had carried. He ran out of line some ten yards short of the crest of the col. The porters, having heard the men approach, peered nervously over the edge. It was 4:00 p.m.—dangerously late.

Norton, who spoke Tibetan, coaxed the porters into trying the ten-yard descent to Somervell on their own. Two men made it safely, but the other two fell, slid and tumbled, then came to rest in precarious spots a short distance from Somervell. With no other option, he drove his axe into the slope, untied, fed the rope over the axe shaft, and, simply holding the end of the rope in his hand, sidled toward the trembling porters. With hardly an inch to spare, he grabbed each by the scruff of the neck and hoisted them back to the anchored axe. The worn-out men regained Camp III long after dark.

This debacle demoralized the porters utterly. After May 24, only fifteen of the fifty-five porters were of any use at all. The team dubbed these stalwarts "Tigers," a hortatory epithet that has been current on Everest ever since. In the meantime, however, the party was in such disarray that Norton had no other choice than to order once more a wholesale retreat. By May 25, the team had limped all the way down to Camp I, at 17,900 feet.

"It has been a bad time altogether," wrote Mallory to Ruth on May 27, in the last letter she would ever receive from him. "I look back on tremendous effort and exhaustion and dismal looking out of a tent door into a world of snow and vanishing hopes."

At his most pessimistic, Mallory had never foreseen a rout as complete as the one Everest had dealt his team during the preceding month. Less plucky men might have packed up and gone home at this juncture, with less than a week of May remaining. Instead, the 1924 expedition held what they called a "council of war."

Neither food nor oxygen had yet been carried to Camp IV; only tents and sleeping bags were stocked there. Norton's revised plan was to forget altogether about oxygen, in hopes that two light, fast parties of two men each, supported by porters, could make leaps on three successive days to Camps V and VI and then to the summit. The plan, of course, was pie in the sky, for as yet no climber had taken a single footstep above the North Col.

Both Somervell and Mallory had developed racking coughs. Mallory described his to Ruth: "In the high camp it has been the devil. Even after the day's exercise . . . I couldn't sleep, but was distressed with bursts of coughing fit to tear one's guts—and a headache and misery altogether."

Yet Norton offered Mallory a place in the first pair, arguing that "though he had so far borne the brunt of the hardest work, yet the energy and fire of the man were reflected in his every gesture." His partner would be Geoffrey Bruce, who at the moment, Mallory wrote, was "the only plumb fit man" in the party.

At last the weather relented, granting the team several "cloudlessly fine and hot" days in a row. Despite their ailments, the climbers moved efficiently up the mountain. Mallory had no illusions about the team's thin chances of summitting: "It is fifty to one against us, but we'll have a whack yet and do ourselves proud," he wrote Ruth. Yet he closed his last letter with a jaunty vow: "Six days to the top from this camp!"

On June 1, for the first time, climbers set off upward from the North Col, as Mallory, Bruce, and eight porters intended to establish Camp V at 25,300 feet. The day was again sunny, but above the col a bitter wind out of the northwest swept the face. Some 300 feet short of their goal, the porters flagged. Four of them had to drop their loads and head down, while the other four stumbled up to the stony slope where Mallory had already begun to build makeshift tent platforms. In a heroic effort, Bruce and Sherpa Lobsang ferried the other four loads up to camp. In doing so, however, Bruce exhausted himself; it was later determined that he had "strained his heart," and after June 1, he was of little use on the mountain.

That night the two sahibs and three porters slept at V. In the morning, Mallory was ready to push on, but Bruce was too weak to climb, and the porters had, in Norton's phrase, "shot their bolt." There was no choice but to head back down to Camp IV.

There Odell and Irvine were installed in a supporting role, cooking meals for the summit pair and carrying oxygen up to them as they descended. Irvine chafed at his role, writing in his diary, "I wish I was in the first party instead of a bloody reserve." But during the previous week, he too had been unwell: he had had a three-day bout of diarrhea, and on May 24 he recorded, "felt very seedy." The sunburn that had afflicted his fair complexion for more than a month had gotten worse. The men had brought various ointments, including zinc oxide, to smear their faces with, but these remedies apparently did Irvine little good. As early as April 11, he had written, "My face is very sore from wind and sun . . . and my nose is peeling badly."

On May 24, he noted, "face very sore indeed." By June 2, the sunburn was in danger of incapacitating the staunch young man. That night he wrote, "My face was badly cut by the sun and wind on the Col, and my lips are cracked to bits, which makes eating very unpleasant."

A day behind Mallory and Bruce, Norton and Somervell formed the second summit party. Rather than appoint himself to this team, which would seize the apparent last chance for the summit, Norton had asked Mallory and Somervell to determine who Somervell's partner should be. From among Odell, Irvine, Hazard, and Norton, they had nominated Norton. It would prove a wise choice.

Norton and Somervell left the North Col with six carefully selected Tigers on June 2. Still the weather held. They carried their own tent and sleeping bags, for if the plan had worked Mallory and Bruce would at the moment be pushing on to establish Camp VI, and all four Englishmen would need tents and bags at both V and VI.

In *The Fight for Everest*, Norton gives a detailed description of the clothing he wore that day—a state-of-the-art wardrobe for 1924. It makes for a startling contrast with the down suits and plastic boots of today's Everest climber:

> Personally I wore thick woollen vest and drawers, a thick flannel shirt and two sweaters under a lightish knickerbocker suit of windproof gaberdine the knickers of which were lined with light flannel, a pair of soft elastic Kashmir putties [ankle wraps, the predecessors of modern gaiters] and a pair of boots of felt bound and soled with leather and lightly nailed with the usual Alpine nails. Over all I wore a very light pyjama suit of Messrs. Burberry's "Shackleton" windproof gaberdine. On my hands I wore a pair of long fingerless woollen mits inside a similar pair made of gaberdine; though when stepcutting necessitated a sensitive hold on the axe-haft, I sometimes substituted a pair of silk mits for the inner woollen pair. On my head I wore a fur-lined leather motor-cycling helmet, and my eyes and nose were protected

by a pair of goggles of Crookes's glass, which were sewn into
a leather mask that came well over the nose and covered any
part of my face which was not naturally protected by my
beard. A huge woollen muffler completed my costume.

Neither man wore crampons, for despite Irvine's tinkering, no one had
yet figured out a way to strap these invaluable spikes to one's boots
without cutting off circulation to the feet.

On the way up, Norton and Somervell were dismayed to meet one
of Mallory's Sherpas descending. From him, they learned of the first
party's turnaround, then crossed paths with their friends as they
despondently clumped down to the North Col. Continuing with only
four porters, Somervell and Norton reached Camp V at 1:00 p.m.,
where they settled in to cook and get warm.

Lower on the mountain, the men had cooked on Primus stoves
using liquid fuel; above the North Col, however, they preferred Unna
cookers that burned a solid cake of Meta fuel made in France. The
chore of making dinner was one all the men detested. As Norton put
it, "I know nothing—not even the exertion of steep climbing at these
heights—which is so utterly exhausting or which calls for more determination than this hateful duty of high-altitude cooking."

Scooping pots full of snow to melt, heating the water to its tepid
boiling point at altitude, filling Thermos flasks with hot water or tea for
the morrow, washing up the greasy pots—and then, "Perhaps the most
hateful part of the process is that some of the resultant mess must be
eaten, and this itself is only achieved by will power: there is but little
desire to eat—sometimes indeed a sense of nausea at the bare idea—
though of drink one cannot have enough."

In the morning, the men did not get off until 9:00 a.m., so difficult
was it for Norton to persuade three of the four porters to continue. "I
remember saying, 'If you put us up a camp at 27,000 feet and we reach
the top, your names shall appear in letters of gold in the book that will
be written to describe the achievement.'"

Despite the late start, the climb on June 3 went smoothly enough;

the weather was still fine, with even less wind than the day before. Somervell's cough gave him so much trouble he had to stop now and then. Even so, the two Englishmen passed their own 1922 high point of 26,000 feet just after noon, and later they exceeded Finch and Geoffrey Bruce's mark of 26,500 feet. Sending the three porters back, Somervell and Norton pitched Camp VI at 26,800 feet, once again shoring up a tent platform by piling loose stones. They were higher than human beings had ever been on earth.

After a month of demoralizing setbacks, of ignominious defeat staring them in the face, the two men dared believe that the summit might be within their grasp. Norton slept well, Somervell tolerably. "Truly it is not easy to make an early start on Mount Everest!" Norton would write. Yet on June 4, the men were moving by 6:40 a.m.

After an hour, the pair reached the foot of the broken cliffs that would come to be known as the Yellow Band. They had topped 27,000 feet, with the summit about 2,000 feet above them. Moving diagonally up and right, Norton and Somervell found easy going on ledges that led one to the next.

It was here that Norton purposely diverged from the ridge route that had always been favored by Mallory. To his eye, a long, gradually ascending traverse toward what would come to be called the Great Couloir afforded the best line on the upper north face. The day remained perfect, though the men climbed in bitter cold.

Yet now, with the top tantalizingly close, the men began to succumb to the awful ravages of altitude. Somervell's cough had grown alarming, necessitating frequent stops. Norton had made the mistake of taking off his goggles when he was on rock: at 27,500 feet, he started seeing double. Without oxygen, the men were slowed to a crawl. "Our pace was wretched," Norton later wrote. He set himself the goal of taking twenty steps without a rest, but never made more than thirteen: "we must have looked a very sorry couple."

By noon, however, the two men were approaching the top of the Yellow Band. They were some 500 or 600 feet below the crest of the summit ridge, well to the west of the First Step. All at once, Somervell announced that he could go no farther, but he encouraged his partner to continue alone. With weary, careful steps, Norton pushed on, traversing farther right along the top of the Yellow Band. He turned two corners, the second directly below the skyline feature the team had named the Second Step—"which looked so formidable an obstacle where it crossed the ridge," Norton presciently wrote, "that we had chosen the lower route rather than try and surmount it."

Beyond the second corner, the going abruptly got worse, as the slope steepened and the downsloping "tiles" underfoot grew treacherous. Twice Norton had to backtrack in his steps and try another approach. Still he pushed on, at last reaching the Great Couloir.

There, suddenly, he waded through knee- and even waist-deep unconsolidated snow. In a moment, the full terror of his predicament came home to him:

> I found myself stepping from tile to tile, as it were, each tile sloping smoothly and steeply downwards; I began to feel that I was too much dependent on the mere friction of a boot nail on the slabs. It was not exactly difficult going, but it was a dangerous place for a single unroped climber, as one slip would have sent me in all probability to the bottom of the mountain. The strain of climbing so carefully was beginning to tell and I was getting exhausted. In addition my eye trouble was getting worse and was by now a severe handicap.

Norton turned around. He was only 300 yards west of Somervell, and 100 feet higher, but, as often happens when a climber acknowledges defeat, a kind of mental collapse now seized the man. As he approached his partner, facing a patch of snow thinly overlying sloping rocks—ground he had walked easily across perhaps half an hour before—he lost his nerve. Norton pleaded for Somervell to throw him a rope. Once tied in, he accomplished the crossing.

The expedition would later fix Norton's high point as 28,126 feet—

only 900 feet below the summit of the world, which stands 29,028 feet above sea level. Unless Mallory and Irvine reached a greater height four days later, Norton's altitude record would stand for the next twenty-eight years. His oxygenless record would last twenty-six more, until Peter Habeler and Reinhold Messner summitted without gas in 1978.

Starting down at 2:00 p.m., the men stayed roped together all the way back to Camp VI. Along the way, Somervell dropped his ice axe and watched as it bounded out of sight. At VI, he replaced it with a tent pole.

By sunset, the men, now unroped, had reached Camp V. Rather than spend a miserable night on one of its sloping, inadequate tent plat-forms, the duo pushed on down into the dusk, aiming for Camp IV. And here, Somervell nearly lost his life. Glissading ahead, Norton noticed that his partner had stopped above. All during the expedition, Somervell had painted skillful watercolors of the scenery (a number of the paintings were published in *The Fight for Everest*). His thinking addled by altitude, Norton now guessed that his friend had stopped to make a sketch or painting of the mountains bathed in their twilight glow. In fact, Somervell's worst coughing fit so far had seemed to lodge some object in his throat that threatened to choke him. At last he coughed it loose in an explosion of blood and mucus. It was later determined that Somervell had coughed up the lining of his larynx.

As Norton staggered down to the North Col in the last light, Mallory and Odell came up to meet him and guide him through the crevasse-riven shelf just above camp. One of the men shouted that he was bringing an oxygen cylinder. Norton yelled back, again and again, in a feeble wail, "We don't want the damned oxygen; we want drink!"

So might the 1924 expedition have ended, with an extremely gallant stab by Norton and Somervell that had established a new world alti-tude record. The monsoon would be upon the mountain any day now. Yet as he regained the North Col, Norton learned that Mallory had decided, in the event of the second attempt failing below the summit, to make one last push—with oxygen. After descending himself from Camp V on June 2, Mallory had organized a porter carry from Camp

III that had wrestled a quantity of bottles up to the North Col. Norton expressed his approval; privately, he "was full of admiration for the indomitable spirit of the man." He demurred only in wishing Mallory had chosen Odell for his partner rather than Irvine.

In the middle of the night of June 4–5, Norton woke up with a terrible pain in his eyes, to find that he had gone snow-blind. He could do nothing the next day to help his friends organize their assault except talk to the porters in their own language. The key to communicating with these vital allies above Camp IV on the two previous attempts had been Norton's and Bruce's competence in their language. Mallory had a "smattering of Hindustani," but Irvine spoke scarcely a word of any tongue the Sherpas understood.

At 7:30 in the morning of June 6, Norton said goodbye to the summit pair. "My last impression of my friends was a handshake and a word of blessing." Still blind, he could not watch the men move off among the snow humps and crevasses toward the north face. Later that day, Norton went down to Camp III, so helpless that six porters had to take turns carrying him along the moraine. During the next four days, wrote Norton, "we were to pass through every successive stage of suspense and anxiety from high hope to hopelessness," until Camp III would eventually lodge in his memory as "the most hateful place in the world."

Noel Odell, the sole climber left fit enough to serve in support, would spend eleven days at or above the North Col, a performance, as Norton later put it, with "no equal in our short record of high climbing." Odell too was full of admiration for Mallory's indomitable will. As was characteristic of the man, Odell bore his own exclusion from the summit party with serene magnanimity.

Despite their ailments, using oxygen Mallory and Irvine had come up from Camp III to IV on this last push in only two and a half hours— a time that some of the strongest climbers in the 1990s would be proud of. Up till the last minute, Irvine had fussed with the oxygen sets, jury-rigging final adjustments.

His spirit must also have been indomitable, for he cannot have gotten much sleep during his last nights on the North Col. The final diary entries reveal just how badly Irvine was suffering from his sunburn. On June 3: "A most unpleasant night when everything on earth seemed to rub against my face, and each time it was touched bits of burnt and dry skin came off, which made me nearly scream with pain." June 5, on the eve of departure: "My face is perfect agony."

Despite having slaved for more than a month to improve the oxygen apparatus, Irvine told Odell that "he would rather reach the foot of the final pyramid without the use of oxygen than the summit by means of its aid! He thought that if it were worth while doing at all, it was worth while doing without artificial means." Such a purist sentiment would scarcely be voiced again for the next fifty years.

At 8:40 a.m. on June 6, using oxygen, with eight lightly burdened porters going without, Mallory and Irvine left the North Col. Odell took a picture of the two: by his own admission a hurried snapshot, the men's features unrecognizable as they putter with gear, it has nonetheless been reprinted hundreds of times over, for it is the last photo taken of either man—unless there are images lying dormant in the celluloid inside Mallory's Vestpocket camera, lost somewhere still on Everest.

A clear morning deteriorated into a cloudy day with evening snow. At 5:00 p.m., four of the porters returned from the north face, with a note from Mallory, ensconced in Camp V: "There is no wind here, and things look hopeful."

The next day, as planned, Odell and a Sherpa climbed to Camp V. Soon after they got there, the remaining four porters descended from above, bringing another message, this one from Camp VI at 26,800 feet:

Dear Odell,—

We're awfully sorry to have left things in such a mess—our Unna Cooker rolled down the slope at the last moment. Be sure of getting back to IV to-morrow in time to evacuate before dark, as I hope to. In the tent I must have left a compass—for the Lord's sake rescue it: we are without. To here on 90 atmospheres for the two days—so we'll probably go on two cylinders—but it's a bloody load for climbing. Perfect weather for the job!

Yours ever,
G. Mallory

To the end, Mallory was dogged by his forgetfulness and mechanical ineptitude. The loss of the cookstove was ominous, for unless the men had already filled their Thermoses with water or tea before it "rolled down the slope," they would be hard put to melt any snow for breakfast or to carry on the climb. Not having a compass (Odell in fact found the instrument in the tent at V) would be less consequential on summit day, unless the pair were engulfed in a white-out. The "90 atmospheres," Odell knew, amounted to a flow of about three quarters of the rig's capacity. At that rate, each bottle ought to have lasted at least four hours. If the men carried two cylinders apiece on June 8, they should have been able to climb for eight hours breathing gas.

With the message to Odell was the one to John Noel, exhorting the men lower on the mountain to start looking for Mallory and Irvine "either crossing the rock band under the pyramid or going up the skyline at 8.0 p.m." Odell read this note, assuming at once, as all historians have, that Mallory meant 8:00 a.m. on June 8.

After sending the five Sherpas down, Odell spent a peaceful night alone at Camp V. The Sunset transported him, as he gazed in three directions at distant peaks sharply etched in the clear air, including the massive sprawl of peaks surrounding Kangchenjunga, the world's third-highest mountain, 100 miles to the east. "It has been my good fortune to climb many peaks alone and witness sunset from not a few," he later wrote, "but this was the crowning experience of them all, an ineffable transcendent experience that can never fade from memory."

Odell started out to climb to Camp VI at 8:00 a.m. on June 8. The day had dawned clear, but by mid-morning "rolling banks of mist commenced to form and sweep from the westward across the great face of the mountain." The wind, however, was light. The day seemed propitious for a summit climb. "I had no qualms for Mallory and Irvine's progress upward from Camp VI," Odell reported, "and I hoped by this time that they would be well on their way up the final pyramid."

Still climbing without oxygen, Odell was by now so completely in his element that, rather than take the shortest approach to Camp VI, he wandered about the north face, appraising its geology, discovering his beloved fossils. Just after noon, he climbed the "little crag" at 26,000 feet, stared at the skyline ridge, and made his legendary sighting. There, some 2,000 feet above him, he watched as the lead figure quickly climbed to the top of a step on the ridge, then waited as the second figure followed, both men "moving expeditiously as if endeavouring to make up for lost time." Then the clouds moved in again, blocking his view.

It was 12:50 p.m., five hours later than the 8:00 a.m. appearance Mallory had seemed to predict in his note to John Noel. Odell now felt a mild alarm, but he listed to himself all the reasons that could have contributed to his friends' delay. (Curiously, few commentators in the last seventy-five years have wondered whether Mallory's 8:00 a.m. prediction might have simply been the final example of his underestimating the mountain. No party had yet managed to leave a high camp on Everest before 6:30 a.m., and the skyline ridge lay more than 1,200 feet above Camp VI.)

In the midst of a snow squall, Odell reached VI at 2:00 p.m. There he was disappointed to find no note from Mallory chronicling the pair's departure, and further disturbed to see pieces of oxygen apparatus strewn about the tent. Yet he would not conclude from the debris that Irvine had made desperate last-minute repairs; instead, he rationalized that his protégé might simply have "invented some problem to be solved even if it never really had turned up! He loved to dwell amongst, nay, revelled in, pieces of apparatus and a litter of tools."

Odell did not notice that Mallory had left his flashlight in the tent—yet another instance, and a potentially weighty one, of his absentmindedness. The flashlight would be rediscovered by members of the 1933 Everest expedition, who turned on its switch and found that it still functioned nine years after it had been left there.

Hoping to find his friends on their way down and guide them back to Camp VI, Odell climbed another 200 feet in dense clouds, whistling and yodeling to signal his presence. Then, realizing that it was too early to expect the pair's return, he made his way back to Camp VI. Just as he got there, the squall ended and the mountain cleared again. Now, however, Odell could see nothing, although warm afternoon light bathed the mountain's upper slopes.

He lingered until 4:30 p.m., then, in obedience to Mallory's note, started back down the mountain, not before leaving Mallory's compass, which he had retrieved from Camp V, in "a conspicuous place in the corner of the tent by the door"—less, one suspects, to enable his friends to navigate down to the North Col than as a charm against the fates. Odell reached Camp V at 6:15 p.m., then, glissading much of the way, descended the 2,300 feet to the North Col in the astonishing time of thirty minutes.

Among the Englishmen, there was only Hazard there to greet him. The others, still weakened by their ordeals of the last few days, were convalescing at Camp III. On the evening of June 8, everyone stared for hours at the upper slopes of Everest, hoping to see the beam of a flashlight or even the flaming burst of one of the emergency flares the porters had carried to Camp VI; but they saw nothing. Still rationalizing away his fears, Odell hoped that moonlight reflected off summits to the west might have aided his friends' descent.

All next morning, Hazard and Odell swept the mountain with field glasses, detecting no signs of life. Unable to bear this idle vigil, at noon Odell started up the north face again with two Sherpas. The well-rested Hazard did not even consider joining him, for he had reached his limit at 23,000 feet.

The three men reached Camp V that afternoon, then spent a sleepless night as a nasty wind threatened to tear the tents loose. On the morning of June 10, with the wind still fierce and cold, the two Sherpas were incapable of continuing. Odell sent them back down to the North Col, then set out alone to climb to Camp VI. For the first time, he breathed bottled oxygen in hopes it would aid his performance, but, true to his ingrained skepticism, turned off the apparatus partway up and "experienced none of those feelings of collapse and panting that one had been led to believe ought to result." Lugging the useless contraption on his back, Odell marched on up to VI, reaching it at midday.

Odell's own account does not dwell on the terrible shock of his discovery. In the most understated fashion, he mentions simply that "I found everything as I had left it: the tent had obviously not been touched since I was there two days previously." Dumping the oxygen set, he at once pushed on above to search for some trace of his companions, even as the weather deteriorated.

In a state of heightened awareness that the dawning tragedy had spurred in him, Odell was now granted something like a revelation:

> This upper part of Everest must be indeed the remotest and least hospitable spot on earth, but at no time more emphatically and impressively so than when a darkened atmosphere hides its features and a gale races over its cruel face. And how and when more cruel could it ever seem than when balking one's every step to find one's friends?

Odell struggled on for almost two hours, finding nothing. Back at Camp VI, he crawled into the tent to take shelter from the gnawing wind. Then, during a lull, he dragged two sleeping bags up to a precarious snow patch above the tent and laid them out in the form of a T. Four thousand feet below, looking with field glasses, Hazard saw the prearranged signal and knew the worst.

At last Odell closed up the tent and headed down. As he took one more look at Everest's distant summit, his revelation of the utter inhumanity of the great mountain reached a spiritual pitch:

> It seemed to look down with cold indifference on me, mere

puny man, and howl derision in wind-gusts at my petition
to yield up its secret—this mystery of my friends. What right
had we to venture thus far into the holy presence of the
Supreme Goddess . . . ? If it were indeed the sacred ground
of Chomolungma—Goddess Mother of the Mountain
Snows, had we violated it—was I now violating it?

In that freighted moment, chilled to the soul by the mountain's indif-
ference, Odell all at once heard the siren's song:

And yet as I gazed again another mood appeared to creep
over her haunting features. There seemed to be something
alluring in that towering presence. I was almost fascinated. I realized that no mere mountaineer alone could
but be fascinated, that he who approaches close must ever
be led on, and oblivious of all obstacles seek to reach that
most sacred and highest place of all. It seemed that my
friends must have been thus enchanted also: for why else
should they tarry?

Lower on the mountain, Odell's teammates had passed these last few
days in an agony of ignorance. In hopes of curing his throat problems,
Somervell had descended all the way to Base Camp. On June 11, he
wrote in his diary, "No news. It is ominous." And the next day, after
several comrades had arrived with their tidings: "There were only two
possibilities—accident or benightment. It is terrible. But there are few
better deaths than to die in high endeavour, and Everest is the finest
cenotaph in the world."

By June 12, the whole expedition had gathered at Base Camp. Wrote
Norton later:

We were a sad little party; from the first we accepted the loss
of our comrades in that rational spirit which all of our generation had learnt in the Great War, and there was never any

tendency to a morbid harping on the irrevocable. But the tragedy was very near; our friends' vacant tents and vacant places at table were a constant reminder to us of what the atmosphere of the camp would have been had things gone differently.

The men might accept the loss of Mallory and Irvine, but they could not resolve the mystery of what had happened to them. As they retreated from Mount Everest, they speculated ceaselessly as to how their friends had met their end. For the rest of their lives—John Noel the last to die, just short of his one hundredth birthday—they would continue to wonder and speculate, turning over and over like potsherds the fragmentary clues they had to base their guesses on.

Tombstone White

by Mark Jenkins

Mark Jenkins (born 1958) has written books about his 8,000-mile bicycle trip across the then-Soviet Union and his first kayak descent of Africa's Niger River. His column in Out-side chronicles his other exploits around the globe. Here Jenkins faces a blizzard on the Matterhorn—which, he points out, has claimed more lives than Everest or McKinley.

W hen we left the moraine and crossed onto the glacier, we discovered it was speckled with black stones that had plummeted down the Matterhorn's east face. Some were small as fists, some big as barrels, but all had fallen thousands of feet at a fatal velocity. The glacier was gravity's missile range, and we were moving across it as quickly as we could when we spotted something strange on the ice. We didn't know what it was at first—or didn't want to know. From a distance it appeared as a twisted blue lump with blond hair. I approached holding my breath.

It was just a backpack. The impact of the fall had burst the nylon sack like a water balloon, strewing its contents across the glacier. A 35mm camera with a smashed lens. A down coat tied in a bundle with string. Wool socks. A woman's wool sweater melted into the ice. The pack had crashed here days, maybe weeks, earlier. The blond locks were loops of rope that slumped half out of the pack.

John knelt beside the shredded pack. He was thinking what I was thinking: *And the person who was wearing the pack?*

"Perhaps she took it off to rest," I said, "and the pack just slipped over the edge."

We continued up the Furgg glacier to the icefall and decided to climb straight up the middle rather than hike the big loop around the end. Foreshortening is the mother of all optimism, and shortcuts seldom are (short, that is). But certain kinds of people—mountaineers in particular—have a tendency to choose the hope of the unknown over the reality of the well-trodden. Halfway up we became lost in a labyrinth of wide-mouthed crevasses and leaning seracs, and had to rope up and slow down. We began to zigzag, searching for the firmest-looking snowbridges.

A chopper suddenly appeared overhead and made passes back and forth above the icefall. We were afraid the pilot thought we wanted to be rescued. Then the chopper arced backward and landed on the mountain far below us. Minutes later it flew over us again, this time with an orange-suited human harnessed to a cable swinging beneath the aircraft. The chopper gradually lowered the person onto the Matterhorn's face, right at the top of the icefall. We got out the monocular. The chopper backed away from the wall, the cable dangling like an empty fishing line. For the next few minutes the chopper circled, and then it dropped back in against the east face and hovered briefly. When it flew back into the blue sky, there was another human harnessed to the end of the line, a limp body with limbs hanging in unnatural positions.

The year before, I had come to Zermatt to climb the north face of the Matterhorn and it had snowed for six days straight. I thought I could still cajole a local climber into making a quick trip up the Hornli Ridge, the mountain's autobahn, the route climbed by unskilled hordes every summer. But no climber was interested. I tracked down several guides, all of whom shook their heads. One of them ended our conversation saying, "No one. No one. No one guide Matterhorn when it snows."

I hiked up beyond the Hornli hut alone and found more than a foot of snow on the route and the rocks so slippery it was as if the mountain had been coated in grease. I descended, chastened.

Now, a year later, I was back with a partner, John Harlin. The north face was loaded with avalanche-prone, unconsolidated snow, and John had climbed the Hornli Ridge on a previous trip, so we decided to attempt a traverse: trek halfway around the mountain, crossing from Switzerland into Italy, ascend the Italian Ridge, cross over the 14,690-foot summit, and descend via the Hornli. The hike over to the south side of the mountain would give us a chance to acclimatize and the weather a chance to shape up.

After the chopper disappeared with the body (we later learned it was that of a Polish climber who had fallen off the Hornli Ridge), John and I finished the icefall, topping out on the Furggen Ridge. We spent the night there, at 10,957 feet, in the Bossi *refugio*, a tiny, dirty, round-topped aluminum hut that is depressingly similar to a sheepherder's trailer. We boiled soup and spoke softly, reassuring each other that the man had died because he had made a mistake, a mistake we wouldn't have made—the bedtime lie that consoles all climbers.

By morning it was colder, the barometer was sinking, the mountain lost in mist. We dropped down onto the stone-speckled Cervino glacier, crossed below the south face, and started up the Italian Ridge just as it began to snow. Soon we were in a full-on blizzard, wet snowflakes as big as leaves. What was supposed to be a simple scramble up to the Carrel hut at 12,562 feet on the Italian Ridge turned into a half-desperate dance over slick rocks skidding out from under our feet. The thick chain hanging down the Whymper Chimney, placed there to aid in the ascent of the rock corner, was encased in ice. When we got to the hut our eyelids were frozen open and our jaws frozen shut.

There was an experienced Czech team inside. They showed us a journal that documented all the ascents they'd done across Europe. You could feel the vertigo in the photos. They had been waiting out the weather for several days; periodically one of them would step outside, then come back in covered with snow and cussing flamboyantly, making his teammates laugh.

The blizzard continued through the afternoon and into the evening, as one team after another kept arriving at the Carrel hut. The door would burst open and a blast of snow would blow in a frost-covered climber, crampons on his feet, an ice ax in each hand, beard crusted white. Stabbing his crampons into the wooden floor, he would flip a glazed rope over his shoulder, brace himself, and begin reeling his partners—one by one, each an abominable snowman—into the hut. By nightfall there were 20 climbers crowding the shelter and the walls were covered with wet clothes. Outside, the storm intensified, furious that we had found someplace to hide.

In the morning the storm was gone, the sun was up, and the mountain was buried in snow. We all slept in, assuming the mountain was unassailable. One more check mark on the "failed" side of the ledger. It's a part of mountaineering: you have to get used to it, even though you never do because if you did you'd quit.

A French guide announced that the Matterhorn could not be climbed. He was taking his two clients down immediately. I asked him what he thought about the chances of the mountain coming back into condition in a few days, and he replied that in a few days the sun would turn the snow to ice and the mountain would become coated in sheets of verglas and thus *traître extremement!*—extremely treacherous. Furthermore, the weather forecast called for another storm sometime in the next two days.

A snow-plastered mountain, a French guide's knowing opinion, and a bad forecast. That was it. That was enough.

The French guide and his clients went down. The Czech team went down. Two Spanish teams and two other Czech teams that had arrived the evening before went down. Everybody went down but John and me and a Czech father-and-son team that had arrived so late the night before they were spending the day in their sleeping bags.

John and I watched the retreat. Going down wasn't easy. The Carrel hut is perched high on a thin ridge of the mountain, the emptiness of the west face dropping off to one side, the blankness of the south face to the other. The climbers rappelled right off the hut stanchions, sliding into space. We stood on the airy steel veranda of the Carrel hut, staring down, watching the string of descending climbers, wondering why the hell we weren't following them.

Jean-Antoine Carrel is the climber who was forgotten once Edward Whymper successfully climbed the Matterhorn on July 14, 1865. Carrel, born in 1829 in Breuil, the Italian hamlet below the peak's south face, was one of the Alps' first mountain guides and the first man possessed with the vision and the will to try to climb the Matterhorn. His initial attempt was in 1857; he tried again in 1858 and 1861. He made three more attempts in 1862, two of them with Whymper. Whymper and Carrel were both friends and rivals. Carrel, the tough former soldier and stonemason; versus Whymper, the 25-year-old English artist, the climbing rookie who burned with the desire to reach the top of the stone dagger that had been pronounced unclimbable.

There were 17 attempts made on the Matterhorn, eight of them by Whymper himself, before the Englishman pulled it off. It was a battle of egos and shifting loyalties. Carrel considered the Matterhorn his mountain, jealously coveted the summit, and viewed Whymper as an interloper. Whymper believed Carrel to be the best climber in the Alps and had actually arranged to hire him for what turned out to be his successful ascent. But during the week of Whymper's planned attempt, bad weather intervened, and Carrel secretly agreed to guide a four-man all-Italian team, leaving Whymper out in the cold. When the Englishman discovered that Carrel was attempting the mountain from the Italian side, he quickly cobbled together a seven-man team in Zermatt to make an attempt from the Swiss side.

On the summit day, Whymper's party ascended the Hornli Ridge, while the four-man Carrel team climbed the Italian Ridge on the opposite side of the mountain. Carrel had gotten a late start, and the Italian Ridge is the more difficult route, but Whymper won the race by only 600 feet. When he stood on the summit he could see Carrel and his companions below, and the Englishman rolled a few stones to get Carrel's attention. Devastated. the native guide turned back, only to return three days later, with a new team, to successfully complete the first ascent of the Italian Ridge and the second ascent of the Matterhorn.

Whymper's victory had exacted a great cost. During the descent, four members of his group fell to their deaths. One man, Douglas Hadow, slipped, pulling off three others. Whymper and his two guides, Peter Taugwalder Sr. and Peter Taugwalder Jr., caught the fall, but the rope snapped and Michel Croz, a Chamonix guide, and the English climbers Charles Hudson, Douglas Hadow, and Francis Douglas fell 4,000 feet.

In Zermatt, Taugwalder Sr. and Whymper were accused of cutting the rope. The Swiss authorities conducted an inquest. After three days. Whymper and Taugwalder were exonerated, but the controversy continued. The *Times* of London denounced the ascent and deplored the utter uselessness of the sport of mountaineering. Queen Victoria considered outlawing the climbing of mountains. European newspapers published denunciatory editorials by writers who had never set foot on any mountain, let alone the Matterhorn. England was in an uproar over the disaster and everyone had an opinion. (Sound familiar?)

In 1871, Whymper gave his account of the story in a best-selling book titled *Scrambles Amongst the Alps*. Whymper would be famous for the rest of his life, although he hardly climbed in the Alps again. He went to Greenland, then to the Andes with Carrel, then to the Canadian Rockies.

Deaths of a putatively heroic nature seem to have a bizarre magnetism, particularly for those who have never witnessed the horror of dying. In Whymper's wake, suddenly everybody wanted to climb the Matterhorn. (Sound familiar?) In 1871 an English adventuress named Lucy Walker became the first woman to summit the mountain. The

Zmutt Ridge was climbed by the famous English alpinist Albert Frederick Mummery in 1879. In 1881, 23-year-old Teddy Roosevelt climbed the mountain. In 1911, the Matterhorn's last remaining unconquered ridge, the Furggen, was summited. The north and south faces fell in 1931.

Thousands have attempted the Matterhorn and more than 450 have died—more than on Everest or McKinley, Rainier or the Grand Teton. Technically, both the Italian Ridge and the Hornli Ridge are far more difficult than the trade routes up these other peaks. Whymper and Carrel's achievements are a testament to the skill, courage, and determination of mountaineering's early pioneers.

After turning tail on the Matterhorn the first time, I took a walk through the Zermatt cemetery, the graveyard of the Matterhorn. There are tombstones with ice axes and ropes sculpted into the rock, tombstones with real axes and crampons bolted onto the stone, even a tombstone in which a crucified Christ is adorned as a climber, ax and rope hanging from his body. These are the graves of too many who attempted the Matterhorn and paid for it with their lives. (Jean-Antoine Carrel, who perished in a blizzard on the mountain in 1890, is notably absent; his final resting place is Valtournanche, in the shadow of the mountain's Italian side.)

Whymper ends *Scrambles Amongst the Alps* with this admonition: "Climb if you will, but remember that courage and strength are nought without prudence, and that a momentary negligence may destroy the happiness of a lifetime. Do nothing in haste; look well to each step; and from the beginning think what may be the end."

Walking past those tombstones at dusk, with their hats of fresh powder, I understood why they don't guide when it snows on the Matterhorn.

John and I shoveled the snow off the bench outside the Carrel hut and took turns staring up at the Italian Ridge with the monocular. It didn't look that bad. It really didn't. There was a lot of new snow, but it was melting fast.

Sometimes it doesn't pay to think too much; other times thinking will save your life. It's case by case. The hard part is knowing what is reality and what is just the confusion of opinion, hearsay, and the constant three-way battle in your head between Mr. Ego, Mr. Fear, and Mr. Rationality. If you can't sort it out, you can get killed. You can get killed even if you do sort it out.

By noon we couldn't stand it anymore.

"We could just run up a few pitches and see how it goes," John blurted out.

"Right," I chimed. "If it's bad, we can rap right back down."

To forestall an imprudent attempt on the summit, neither of us took food or water. John even left his headlamp behind. We were going for a little reconnaissance, nothing more.

With all the snow and us not knowing the route, we moved cautiously but steadily, and in three hours we found ourselves atop Tyndal Peak with only the last rock between us and the summit. We were standing right where Carrel had been—only a few hours from the top—when Whymper had summited. We cursed our own late start. We cursed the unwarranted foreboding we had allowed into our hearts. We cursed our prudence for tricking us into leaving behind food and water. We turned and descended to the Carrel hut.

The next morning we were up at four, cruising the lower portions of the Italian Ridge at six, attacking the icy summit block at eight, snapping pictures on the hanging ladder at ten, standing on the summit at noon. Then, with perfect timing, the storm hit.

It was colder than the storm two days before. Winds that could have knocked us off our feet, bullets of snow, zero visibility. The mountain was instantly sheeted with ice, making it impossible to downclimb. We started to rappel, one anchor down to the next. The first rap off the summit we ran into a three-man Italian team that had also summited. The day before, one of their teammates had turned around, taking their second rope with him. Their one rope, doubled, didn't reach between the rappel anchors, so they were each rapping off the end of the rope and then soloing down to the next anchor—dangerous behavior, given the conditions.

Sometimes your own random good fortune can be another's salvation. Someone had left a climbing rope in the Carrel hut and John and I had taken it with us, just in case we needed an extra. The Italians would have hugged us if we hadn't all been clinging to the side of the mountain.

It took John and me almost five hours to make it down to the Solvay emergency hut at 13,133 feet on the Hornli Ridge. We were soaking wet and shivering. It wasn't a true emergency, but we didn't want it to become one.

"Well, John," I said, plucking the icicles from my eyebrows, "should we stay or should we go?"

"Tomorrow it could be storming even harder."

"Tomorrow the sun could come out."

"Mark, we can make it down tonight."

"If we get off-route it'll be a cold bivy."

In the end, we decided to humbly stay the night, our fourth on a mountain that is supposed to be climbed in one day. The Italians came stumbing in an hour later.

In the morning it was clear and sunny. We descended to the Hornli hut, a comfortingly huge hostel-cum-restaurant, where the Italians bought us beers, and we all sat in awe of the gleaming gothic cathedral of the Alps.

Other teams had been going up the mountain as we were coming down. A speedy Austrian team. A somber, silent German team. An American talking to his wife on a cell phone, maintaining he was doing just fine. (She was saying he was way behind schedule for the little distance he'd ascended and should turn around. She was right.) And a Japanese team. The Japanese were all bunched together except for one guy in silly nylon boots and ill-fitting clothes, climbing clumsily and unroped, apparently trying to stay ahead of his teammates.

Several hours later he died falling off the Matterhorn.

The Other Side of Crazy
by Michael Finkel

Michael Finkel (born 1969) has volunteered to be an avalanche victim, kayaked down the Congo's unmapped Chinko River, bicycled 5,000 miles across the U.S. and competed in the World Lumberjack Championships. But none of those experiences scared him more than his 1997 snowboarding trip to Alaska's Chugach Mountains.

Nothing in the Lower 48—not the precipices of Squaw, not the chutes of Jackson, not the steeps of Stowe—has prepared me for the sight I encounter driving south on Alaska's Richardson Highway, heading toward the port city of Valdez. Here, just after the road begins its long climb toward Thompson Pass, the broad, fertile Matanushka Valley abruptly pinches shut, the horizon turns jagged, and the Chugach Mountains vault skyward.

In all my previous alpine experiences the mountains were shaped roughly like pyramids: broad at the base, tapering to a peak. The Chugach have dispensed with the preamble. They hardly taper. They are all peak—three-, four-, five-thousand-foot-high fangs, nearly vertical from all aspects, angled with black slate ridges. Crevassed. Treeless. Stunning.

The truly unusual part, however, is not the shape of the mountains. Fang-shaped peaks exist elsewhere in the world—Nepal, Chile, Antarctica. I have seen photos. But nowhere else on the planet can you look upward at mountains such as these, look up at rock-streaked couloirs with the approximate pitch of the Washington Monument, and see line after line of ski and snowboard tracks.

I have come here with my snowboard. I'm not as strong a snowboarder as I am a skier, but the people I've been invited to join—photographer Eric Berger and professional riders Omar Lunde, Ross Rebagliati, and a woman named Athena who has dispensed with her surname—are all top-shelf snowboarders, sponsored by various and sundry companies, and I thought it might be polite to fit in equipmentwise, if not exactly skillwise.

My group, it turns out, is standing on the side of the road, waving their thumbs. They had arrived this morning, and now, at 8:30 p.m., in the flushed arctic twilight, they've finished riding for the day. There are no chairlifts in the Chugach. The runs are reached, in increasing order of expense, by foot, by snow cat, by airplane, or, for the marquee descents, by helicopter. My group had used a helicopter. They wear expressions on their faces that suggest the early stages of shock.

I ferry the group to our headquarters—a pair of Fleetwood motor homes each the length of a city block, complete with kitchen, bedroom, and an electric step that automatically extends every time you open the door. The RVs are painted rotten-apple brown and are trimmed with bands of pink and teal, like ski sweaters from the '70s. Eric had rented them in Anchorage. They are stationed in what is officially known as the Alaska West Air parking lot but is widely referred to as the Ghetto.

The Ghetto is one of two mud-and-gravel patches that house all the services for skiing or snowboarding the Chugach. The other is the Tsaina Lodge parking lot, four miles to the north. Thompson Pass is no threat to St. Moritz. The nearest hotel is 30 miles away, in Valdez. The Ghetto is composed of a scattered collection of mobile homes, recreational vehicles, beater pickup trucks, pup tents, and mufflerless vans reeking of dope. Tucked in back is a white-and-red Bell Long Ranger helicopter and a 1954 DeHavilland Beaver. There are barbecues and lawn chairs and Frisbees and a pair of portable toilets. Several guys are standing in a circle playing hackey sack. Two people are shooting BB guns at the portable toilets. Some attempt to form groups for the next day's helicopter rides. Others try to scam rides by telling Eric they're good enough to be photographed. They'll ride anything, they say. Anything. They are junkies.

I can't blame them. Despite heavy coverage from filmmakers and magazine writers, the Chugach Mountains still represent the last great frontier of North American skiing and snowboarding. Most mountains in the area haven't yet been tracked. Entire subranges haven't even been named. First-ever descents are a daily occurrence.

Helicopter skiing did not begin here until 1990, when, in the wake of the disastrous Valdez oil spill, the region was seeking sources of revenue that didn't rely on healthy runs of fish. The next year, the World Extreme Skiing Championship was established, and soon every brand-name rider and skier in America made a visit. Word got around: bottomless snow, ridiculous steeps, no rules. Pilgrims began arriving. Some weren't as good as they thought they were. A few died.

Now the area is slowly maturing. The helicopter services have recently decided to make guides mandatory. Even so, no matter how skilled you are, if you're seeking to push your limits, the Chugach is the place to be.

In the morning, I put on my climbing harness and my avalanche transceiver. I pack my shovel, ice ax, and first-aid kit. Eric has hired the services of H_2O Heli Adventures, one of the region's three flying and guiding operations. Our guide is veteran Chugach rider Dan Caruso. The sky is a cloudless, wet-paint blue. Eighteen inches of snow have fallen in the past week. We are going where no one has touched it, to a remote area called the Books.

Through the bubble of the helicopter I have a front-row view of a dozen glaciers, choppy and cracked and melded with the flanks of the mountains. Glaciers may move only a few inches a year but the impression they prompt is of raw, tumbling speed. Sheer slate walls, thousands of feet of opaque rock, rise vertically from the ice. Impossible-seeming cornices jut off windblown summits like the bills of baseball caps. I grasp a new understanding of the term knife-edge ridge. I see no place to land.

For all practical purposes, there isn't. Snowboarding the Chugach, though, is hardly practical. Picking a run is a seat-of-the-pants proposition. The guide looks out the window, spots a good face to ride, then asks the pilot if it's possible to put the helicopter down atop it. We hover over one spot, then another—the ridges are too narrow, too unstable. On our third attempt, we land on a dome of snow no bigger than a pitcher's mound. Gingerly, the six of us exit the chopper and unload our boards. We huddle together. The machine flies away.

From our perch, I can see an uncountable array of peaks. What I can't see, however, is the mountain I'm standing on. In all directions, the slope drops off below my field of vision. It is as if we've landed on a cloud. I feel dizzy. Though it's well below freezing, I begin to sweat. Eric straps on his board and shuffles to the south-facing slope. He peers over, and drops off. Then Omar, then Athena, then Ross.

"How steep is this?" I ask Dan.

"Not very. Forty-five, maybe fifty degrees." Then he disappears, too.

I crawl over to the edge. The slope is so steep it does not seem possible snow could stick to it. Most places it wouldn't. The rare combination of low-elevation peaks, proximity to the sea, surplus of snowfall, and extreme midwinter cold has resulted in a phenomenon whereby snow clings to virtually any surface in the Chugach, no matter the pitch. And only rarely does it avalanche.

My first turn is shaky. I traverse onto the slope on my toeside. While standing upright on my board, I can extend my hand and touch the hill in front of me. This is a new category of steep. For the Chugach, it isn't even a difficult run. I flex my knees, uncoil, and flip onto my heelside. Then, unaccustomed to the steepness, I sit down on the slope. The top six inches of snow slides from beneath my board, exposing a layer that glints in the sun like glass. Everyone else has managed to miss it, but I've found the ice.

I quickly stand up and hop back to my toeside, but this is a mistake—more ice is exposed. It's all around me now. I start to slip.

"Turn!" Dan yells, watching me from below.

But it is too late. My edge loses its bite, and I fall. Ten feet. Twenty. I paw at the slope with my gloves but there's nothing to grab. For a few seconds, my heart does not beat. I think: That's it. I have fallen on a run where falling is not allowed.

Then I stop. Falling, it turns out, is allowed. The ice slick was 30 feet long, and it shot me directly into a winddrift of powder. I'm suddenly thigh-deep in snow.

"Well, you've found the sweet spot," says Dan. He's grinning. "Rip it up."

I rest for a few moments, letting my panic fade. I convince myself that I'd merely been unlucky. I'd done nothing wrong. I start to ride.

In my relatively brief snowboarding career, I have experienced some premium powder in some world-famous places. But here, in Alaska, this early May snow I've nearly killed myself getting to is far and away the finest. My board cuts three-foot furrows, spindrift swirling about me, catching the sun. Everything is silent. The snow is light as down. I don't so much ride as float. I ease out slow, rounded arcs—safe, savoring. My rhythm feels hypnotic. The run is 4,000 vertical feet.

After two more runs and no more ice, we return to the Ghetto and unwind. We tell stories about the powder to the others in the parking lot. In the morning, though, reality strikes: I get the bill. The price is steeper than the terrain—my three runs cost $331. This is beyond the means of most people who are not regularly pictured in *Forbes*, so I decide to spend my second day doing things the cheap way. I'm going to hike.

Finding a partner is simple—the Ghetto houses no shortage of the dedicated but destitute. His name is Chris, a boarder from Massachusetts who is spending the winter in Valdez, eating peanut-butter sandwiches ("Can't afford jelly."), camping out ("Can't afford hotels."), and hiking the mountains ("Can't afford helicopters."). We drive down the pass in Chris's Westphalia, looking at possible road runs. There are thousands of them. We choose an obvious one: a large chute, wide as the highway, cupped between two rocky foothills a short slog from the road. If this run were anywhere near my hometown there would be 200 people scrambling up it every weekend. The thing would be a mogul field. But we are in Alaska. The chute is untracked.

The climb takes two hours. With my board slung across my back, I kick steps up the left edge of the chute. Kick, stop, breathe. Kick, stop, breathe. I hum to myself. Sometimes, when I stray too close to the rock wall lining the chute, I encounter a patch of rotten snow and sink to my hip. Within half an hour, I'm down to my T-shirt. Every now and then a helicopter swoops across the sky, but I'm not jealous. I'm earning my turns. I feel superior.

Two bald eagles soar overhead—it's mating season, and the Valdez area is practically congested with eagles. All along the road they perch on the top of black spruces, transmitting wide-eyed, challenging stares. When one launches, it is a soundless explosion of energy. The tree shakes for nearly a minute. The pair above me ride the updrafts, circling higher and higher in the brilliant sky until they disappear. Not once do they flap. Now I'm jealous.

At the top of the chute, there is a patch of burgundy wildflowers and a rusty shotgun shell. I sniff the flowers, pocket the shell, and strap on my board. The temperature at the lower elevations has been too warm to preserve the powder, but the snow has congealed into smooth spring corn. I ride the couloir without stopping, leaning into the turns with exaggerated body movements, arms outstretched, wind rippling through my hair, inscribing a broad helix the length and breadth of the couloir. Chris does the same. I'd like to think the eagles were impressed.

Back at the Ghetto there is a group of riders sitting in white plastic lawn chairs, finishing a Doritos and 7-UP lunch, and pointing at the mountains, talking big behind their Oakleys.

"How about the south side of New World?"

"No way, man. Got tracks on it."

"Main line off Cold Smoke?"

"Been there, done that."

"West face of Python?"

"That's an idea."

An airplane ride is swiftly organized. The DeHavilland Beaver seats eight; there's a couple of spots available. Thirty-five bucks a ride. What the hell? I jump in. The engine clatters to life. The pilot, whose name is Tom, makes an announcement: "There's no movie on this flight, but if any of you care to step onto the wing, I'll show you *Gone with the Wind.*" We rumble down the packed-snow runway.

Five minutes later we land on a flat glacier 3,000 feet above the Ghetto. It's late in the afternoon and the sun is dropping behind the Worthington Glacier, across the valley, causing the ice to glow as if lit from within. I ride and ride and ride, the fattest turns possible, turns that would gobble up an entire Vail back bowl with a single arc, and still I don't cross another track. I feel like the ultimate powder pig. I love it. The run returns me to the road, where I flash my thumb and catch a ride home.

The next day, I turn the tables again. Once more, I decide not to join Eric and the pros. Instead, I drive to the Tsaina Lodge and book a day with Valdez Heli-Ski Guides, the company owned by husband-and-wife extreme skiers Doug Coombs and Emily Gladstone. Their service is reputed to offer the best access to the Chugach's wildest descents. It is not cheap. A six-run day costs $450. The waiver I'm given includes a detailed questionnaire:

Are you comfortable on 45-degree slopes?

This is steeper than virtually every lift-served run in the United States. "Yes," I write.

Fifty-five degrees?

This is so steep you'd have to climb up it with crampons and an ice ax. I have never ridden a 55-degree slope. But I'm feeling confident. "Yes," I write.

Sixty?

This is practically an elevator shaft. "Yes."

I am paired with four alarmingly adrenalized Chugach fanatics, including our guide, a lanky, bushy-bearded Montanan named Jerry Hance. There is another snowboarder, also named Mike, who'd come from southern California to spend a month here. The other two skiers are Jade, from Hawaii, and Jeff, a Taos ski instructor. We ride a snappy A-Star chopper into the mountains, flying over a network of bear tracks and a pair of mountain goats clinging to a thin ledge, before landing on a ledge of our own. The first run is disappointing, a short shot on wind-crusted snow.

The second run is the scariest experience of my life. The pilot, a middle-aged, gray-haired man named Walt who initially appeared to be the very essence of sanity, turns out to be the helicopter version of Evel Knievel. He hovers above a summit knob that doesn't contain enough real estate to plant a phone booth. One half of one runner is touching snow when we're given the exit signal. We leap from the chopper and grab hold of an outcropping of rocks until Walt flies away.

I stand up, then instantly squat back down. The first run of the trip, when I'd slipped on the ice, was merely terrifying. This is something else entirely.

"This is extreme," says Jerry. Everyone but me seems thrilled.

We are on a run called Flatiron, which is anything but flat. It has not been descended in four years. This is understandable. Save for one narrow ribbon of snow, the summit ridge drops off into vertical cliffs. Extreme—you fall, you die. Simple as that. My breathing becomes labored. *This is beyond crazy*, I think. *This is stupid.*

"Watch for hidden ice," says Jerry.

I think about my previous encounter with ice. "What if I find it?"

"Don't," says Jerry. "Don't."

Once again, I let everyone else go first. I try to focus. If this section of the run were at a ski area, without the cliffs, I'd ride it no problem. But now that the penalty for a mistake is my life, I can't move. So I swallow my pride, put my hands on the ground and gingerly sideslip down the ribbon, obliterating everyone else's neat tracks, to where the group has gathered overlooking the main face of Flatiron. I look down.

It's about 60 degrees. Crevassed in a series of broad frowns. Peppered with loose rock. Wide, though. We stand silently for a moment, gathering confidence. On a nearby peak a few boulders, loosened by the intense sunlight, clatter down a cliff. Echoes rumble up from the valley floor.

I ride the run. Not well, not smoothly, but I ride. I am focused so intensely on my turns there is not a single extraneous thought in my head. My whole world is the next carve. Extreme riding, I realize, is meditation for madmen. The run is so steep the top three inches of snow peel away and slide down with me. The sensation is of riding over a waterfall. I can't look at my feet. And I can't look at the horizon: I am on the steepest pitch imaginable and the run *still* rolls away beneath me. So I ride in my own focused bubble, one careful turn at a time.

I ride 5,000 vertical feet before my concentration breaks. Then I nearly die. At the bottom of Flatiron, running completely across the slope, is a narrow crevasse, called a bergschrund, where the valley glacier has peeled away from the mountain. Jerry's instructions, insane as they sound, are to gather up speed and jump across the bergschrund. After that the run would essentially be over, and we could ride freely to the helicopter's landing zone.

From my final stopping point, the bergschrund looks no more than a foot wide. A foot—easy. So I do not gain much speed. I approach the crack almost leisurely. It is not until I am right at the lip that I realize my miscalculation. The bergschrund is not one foot wide. It is not two or three. It is five feet wide. At the last instant, I instinctively yank my front foot upward and launch myself forward. I look directly into the center of the Earth. It is a luminescent pit of jade-blue ice. Bottomless. They won't even bother to retrieve my body.

I land with the front half of my board on the snow, the rear half hanging over the abyss. I tumble forward, flip once, twice, three times, and slide face first on the cold, wet snow.

I consider quitting for the day, but Jerry promises we won't be doing anything that intense again. So I stay for the final four runs. Though all are far harder than anything I'd ever ridden in the Lower 48, they are a comparative breeze. We even complete a first-ever descent, which I'm allowed to name. The run is short and feisty, so I call it Napoleon. We ride Napoleon twice, waist-deep in snow on a slope that's waited all eternity to be carved, leaving behind tracks befitting the honor. I begin to feel comfortable with the terrain. Odd as this seems, by the time we've flown back to the Tsaina Lodge, instead of savoring my safe return I find that I'm nearly ready to push myself again.

So I hang out in the parking lot. And sure enough, just before sunset, there's talk of skiing the north face of Diamond Peak. Diamond is one of the Chugach's premier shots: a vertical mile of unending steepness. A helicopter needs to be filled, pronto. The excitement in the Tsaina Lodge parking lot is palpable. People are buzzing on adrenaline. It's contagious; I'm susceptible. I stand on a rock and look up at the peak, lit in salmon-tinted light by the waning sun. Gorgeous.

Jade comes over. "Five thousand more vertical," he says. "The conditions are pristine."

I'm tempted. I can't help it. "Is there some exposure?" I ask.

"Some."

"How much is some?"

"Well, there's a few no-fall turns."

"Oh."

"Flatiron was all no-fall turns. You'll be half as scared this time. You'll see."

I stare over the roof of the Tsaina, over the spruces, up at Diamond Peak. It is a painful decision. "I don't think I'm a good enough snowboarder yet," I say.

"Well," Jade says to me tersely, "at least you know your limits."

Then he leaves to find someone else willing to ride. This is Valdez—his task is easy. The helicopter soon departs, and I'm alone in the parking lot. The brave are flying to the mountain, the meek are at the bar. I want to be up there, I think, with the pioneers, adventuring, challenging myself, *living*. But overriding all my machismo is a basic truth: I don't want to die.

from My Quest for the Yeti
by Reinhold Messner

Climbers know Tyrolean Reinhold Messner (born 1944) as the boldest mountaineer of his generation. He was the first person to solo Everest, and the first to climb all 14 of the world's 8,000-meter peaks. Messner, an indefatigable explorer, in 1985 became lost in the wilds of Tibet—where he had this terrifying encounter with a beast who may or may not have been one of the legendary yeti.

The waters of the Mekong River, swollen from the melting snow, had forced me deeper into one of the countless Tibetan valley rifts. There was no choice—I would have to fight my way through the churning waters. I found what looked to be the best spot and waded in. With every step the powerful current threatened to sweep my legs out from under me. After finding a firm foothold and shifting my weight to one leg, I would muster all my strength and lift the other leg. Progress was slow, but eventually I found myself standing in the middle of the raging waters, leaning on a branch braced against the current, trying not to panic. Turning back now was impossible.

The opposite bank, a dark strip stretched between coniferous trees and glistening black rock, was only a stone's throw away. The frigid water was gray as fog, and the spray tasted of rock and dirty snow. I was glad I had kept my boots on. Seven of my toes had been amputated in 1970 after an expedition to Nanga Parbat, the eight-thousand-meter mountain in northern India, and the boots helped me get a stronger foothold between the stones.

Positioning myself for my next step, fixing my eyes on a rock that lay on the opposite bank, I slid my right foot into a gap between two stones beneath the seething waters. The trick was to find my balance and then simply place my trust in the riverbed. I inched my way forward, upstream, diagonally against the current.

The water was so cold that I could not feel my legs below my knees, but my face was covered with sweat. My arms were exhausted from gripping the branch and from flailing to keep my balance. Finally I reached the dark bank, exhausted but exhilarated.

My exact location was difficult to pinpoint. I had come from Qamdo in eastern Tibet and was trying to make my way south to Nachu. I had crossed the valleys of some of Asia's greatest rivers: the Yangtze, the Mekong, and the Salween. The mountain ranges towering over the river valleys were so craggy and steep that people had managed to settle in only a few places. I often trekked for two days without encountering a single soul.

Once you get off the roads in eastern Tibet the mountains become completely impregnable. With a yak caravan or with some sturdy Tibetan ponies you might manage to reach certain locations. Trekking alone and on foot meant sacrificing every comfort. I had a sleeping bag, a flashlight, some bacon and hard bread, a pocketknife, a waterproof cover, and a camera. But no tent. Whenever I couldn't make it to a village by sundown, I slept in the open, in a cave, or under a tree.

Sitting on a dry rock above the riverbank, I took off my shoes, wrung out my socks, and slowly began to warm up a little. The bubbling water now sounded soothing. An incredibly dense forest lay before me. I would need to cross it by sundown, and the sun's rays were already slanting. After putting my wet socks and shoes back on, I heaved my rucksack back onto my shoulders. It seemed much heavier than it had when I crossed the surging glacial waters.

I had not come to Tibet this time to climb a mountain or to cross a desert. Instead, I wanted to follow the route the Sherpa people had taken in their flight from the lands of Dege, across Qamdo, Alando, Lharigo, Lhasa, and Tingri, then all the way to the Khumbu territories—a migration that still echoed through many Sherpa legends though it had occurred centuries ago. By retracing the Sherpas' journey, I hoped to discover how closely the legend corresponded to reality.

Dense rhododendron bushes and barberry thickets made progress almost impossible. The undergrowth was as impenetrable as a tropical rain forest. I tried to remember which direction the natives of the last village had told me to take. One yak herdsman had hinted that following the wrong riverbed could lead one into falling rocks and avalanches.

The forest was silent—not even a breeze stirred the air. White tufts of cloud floated high above the slanting peaks of the conifer trees. In the sky above the gorge, which seemed close enough to touch, a few birds hovered, as if lost.

A little daylight was still left and the weather was good, so I kept climbing. Trekking became easier the deeper I went into the forest. Rocks and tree trunks of centuries-old Himalayan cedars were less daunting than the hydrangeas, woody weeds, clematis, rhododendron, and maple thickets that clogged every trail near the river. I am usually not prone to fear, but on this day I was apprehensive about finding a trail, a clue, some reassurance. Whenever I had to climb a steep rock, I stopped, my arm propped on my knee, trying to catch my breath and calm my racing pulse. Looking down into the ravine reminded me that this was the edge of the world. I could only hope I was heading for the village of Tchagu.

During all the weeks of trekking I had somehow managed to find paths and trails. Sometimes I tagged along with yak caravans. There had always been somebody to tell me what route to take when I set off alone for the next village. But the Alando region, where I had expected to find a settlement, was deserted—not a hut to be seen, not even the crumbling walls of abandoned homes or the remains of campfires, and therefore not a soul to tell me which way to go.

I sat on a moss-covered rock, took a map out of my backpack, and looked at the tangle of red and blue lines between which were a mass of numbers and place names. Trying to pinpoint my exact position on the map was, however, hopeless. Get lost here and nobody will find you. I folded up the map and sat staring into the high mountain world from which I had come. I have been through this before, I told myself. There were times when I had trekked for sixteen hours straight with barely enough food to keep me going.

The sun's rays no longer penetrated the tall trees; it had become so cold that the skin beneath my sweat-drenched shirt tightened. Deep in the ravine, the meltwater, which would soon reach its high point, flowed smoothly. I had to find a settlement by sundown, or at least reach the high pastures beyond the forest.

The peaks in the east shimmered in the fading light of the evening sun. Dusk was spreading over the forest floor. Barely visible through the trees and the underbrush, I saw what looked like a mountain path not ten feet away from where I had been sitting. I began climbing faster, my pace almost mechanical, and emerged from the verdant undergrowth into a clearing. This was unquestionably a mountain path—the trail I had anxiously been searching for for so long. I followed it without hesitating, making my way up toward where I thought Tchagu must be. My exhilaration grew with every breath.

Then, suddenly, silent as a ghost, something large and dark stepped into a space thirty feet ahead among the rhododendron bushes. A yak, I thought, becoming excited at the thought of meeting some Tibetans and getting a hot meal and a place to sleep that evening. But the thing stood still. Then, noiseless and light-footed, it raced across the forest floor, disappearing, reappearing, picking up speed. Neither branches nor ditches slowed its progress. This was not a yak.

The fast-moving silhouette dashed behind a curtain of leaves and branches, only to step out into a clearing some ten yards away for a few seconds. It moved upright. It was as if my own shadow had been projected onto the thicket. For one heartbeat it stood motionless, then turned away and disappeared into the dusk. I had expected to hear it make some sound, but there was nothing. The forest remained silent:

no stones rolled down the slope, no twigs snapped. I might have heard a few soft footfalls in the grayness of the underbrush.

I stared, first amazed, then perplexed, at the spot where this apparition had stood. Why had I not taken a picture? I stood stock-still, listening to the silence, my senses as alert as those of an animal. Then I crept into the undergrowth from which the creature had emerged only to disappear again, noting everything that moved, every sound that rose above the murmur of the lightest breeze, every scent different from that of the forest floor. There in the black clay, I found a gigantic footprint. It was absolutely distinct. Even the toes were unmistakable. To see that the imprint was fresh I touched the soil next to it. It was fresh. I took a picture and checked the soil around it. My shoes didn't sink in nearly as deeply as had the creature's bare soles.

Staring at the black clay, I suddenly remembered the famous photograph of a footprint Eric Shipton had taken in 1951 at the Melting Glacier, located between Tibet and Nepal. This photograph was commonly considered the best proof that the creature known as the yeti existed. Like all Himalaya climbers, I knew the yeti legends well enough. They are told throughout Sherpa country. But I would never have imagined that a real, living creature might be connected to this legend. I knew large parts of Tibet and the Himalayas pretty well, yet even in those remote places where we mountain climbers, with our modern equipment, can survive for months at a time, I had never seen anything resembling such a creature.

The yeti legend drew strength from the drama of the Himalayan landscape—the peaks, glaciers, snowstorms, and howling winter nights. This was a place where storytelling came naturally—and the oral tradition was alive and well. How often in the kitchen tents of the base camps had the Sherpas told me of the yeti—of the girls it had abducted, of the yaks it had killed in a single blow, of the enormous footprints it had left behind in the snow. I had only half listened in the smoky gloom of the tent, crouching between the equipment and the boxes of supplies, as the Sherpas recounted tales of a dangerous giant, paying full attention only when one of them named real place names or spoke of someone who had actually either encountered a yeti or climbed in pursuit of one. But when I asked for specifics, fathers would turn into grandfathers, villages into regions, and definite facts into blurry maybes. My mind would turn to more concrete concerns.

Yeti legends—spreading over the Himalayas and Tibet like the waters that rush down from the mountains in the summer—had trickled into every village, every household. The Sherpas may have brought the legends back with them from Nepal, Sikkim, and Solo Khumbu. Members of the first Western expeditions to the Himalayas had heard them, and they got picked up in newspapers and books. In less than a century, news of a mysterious creature had spread throughout the world. Today millions of people in the West have some notion of the yeti. For most, it embodies a longing for some mirror to our prehistoric past, a mirror into which we can look and shudder in awe and horror. Yeti stories inevitably boost sales of newspapers and tabloids.

As I continued up the mountain path, looking for tracks, it suddenly struck me that no one on this trip had mentioned the yeti. No one had warned me—seriously or in jest—that something might be afoot in the ravines beneath the mountain peaks. Perhaps the yeti craze had never reached regions where words like *Neanderthal* or *King Kong* were utterly foreign.

That evening I saw four more footprints. The animal was moving up the mountain and climbing farther up into the forest. If it was an animal. Had it been a bear, there would also have been imprints of its forepaws, and the tracks of snow leopards were, I knew, much smaller.

The icy mountain wind blew harder, and the birdsongs high up in the trees became softer and more intermittent. Climbing faster, I could hear nothing but my breathing and the echo of my steps.

The path up to the tree line was arduous, and I was worried that at any moment it would peter out. A gurgling noise came from farther up—whether it came from the ravine through which the river was tumbling or was produced by wind blowing through the treetops that towered into the night I could not tell. By now darkness had fallen. My

plan had been to hike till sunset and then bivouac, but the idea of settling down among the roots of a giant cedar to wait for morning did
not appeal.

So I pushed on. Sometime between dusk and midnight I came out
of the forest into a clearing. Bright moonlight filled the valley before
me. Black mountains cast sharp shadows on the slopes. The snaky coils
of the mountain trail, which ran over the rises and dips of the pasture,
disappeared into the darkness of a moraine. Not a single hut was to be
seen. No scent of animals in the air. No dots of light.

Making my way through some ash-colored juniper bushes, I suddenly heard an eerie sound—a whistling noise, similar to the warning
call mountain goats make. Out of the corner of my eye I saw the outline of an upright figure dart between the trees to the edge of the
clearing, where low-growing thickets covered the steep slope. The
figure hurried on, silent and hunched forward, disappearing behind a
tree only to reappear again against the moonlight. It stopped for a
moment and turned to look at me. Again I heard the whistle, more of
an angry hiss, and for a heartbeat I saw eyes and teeth. The creature
towered menacingly, its face a gray shadow, its body a black outline.
Covered with hair, it stood upright on two short legs and had powerful
arms that hung down almost to its knees. I guessed it to be over seven
feet tall. Its body looked much heavier than that of a man of that size,
but it moved with such agility and power toward the edge of the
escarpment that I was both startled and relieved. Mostly I was stunned.
No human would have been able to run like that in the middle of the
night. It stopped again beyond the trees by the low-growing thickets, as
if to catch its breath, and stood motionless in the moonlit night
without looking back. I was too mesmerized to take my binoculars out
of my backpack.

The longer I stared at it, the more the figure seemed to change shape,
but it was similar to whatever it was I had come across farther down
the trail—that much I knew. A heavy stench hung in the air, and the
creature's receding calls resounded within me. I heard it plunge into
the thicket, saw it rush up the slope on all fours, higher and higher,

deeper into the night and into the mountains, until it disappeared and all was still again.

I stared into the depths of the night sky. My hands were shaking. The Sherpas used to say that whistling meant danger, and that to escape a yeti one should move downhill as quickly as possible. How could anyone run through the thickets and the underbrush as fast as that creature had? It had disappeared over the moonlight-flecked slopes without stumbling once, as if driven by some monstrous fury.

The thought that my mysterious counterpart might reappear sent chills down my spine. Escaping by fleeing—up or down the mountainside—was clearly futile. I would have broken both legs and made myself into easier prey than I already was. I took out my flashlight and continued up the trail, stopping to listen and look behind me. I felt watched.

The trail ended in a mountain torrent. I longed for a safe place to spend what remained of the night, but crossing the stream in the darkness was impossible. There was no bridge, and from what I could tell, the water would come at least up to my hips. I heard large stones rolling in the torrent and saw silvery white crests. Frost had covered the rocks on the banks of the glacial torrent. I knew the current would only ease in the late morning, before more ice began melting high in the glacier regions. That would be the best time to cross to the other side. I decided to return to the meadow.

Lonely and dead tired, I looked for a place to camp and found some rocks that, over decades, the waters had piled into a natural dam. I didn't have much of a choice. A little farther down the valley I could see a riverbed and hear the water I had crossed late that afternoon.

A metallic sheen lay on the rocks and weeds as I rolled out my thick foam-rubber mat. I constructed a little barrier of rocks between my campsite and the open meadow—a semblance of shelter—and slipped into my sleeping bag. My head propped against my half-empty backpack, I stared into the night sky. Every time I closed my eyes, I imagined the outline of a monster glaring down at me, so I kept them open. The moonlight was visible only on the slopes higher up in a side valley.

I heard the whistling call again. I jumped up. It could not have been the wind. The creature had come back. I peered down into the dark valley, then at the torrent across the slope. I could hear my heartbeat and the hissing and bubbling of the water—or was that the whistle? Had the call come from far away or nearby?

I stuffed my sleeping bag into my backpack and set off up the mountain, following the path along the bank of the stream. Somewhere there had to be a crossing where even at night I could reach the other side.

To my surprise and delight I did find a footbridge. I edged my way over the wooden planks high above the stream, then continued up the opposite slope, snaking my way over stones and boulders to a ridge from which I could see more mountain pastures—and also a few huts. They seemed abandoned; no lights burning anywhere. The village was surrounded by thornbushes and stone barriers and looked eerie and desolate. Piles of firewood stood like sentries in front of the houses. As I approached, I made as much noise as possible. I wanted to be heard. It is dangerous for a stranger to suddenly turn up in a mountain village in the dead of night. He might easily be mistaken for a thief. *Tashi delek!* I called out—first softly, then more loudly. Still nothing stirred. Again I called out *Tashi delek,* the Tibetan greeting. Again nothing. No sound, no light, no sign of life. Was this Tchagu?

Still calling, I walked slowly along a narrow cattle path, peering between the piles of firewood into the forecourts and the low-lying huts behind them. Fear and fury made me call louder. Why did nobody answer?

The only sign of life was the cold stench of horse manure, decay, and urine. Tchagu was no more than a line of derelict huts, a way station without hope—two dozen or so, all of them alike, each with a stone foundation and a wooden saddle roof. Between them darkness yawned. Narrow ladders propped up next to the low doors led to lofts that opened toward the path. The huts looked equally dilapidated. I had no choice but to choose one. Forgetting all my routine precautions, I entered a courtyard through an opening in a pile of firewood and looked for a dry place for the rest of the night.

As I neared the door of the hut, a black mass with snarling teeth and four eyes came flying at me. I grabbed a branch out of the woodpile behind me and retreated back down the path. A Tibetan mastiff. Soon other dogs joined in. I had Tibetan mastiffs back home in Austria. Brown patches next to their eyes make it look as if they have four eyes. These dogs are big and they are dangerous.

I swung the long, thick branch like a club, ready to bludgeon any slavering dog that got too close. I stood with my back to the stone barrier that separated the village from the fields behind it. The ferocious pack was closing in on me from all sides—first seven or eight, then more and more. They tumbled over each other, so that only their black muzzles were visible. I alternated between murmuring softly to them and shouting. Not one was smaller than a German shepherd. Whenever a dog came too near, I struck at it. By now the whole pack was snarling, howling, and barking so loudly that in desperation I also started yelling.

The villagers had to wake up now, I thought. But no one came. I slowly crept back down the same path I had come, my back against the stone, looking left and right. The dogs followed me till I staggered out into an open meadow at the edge of the village. There the dogs' fury suddenly dissipated, and they trotted back to the huts, snarling, whining, snapping at each other.

Where was I to go now? I didn't want to head back down into the valley. The scare this pack of half-starved dogs had given me paled in comparison to the horror of my earlier nocturnal encounter. That creature, whose lair was somewhere in these valleys, was ten times more powerful and massive than any dog. I could not make my way over the mountains in the dark, and I was also too exhausted to continue climbing. I had no choice but to slink quietly back to the huts—whose inhabitants had probably taken their yak herds up into the mountain pastures. Tchagu, the dog-ridden hole, was my only hope.

I followed the cattle path back between the stone barrier and the woodpiles to the dwellings. I passed the holding pens without attracting the dogs, entered one of the courtyards through a low opening between

piles of firewood, and walked toward the house: The door was pad-
locked. I decided to climb up the ladder to the open loft. Crouching
between the floorboards and the shingles, I groped my way to a stone
fireplace. Hunched over my backpack, I listened to the stillness of the
night. Looking over my shoulder one last time, I stripped down to my
underwear and crawled into my sleeping bag. A few minutes later, before
my heartbeat and my breathing had even slowed, I fell asleep.

I sat up, torn from a deep, dreamless sleep. I thought I had heard voices.
Bewildered, I peered out of the loft's triangular-shaped opening onto a
ridge under the starry Himalayan sky. I had not been mistaken. I could
hear steps, murmuring, and hissing. Someone was barking orders. A
shower of stones came pelting onto the floorboards next to me.

Startled and still half in my sleeping bag, I crawled behind the fireplace for cover. Now there were more voices below and they grew
louder. I couldn't stay hidden up in the loft. I had to come down before
they dragged me out and beat me to death.

I crouched by the loft opening, almost naked, clutching my sleeping
bag and clothes under my right arm, holding my backpack in my left.
I hesitated for a few seconds in the moonlight at the top of the
stepladder, but when I saw the grimy faces of men swinging cudgels
and torches, I immediately climbed down from the loft into the courtyard. They grabbed my belongings before my feet even touched the
ground, and one of the men held up a lantern to my face. I stood
before them—thin, bleary-eyed, making submissive gestures—
confronted by their anger, their cudgels, and their curiosity. I must have
looked pitiful. The horde of wild and ragged men first started murmuring, then broke out into laughter. They weren't glaring at me anymore. Some of them whispered among themselves, others shouted
questions at me I didn't understand. They began slipping swords and
knives back into the leather or silver sheaths that hung from their belts.

I started stammering to them about my encounter with the yeti. I
knew just about enough Tibetan to ask for some buttermilk and a place
to sleep, so to describe what I had seen I used gestures and fragments

of pidgin English, Nepalese, Urdu, and Tibetan. Miraculously, they understood my tale and knew right away what I was talking about.

Frantically, I told them all I could. The beast had walked on two legs, looked much stronger than a man, and was as tall as the stepladder up to the loft. It whistled by blowing air between its tongue and its upper jaw (I tried to imitate this for their benefit). And the stench! (I pinched my nose.) Even its tracks smelled like a mix of frozen garlic, rancid fat, and dung.

Two tall, gaunt Tibetans, their faces half-hidden beneath wide, broad-brimmed hats, motioned for me to follow them into their house. I had managed by then to put on my pants and my shirt. Grabbing my sleeping bag, I followed them between the walls and the woodpiles into a courtyard full of baskets and horse manure. Bending down, I entered the hut through a narrow door. One of the men pointed with his wooden club to the sleeping area near the fireplace while the other man bolted the door from the inside. I rolled out my mat and my sleeping bag. The first man put some wood in the fireplace and knelt on the floor to blow on the embers. Dull sparks and smoke billowed up, and then the fire started. In the pleasant glow of the flames the scattered objects in the room no longer looked like a confused jumble. Yak-hair ropes hung from the walls next to leather straps and an ornamental saddle. Piles of furs, stuffed sacks, and a few wooden racks lay on the floor. These racks were hauling saddles for the yaks. Two pots stood in the corner—a large one of hammered copper for water, and an aluminum one for buttermilk.

I was too tired to feel hunger, but my tongue and throat were parched from days of breathing through my mouth and from the fear of the past few hours. I begged them for some buttermilk.

One of the men put a wooden bowl in front of me filled with a grayish mush containing particles of soot. I downed it without bothering to spit out the soot. The other man was slowly and reverently pounding butter tea in a knee-high cylinder, all the while glancing over at me. They wanted to know how I had come here from Dege and why the Chinese hadn't locked me up. I laughed and showed them a document, a sort of permit, which had been issued in Lhasa, but which they couldn't read.

"There was a storm in Dege, with thunder and lightning," I tried telling them in my broken Tibetan. "I sheltered with a Tibetan family in a hut by the roadside. At midnight the floodwaters came. Loudspeakers shouted orders. People were screaming. But only a couple of houses below the road from Chengdu to Lhasa were flooded. And as the cleanup began, I escaped the Chinese."

"Escaped?"

"Before dawn. The Chinese had already locked me up once for a whole week."

One of the men shook the steaming butter tea into the wooden bowl I had eaten from. I continued with my tale.

"The road to Qamdo was cut off, so I had to walk. I spent the night in roadside inns or in the tents of yak nomads. Twice in stables. I walked for days in the rain. I hid during the day and walked through the night. The forests everywhere have been cut down and the old caravan roads were either washed away or so muddy that I often slipped and fell."

I pointed with some pride at my dirty trousers. My hosts laughed.

"Most of the time I ate *tukpa* [soup]. I drank *sho* [yogurt] and water from the springs. The day before yesterday I crossed the Shaka-La River with a yak caravan. The drivers threw my backpack onto a yak's back between two sacks, and I followed behind. After traveling down a steep slope we stopped to rest, and they offered me *tara* [buttermilk], *tsha* [tea], and *tsampa* [barley flour]. Then we went our separate ways, and I got as far as the Tokatchu monastery. "

"*Tsampa?*" one of them offered. I shook my head. I wanted to sleep. The two looked at me expectantly and continued throwing twigs into the fire. They wanted to know how I had managed to escape the monster.

"Right after I left Alado, I found the path again. The creature came out of the underbrush. His head was almost as big as a yak's, but without the horns, and with dark fur. He rose on his hind legs, turned, and disappeared. His back was red."

"*Chemo?*" both men asked with one voice, uttering this word with such fear in their voices that my encounter now suddenly seemed even more terrifying. But their fear was also tinged with respect. They were obviously surprised that I had managed to survive my long trek through the darkness. "Chemo!" one of the men whispered, and shaking his head, he poured me some more butter tea. He wasn't wearing shoes.

"Chemo," I repeated. "Is that a bear?"

No, no, my hosts gestured. They told me *tom* is the word for bear, and that the tom live farther down the mountain, in the forests. Tom have shorter legs, a white patch shaped like a half-moon on their chest, and are otherwise black. They are dangerous, said my hosts, but they're not chemos. The way they said *chemo* again indicated to me both fear and veneration. Was this, I wondered sleepily, the phantom we in the West call the abominable snowman?

I must have dozed off in the middle of the conversation. In my sleep I could hear the crackling of the firewood in the fireplace, then the voices died down and the world fell silent.

a c k n o w l e d g m e n t s

Many people made this anthology.

At Thunder's Mouth Press and Avalon Publishing Group:
Neil Ortenberg and Susan Reich continued to offer vital support and expertise. Dan O'Connor, Ghadah Alrawi and Matthew Trokenheim also were indispensable.

At Balliett & Fitzgerald Inc.:
Tom Dyja and f-stop Fitzgerald lent intellectual and moral support. Sue Canavan designed the book and Patti Ratchford put in overtime designing the cover. Maria Fernandez oversaw production with scrupulous care and attention—with help from Paul Paddock.

At Shawneric.com:
Shawneric Hachey handled permissions, found photographs and scanned copy—all with his usual aplomb.

At the Writing Company:
Associate editor Nate Hardcastle played an essential role in finding the selections for this book. He drafted introductions to the selections, and lent his keen editorial eye to many other delicate tasks. John Bishop provided research assistance and helped coordinate the final stages of the book's production. Nat May proofread copy. Taylor Smith, Mark Klimek, Lee Rader and Deborah Satter also helped with the book, and took up slack on other projects.

Among friends and family:
Jennifer Willis lent me her judgement—again.
Will Balliett made it a pleasure—again.

Finally, I am grateful to the writers whose work appears in this book.

b i b l i o g r a p h y

The selections used in this anthology were taken from the editions listed below. In some cases, other editions may be easier to find. Hard-to-find or out-of-print titles often are available through inter-library loan services or through Internet booksellers.

Anker, Conrad and David Roberts. *The Lost Explorer*. New York: Simon & Schuster, 1999.

Finkel, Michael. *Alpine Circus*. New York: Lyons Press, 1999.

Hanson, Neil. *Custom of the Sea*. New York: John Wiley & Sons, 2000.

Lundy, Derek, *Godforsaken Sea*. New York: Anchor Books, 2000

Marriott, Edward. *Savage Shore*. New York: Henry Holt & Company, 2000.

Messner, Reinhold. *My Quest for the Yeti*. New York: St. Martin's Press, 2000.

Montgomery, Sy. *Journey of the Pink Dolphins*. New York: Simon & Schuster, 2000.

National Geographic Adventure. May/June 2000. (For *Among the Man-Eaters* by Philip Caputo.)

New York Times Magazine, The. June 18, 2000. (For "Desperate Passage" by Michael Finkel.)

Outside. May 2000. (For "Tombstone White" by Mark Jenkins.)

Salon.com. March 28, 2000. (For "Be Your Own Donkey" by Rolf Potts.)

Salon.com. May 26, 2000. (For "Into the Jaws of Destiny" by Bill Belleville.)

Utne Reader. July/August 2000. (For "Being Prey" by Val Plumwood.)

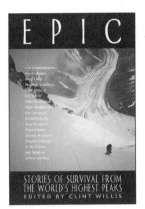

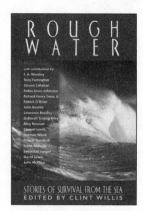

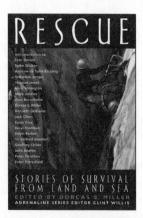

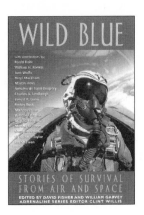

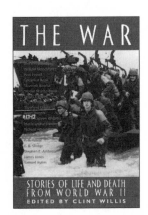

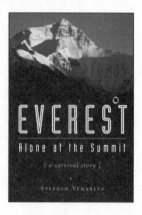

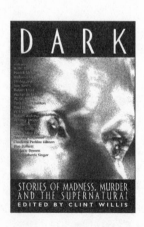